Young People and Political Participation

Jacqueline Briggs

Young People and Political Participation

Teen Players

Jacqueline Briggs
University of Lincoln
Lincoln, United Kingdom

ISBN 978-0-230-29867-5   ISBN 978-1-137-31385-0   (eBook)
DOI 10.1057/978-1-137-31385-0

Library of Congress Control Number: 2016956651

Cover illustration: © Desislava Dimitrova / Alamy Stock Photo X created by Spencer
Harrison from the Noun Project

Printed on acid-free paper

This Palgrave Macmillan imprint is published by Springer Nature
The registered company is Macmillan Publishers Ltd.
The registered company address is: The Campus, 4 Crinan Street, London, N1 9XW,
United Kingdom

To Imogen, John, Mum and my late Dad

ACKNOWLEDGEMENTS

I would like to express my sincere thanks and deepest gratitude to my colleagues whose advice, comments and moral support have been invaluable throughout the research. Particular thanks to my colleagues, Marie Nicholson, academic subject librarian, for her invaluable research support, and to Jill Jameson and Kate Strudwick for their help and advice with regards to statistical data analysis.

I am particularly indebted to the School of Social and Political Sciences at the University of Lincoln, my place of employment—for the aid, advice and assistance given to me. Thank you to Sara Mann for making space in my diary and to Tom Kirman for help with the graphs.

Thank you to Andrew Baird, Jemima Warren and Imogen Gordon Clark, editorial assistants from Palgrave, for their expertise and advice.

Special thanks undoubtedly go to the young people without whom this research would not have been possible.

Last, but not least, thanks to my partner, John, and daughter Imogen, for their support and sacrifice.

CONTENTS

Notes on Author

Jacqueline (Jacqui) Briggs is Head of the School of Social and Political Sciences at the University of Lincoln. She was Vice Chair of the Political Studies Association UK (2011–14), with special responsibility for Education and Skills, and served on the learned society's executive committee for more than a decade. In 2012, she became an Academician of the Academy of Social Sciences. Briggs is a member of the board of the Campaign for Social Sciences; she is also a Fellow of the RSA. The Quality Assurance Agency recently asked Briggs to chair, for a second time, the review panel examining the subject benchmarking statements for Politics and International Relations.

List of Tables

Young People and Political Participation: Is There an Issue About Young People and Politics?

INTRODUCTION

Political youth: is this an oxymoron? It can sometimes be difficult to think of young people as being political animals. Politics is often regarded as an older, or perhaps middle-aged, person's pursuit, when levels of political turnout and participation are analysed. Middle-aged and older generations are, statistically, more likely to turn out to vote and to stand for election than their younger counterparts. Politics, at all levels—European, national, devolved and local—contains relatively few representatives in their late teens, 20s or even 30s. The stereotypical image of a Member of Parliament (MP), for example, has remained relatively static for decades, being predominantly white, male, middle aged and middle class. Against this backdrop, young people may find it hard to relate to politics on a macro level—politics with a large 'P'. The perception is often that politics neither includes young people nor represents young people in both a numeric and a substantive way. They are absent from the ranks of the elected representatives and also their views are either ignored completely or, at least sidelined. Little wonder, therefore, that many young people do seem to regard the political arena as alien territory. This book examines the extent to which these perceptions are correct whilst also assessing topics such as whether young people should be given the right to vote at the age of 16 and 17 and also examining the way in which young people might be seen to be participating in politics in other ways—such as via new social media and through protests and campaigning organisations.

© The Author(s) 2017
J. Briggs, *Young People and Political Participation*,
DOI 10.1057/978-1-137-31385-0_1

This first chapter introduces the topic of young people and political participation. Examination is made of what constitutes youth, the growth and development of youth, historical background, youth as consumers and purchasing power. The rise of youth culture and the duality of youth (whereby young people are regarded both as the future and a source of optimism but also as a troubling phenomenon and a sector of society to be feared) are also assessed. This chapter sets the scene in terms of facilitating understanding of what the concept of youth entails and examining the situation from a historical perspective. It is interesting to note that youth is not a new phenomenon and that notions such as ephebiphobia (fear of youth/teenagers) have existed for a significant amount of time. This chapter provides a logical starting point before proceeding to look at youth in contemporary society.

WHY YOUTH?

Over recent years, there has been a burgeoning literature on young people and politics (cf. Henn et al. Sloam; Tonge and Mycock) and on specific aspects (cf. Ramamurthy, on Asian youth movements; Shephard et al. on youth parliaments). Academics are increasingly finding it a topic worthy of detailed investigation and debate. Certainly, in these relatively early years of the new millennium, it is an interesting topic worthy of subject that has exercised both academics and the media alike. In the past few years, specific events and policies have focused attention upon the extent to which young people are engaged with politics. These include, on the world stage, the Arab Spring that took place in the Middle East in early 2011 and, more specifically, in the UK, the rise in higher education tuition fees to £9000 per year, from September 2012, the cuts of 40 per cent to the Higher Education budget and the so-called riots which took place in August 2011. Also, in the UK, as in some other countries, there has been discussion and a move towards granting the franchise to 16- and 17-year-olds. The fact that 16- and 17-year-olds were given the right to vote in the referendum on Scottish Independence, held on the 18 September 2014, raised the profile of this debate. There are those who believe that it is only a matter of time before this is rolled out to other elections as the momentum gathers pace. It is worth noting that the Conservative Government has declared that 16- and 17-year-olds will not be able to vote in the referendum on continued European Union membership.[1] Ironically, the European Union referendum disenfranchises some young voters in Scotland who were eligible in September 2014 as 16-year-olds but who will not be 18 by 23 June 2016. There are not many young people affected by this but certainly enough for it to be an issue worthy of mention. These events outlined above have, however, all conspired to ensure that youth and politics has become a contentious area of politics.

It is worthwhile examining exactly what is meant by youth and here it is worth noting, as mentioned in the introduction, that the concept of youth is a relatively recent phenomenon. The post-Second World War scenario is often cited as being the onset of youth. Prior to this time, it is claimed that the notion of a youth, as it is understood today, did not really exist. One was either an adult or a child, and the notion of an in-between stage, especially with regards to the idea of being a teenager, did not really exist. It is only after the Second World War and especially from the 1950s onwards, with higher living standards and increasing amounts of disposable income, that the notion of a teenager really began to take off. The idea of an in-between stage of life, after childhood and before the onset of adulthood, was a relatively new phenomenon and meant that businesses would all try to target this sector of society. In part, this was defined for the benefit of education, and the growth and expansion of higher education, in particular, fuelled this process. The late 1950s and the 1960s was an era that witnessed many more people remaining in education beyond the statutory school-leaving age. Whilst it still included an élite, privileged, few who were able to study for a degree, nonetheless, the grammar school system, in particular, and later the comprehensive schooling system saw some from working class backgrounds being able to remain in education and become socially mobile via the attainment of a degree. Certainly, the expansion of higher education helped to perpetuate this in-between stage. For example, in 1950, there were 17,337 people who obtained a university first degree; by 1960 this had risen to 22,426, increasing significantly by 1970 to 51,189. By 1990, this had risen to 77,163 but the real leap occurred by 2000 when the figure was 243,246. The rise was aided by the expansion of the university sector with the transition of former polytechnics into universities and other specific government policies that aimed to increase the numbers of young people staying on for further and higher education. In addition to the rise, there was also a shift in the gender balance. By 2000, there were more women than men obtaining first degrees (133,315 women compared to 109,930 men). The figures for 2011 show this trend has continued, with 197,565 women gaining a first degree as opposed to 153,235 men (See Bolton 2012: 20). Latest available figures reveal that, in 2014, there were 237,690 females and 184,130 males who graduated with a first degree (Higher Education Statistics Agency 2015). Granted some of these numbers will relate to mature students but, certainly, a much larger proportion of young people, therefore, are remaining in higher education for a longer period than hitherto. This potentially impacts the concept of youth in a number of ways. Firstly, it contributes to the extension of time that could be categorised as 'youth' beyond childhood and yet a stage different from the life of adulthood. Secondly, the fact that many more young people than hitherto are remaining in higher education means that they are more likely to become politicised given that universities seek to create critical thinkers and to encourage people to be more questioning, open-minded and, possibly, less accepting of the *status quo*. This could mean that young people who have been to university are more politicised or at least have the potential to become so. It is interesting to consider whether higher education does, indeed, make people more questioning and challenging. In theory, at least, one would expect so. Thirdly, students studying for their first degree have more time not only to reflect on politics but also to actively engage in political activities. This time factor should not be underestimated. Adulthood, often submerged in the world of work, paying the mortgage and raising the next generation, means that many people have neither the time, the energy, nor the inclination to be politically active. Granted, not all young people remain in higher education but, for those who do, it is a potential factor in the politicisation process.

ARE THEY INTERESTED?

In terms of whether young people are actually interested in politics, there has recently been a wealth of discussion and debate. Central to this discussion is whether young people are interested in politics or whether they are apathetic, bearing in mind that apathy may also indicate contentment (Eulau 1963, 1966). Some commentators argue that they are not uninterested in politics but that they are less enamoured with mainstream politics than they are with political issues (cf. Harris et al. 2010). They are, for example, interested in issues such as animal rights and environmentalism. As Nigel Morris states, 'The large numbers of young people moved to march over gay rights, protecting the environment, the Iraq war and tuition fees shows they can be galvanised by single issues' (2014b: 5). Having said this, some commentators and academics question whether young people are actually interested in politics beyond the mainstream. In response to the issue of whether young people are interested in politics, Rowena Mason (2013) cites academic Stuart Fox, who observes that there is a lack of evidence to support the thesis that young people are participating in protest activity (as opposed to mainstream politics) and also academic Maria Grasso, who states rather candidly that no one really knows the extent to which young people are interested in politics. She points out, however, to the perceived lack of division and difference between the major political parties and a move towards occupying the centre-ground as being a political turn-off, that is, not much to choose between the parties (Ibid.). This potentially contributes to a disconnection between young people and the political parties. It will be interesting to see whether the election of Jeremy Corbyn as Leader of the Labour Party redresses this situation. (Corbyn has, for example, declared his opposition to tuition fees.) The actor, writer and comedian, Russell Brand, guest editor of the *New Statesman* states, 'young people, poor people, not-rich people, most people do not give a f*** about politics' (Brand 2013: 26). For Brand, apathy 'is a rational reaction to a system that no longer represents, hears or addresses the vast majority of people' (Ibid.). If young people are apathetic, for Brand, this would seem a rational response to a system from which they are effectively excluded.

YOUTH UNEMPLOYMENT

When assessing levels of unemployment amongst young people and the fact that many of them are part of the NEETS (Not in Employment, Education and Training) (cf. Simmons et al. 2014), it is perhaps surprising that many more young people are not politicised. Not solely down to unemployment but *Generation Υ*, those born after 1982, are likely to grow up to be poorer than their parents' generation. Youth unemployment is a key issue, not just in the UK but also across Europe as a whole. It is claimed that youth unemployment has almost hit the 25 per cent mark, a staggering figure of 24.4 per cent, with one in four young people, across Europe, being out of work.[2] Young people constitute the sector of society worst affected by the high levels of unemployment, with 3.62 million under-25s being out of work. As Russell Lynch asserts, 'Nearly one in four 16 to 24-year-olds across the 17 nations in the single currency is now out of work, according to monthly figures published by the EU's data office, Eurostat'. Moreover, he proceeds to profess that this is worse in some European countries than in others, for example, 'Well over half of those under 25 in Greece and Spain are not in work, compared with more than 40 per cent in Italy' (Lynch 2013: 1). According to Eurostat figures,[3] the youth unemployment level in Greece is 51.1 per cent, Spain 51.7 per cent, Portugal 33.3, Italy 42.0 and France is 24.6. Contrastingly, Germany is only 7.4 per cent as they have not suffered as much from the recession and the austerity measures. On the whole though, these are substantial figures, especially when one thinks about the impact upon a whole generation of young people. Various negative labels have been applied to this cohort of young people, such as the 'lost' generation or the 'jilted' generation. The chances of finding work, with so many others seeking the same, must be minimal and must surely manifest in a tangible sense of despair and disillusionment. In the UK alone, there are more than one million young people who are seeking work. According to Jon Savage, 'In January 2014, unemployment amongst those aged 18–24 was estimated at 18.6 % and, among 16–17 year olds, up to 35.5 %' (Savage 2014: 19). According to a House of Commons briefing paper, '723,000 young people aged 16–24 were unemployed in May–July 2015, which is down 17,000 from the previous quarter and down 32,000 from the previous year' (Delebarre 2015: 2). Even with this decline, given these staggering figures, it might be anticipated that the politicisation of young people will continue apace in the coming months and years. If young people feel that they do not have a stake in society, they are likely to become increasingly disillusioned. Likewise, the perception that it is they, the younger generation, who are increasingly bearing the brunt of the cuts and the austerity measures across Europe as a whole, is likely to perpetuate discontent and possible dissent. The notion of a 'them' and 'us' society with a relative affluent older sector of society is likely to fuel the feelings of unfairness. Andrew Mycock states that 'Unemployment at such a young age undermines self-esteem and also builds resentment. Responses to youth unemployment have been insubstantial though, with too much faith being placed in the private sector to provide short-term panaceas to long-term problems, particularly for NEETS who are also not in education or training' (Mycock 2011, www.opendemocracy.net). This lack of jobs, allied with other factors, such as higher university tuition fees, the increasing difficulty in terms of accessing mortgages and corresponding rising house prices meaning that first-time buyers are particularly disadvantaged, all contribute to exacerbating this situation. In addition, the proliferation of 'zero hours' contracts, pension reforms such as end of final salary pension deals and predictions of retirement in one's 80s potentially have a disproportionate impact on younger people. Furthermore, the reality of politicians and policymakers being middle aged or older may perpetuate the viewpoint that they are primarily legislating in their own interests. It is a fact that the socio-economic backgrounds of MPs, for example, are unrepresentative of wider society, as they do not constitute a microcosm of the wider population. They are an élite group but the question to ask alongside this is whether they constitute a 'dominant' élite. Do they rule in their own interests? If young people arrive at the conclusion that they do, then the levels of discontentment will rise even further. Governments, across Europe, need to take youth unemployment seriously before the levels of resentment and disillusionment rise exponentially. A generation living in despair will inevitably lead to discontent; politicians across Europe ignore this issue at their peril.

POLITICAL ENGAGEMENT

It is certainly the case, therefore, that if one considers issues such as youth unemployment, higher tuition fees and the difficulties of getting on to the property ladder, young people *ought* to be interested in politics and in the politicians whose policies shape and impact their lives. It is difficult to determine accurately whether or not young people are interested in politics. Matt Hartley and Ted Huddleston cite researchers in the UK who refer to '"the millennial generation", a generation of young people who have little interest in politics, particularly party politics, or belief that voting in elections will make a difference, and who consistently hold low expectations of government' (2010: 13). Yet, if they are uninterested in mainstream politics, are they interested in politics *per se*? According to research undertaken by Alexander Hensby, a PhD research student from the University of Edinburgh, 76 per cent of students say they discuss politics, but the question is how is politics being defined? As he states, 'Only 4 per cent claim to "never" discuss politics, with 76 per cent claiming to do so at least "sometimes". Around a quarter of students claim to discuss politics regularly'[4] (Hensby 2013: 4). It does not necessarily mean to say that they are discussing Parliamentary politics or politics at a macro level. Politics is a difficult concept to determine accurately. Certainly, it relates, in part, to the allocation of a finite amount of resources. Difficult decisions have to be made in terms of how those resources will be shared. In the words of the famous American political scientist, Harold Lasswell, and the title of his seminal text on the topic, it is about *Politics: Who gets What, When, How* (Lasswell 1958). If politicians spend more on defence, correspondingly there will less to spend on other areas, such as education or health. There will be winners and losers and, inevitably, therefore, politicians will be unable to please everyone. A wider definition of politics (cf. Adrian Leftwich's work entitled *What Is Politics?* for differing interpretations of what constitutes politics) might include discussion of power relationships, even, for example, who does the washing up at home might be regarded as a political decision, as it entails the concept of power. It depends, therefore, how the notion of politics is being interpreted. Relatively recently, in the UK, there has been a concerted effort to encourage people to understand the relevance of politics to their lives. A cartoon advert shown in newspapers and then animated on television, using voice-overs from actors Jim Broadbent and Timothy Spall, was first used in the 2004 European Elections and then again in the following year's General Election. Focusing upon the theme of 'If you don't do politics there's not much you do do?', the attempt was primarily to reverse the trend of low electoral turnout by trying to get people to make the connection between politics and their daily lives. The price of a pint, the proliferation of road works, sporting achievement and graffiti were amongst the examples presented as indicative of how decisions made by politicians impact the ordinary people. The powerful advert, spanning only 50 seconds, attempted to remind people of how politics affects them. The implication being that it was imperative to turn out and vote so that one's voice could be heard. This multi-million-pound campaign was indicative of a government fearful of low electoral turnout and the question of legitimacy. Whether it had a specific appeal for young people is debatable but it did at least try to get people to make that causal link between political decision makers and their daily lives. This connection is a crucial one for young people, in particular, to make if they are to become politicised.

The disconnect with politics has been well documented and does not just relate to young people (cf. Stoker 2006; Hay 2007). As Gerry Stoker pointed out more recently, 'Not everyone "hates" politics and not everyone is disengaged from it, but there is undoubtedly substantial anti-political sentiment in British society' (Stoker 2011: 11). He proceeds to cite the Hansard 2011 survey which shows, 'Only one third believe the system of governing Britain works well. Only just over a quarter are satisfied with the working of Parliament, the lowest figure so far recorded in the Hansard surveys. Only one in three of us now agree with the statement "when people like me get involved in politics, they really can change the way that the UK is run"' (Ibid.). The perception is that people are unable to make a difference or, at least, that it is very difficult for them to make a difference. There is also a greater degree of cynicism in evidence than hitherto in relation to how politicians are perceived. Having said this, people are not opposed to democracy. Stoker encapsulates this by saying that citizens 'remain convinced by the benefits of democracy but are unconvinced by the role of politics in delivering that democracy' (Ibid: 22). Clearly, all sectors of society, to varying degrees, appear to be disillusioned and disengaged.

The focus of this study is the extent to which young people are disengaged. In answer to this question of whether or not young people are interested in politics, Ben Kisby, author of several works on citizenship and young people, states, 'In general, I think young people are interested in politics. It is true that forms of disengagement from electoral politics, particularly amongst young people, by which I mean roughly 15 to 25-year-olds, are pronounced in historical terms, such as low levels of turnout in elections, membership of political parties and trust in politicians and political institutions. However, the evidence from the UK and Western Europe suggests that young people are not politically apathetic. They have their own views about political issues and engage in democratic politics through various modes of participation'.[5] Kisby goes on to say, 'In particular, there has been a proliferation of youth participation in a myriad of alternative forms of engagement, such as signing petitions, joining boycotts or participating in demonstrations, and in alternative arenas of engagement, such as the utilisation of social media'. This dimension, that is to say the use of social media, is examined in detail in Chap. 4. Kisby proclaims the fact that young people do appear to be participating in politics in ways which differ from what might be regarded as the norm. Muniglia et al. also denote these varied forms of youth participation, 'Young people's participation takes place on all levels; from the local to the global, from informal settings such as groups, networks and communities, to formal structures such as youth organisations, municipal youth councils, school councils and elections' (2012: 5). This difference in the type of political participation is also recorded by Reingard Spannring, who states, 'academics have interpreted the changes not as a decline but as a *transformation*, a shift in the repertoire of political engagement. The decline in traditional forms of participation seems to be partly counteracted by the expansion of new and 'modern' forms of political and social engagement' (Spannring 2012: 39).

It appears, therefore, that young people are participating politically but that they are participating in ways different from traditional forms of political participation. They may be less inclined to vote and to participate in mainstream politics but they are more willing to engage in less conventional forms of political participation. The aforementioned focus upon single-issue campaigns and taking part in direct action, signing petitions and boycotting products and services is an example of this new type of political engagement and involvement. Couple this with the use that young people make of new social media and it becomes clear that young people are participating but in ways which are less conventional than hitherto. Social networking sites such as *Facebook*™ and micro-blogging sites such as *Twitter*™ provide vehicles for young people to discuss and to organise themselves politically. The arena for political engagement and participations has shifted significantly. This might be seen as the democratisation of political engagement. No longer is politics simply the preserve of an élite group but sites such as these provide a platform for people (and young people in particular) to debate, discuss and organise.

OTHER ISSUES

In addition to unemployment, young people are also adversely affected by other factors. For example, a study by the Campaign for Better Transport claims that young people are particularly disadvantaged by government spending policies in relation to transport. This is especially the case given that the 16–24-year-old age group tends to be more reliant on public transport and less likely to have discounted travel than older people. Cuts, therefore, 'have had a significant impact upon the young … [with many] young people not in employment, education or training … often unable to afford to seek work because of rising transport costs' (Topham 2013: 11). Transportation is a key issue as far as young people are concerned, especially for those living in rural communities who, where they do not have easy access to cheap reliable public transport, may find themselves increasingly isolated and ostracised. As the young people interviewed in Chap. 6 elucidate, transport is one of the key issues regularly championed in various young people's forums. They articulated feelings of being 'trapped' and of being unable to afford the high bus fare (see Chap. 6).[6] Certainly, as James Sloam rightly points out, young people have borne the brunt of the austerity measures in the UK and are likely to be 'the first generation since the Second World War who will be worse off than their parents' (Sloam 2013a: 4).

UNIVERSITY TUITION FEES

One of the key factors that undoubtedly has increased the politicisation levels of young people is the introduction of and then the increase in university tuition fees. It appears that once it was established in principle that students should contribute, at least in part, towards the cost of their higher education, there has been no going back. Tuition fees were first introduced in September 1998, following the recommendations of the Dearing Report. Published in July 1997, the findings of the National Committee of Enquiry into Higher Education, Chaired by Sir Ron Dearing, included the premise that students should contribute towards the cost of their tuition. In September 2006, universities were allowed to charge up to £3000 per annum in variable tuition fees, or top-up fees. Critics believe that, in the same manner as prescription fees have continually risen, once that precedent is set, the upward trajectory is inevitable (prescriptions are, however, free in Scotland, Wales and Northern Ireland). Fees have increased from £3290 per annum to £9000 per annum. This increase took effect from the autumn of 2012 and impacted the cohort who started university at that time. Students now were faced with the prospect of paying £9000 per year for each of the three years of their university degree course. The reality is that many young people would now leave university having incurred a minimum debt of £27,000. For some families, the amount of £9000 as fees per year represents a huge reduction on their school fees and so it is not always viewed as an extra cost; for some (albeit a minority) it is a significantly reduced cost. For many, however, this is regarded as a substantial debt with which to commence one's working life, especially given that these early years in the world of work often coincide with the acquisition of a mortgage and, possibly, the expenses incurred with starting a family. A letter to the *Times Higher Education* sums up the predicament quite succinctly, 'Students have always accepted being broke while they study: being broke for the rest of their lives because they studied is another matter entirely'.[7]

Added to this hike in tuition fees would also be costs relating to living expenses, such as accommodation and subsistence requirements. Students could also obtain a loan towards these expenses, thereby adding to the already substantial debts incurred. This was mitigated, according to advocates of the new fees regime, by the fact that graduates now had to be earning at least £21,000 per annum before they would begin to pay off their loan at a low rate of interest. In addition, any outstanding amount still owing beyond a 30-year period after graduation would automatically be wiped clear. Others stated that, rather than seeing this as a debt, in the same way as a mortgage or a credit card, for example, it is better to view it as a tax, akin to a graduate tax, whereby the money is taken off at source from high earners (or at least those earning £21,000 and above). Certainly, the University Central Admissions System (UCAS) data on university applications and acceptances for the 2012/2013 academic year did reveal a significant decline. It is still early days, however, as to whether the new fees regime will lead to a permanent decline in applications and acceptances. Preliminary data reveals that levels are starting to revert to an upwards trajectory with the value of a university degree, with its potential to lead to a graduate job being uppermost in young people's minds. Allied to this, the prospect of three years to immerse oneself in academia, critical thinking and, not to be underestimated, the lifestyle of an undergraduate, remains an appealing proposition. As Sean Coughlan reveals, it appears that 'the massive underlying demand for higher education has snow-ploughed its way through the financial barrier of trebling fees' (Coughlan 2015). Having said all this, the fees increase was not brought in without opposition. The winter of 2010/11 was dubbed the 'winter of discontent' (the same moniker applied to 78/79 but for different reasons). Students organised a series of protests against the proposed increase in university tuition fees and against the abolition of the Education Maintenance Allowance in further education. These included protests held on 10 November 2010, 24 November, 30 November, 9 December, 19 January 2011 and 29 January 2011. One of these protests, held in November 2010, drew support from 50,000 students, and there was also a violent attack on the Conservative Party offices in Millbank. Alastair Hudson believes the tactic of 'kettling' (derived from the German word for cauldron, '*kessel*' meaning to keep the protestors enclosed in a confined area) used on 9 December 2010, and of which he was a part, 'was an exercise in state violence against teenage sixth-form and university students voicing genuinely held concern about their futures and the futures of others' (Hudson 2011: 33). Clive Bloom draws parallels with earlier protests by school children of the late nineteenth and early twentieth centuries. He contends that such protest is not a new phenomenon. 'Starting in 1889, there were waves of national school strikes ... centred on issues such as corporal punishment, the length of the school day, holidays, the school-leaving age, exploitation of "monitors", unpleasant teachers and bullying headmasters or headmistresses' (Bloom 2011: 37). In the contemporary protests, the Liberal Democrats, in particular, also came in for criticism, especially their then leader, Nick Clegg, as prior to the 2010 General Election, they had pledged to vote against rising tuition fees. As the former leader of the National Union of Students, Liam Burns, stated, 'Nick Clegg won the trust and votes of young people and their parents by signing the pledge, but has now lost them once and for all by breaking it'.[8] The fact that the Liberal Democratic Party lost 49 seats in the 2015 General Election and went down from 57 (in 2010) to eight (in 2015) lends credence to this argument.

Not all young people were in favour of the protests. For example, a 17-year-old member of the Youth Parliament (the UK Youth Parliament comprises around 600 young representatives),[9] representing Sleaford and North Hykeham, urged young people not to participate in the protests as the previous protests had not worked, and 'If anything they were counterproductive, as the hijacking of them gave a horrendous, unfair and unjust misrepresentation of the majority of young people in the UK'. Instead, he urged people to complete an online survey being organised by the British Youth Council[10] as a way of articulating their opposition to the proposed fees increase.

As stated, there were a number of demonstrations, protests and even riots. The Parliamentary vote took place on 9 December. There were around 40 occupations across the country. The protests continued into 2011. Some of those young people who were protesting were against the changes to the Education Maintenance Allowance (EMA). They also took part in the demonstrations, so it was having an impact in sixth-forms too. The EMA, aimed at 16–19-year-olds and based on the parental level of taxable income, was introduced across England in September 2004. A number of pilot schemes (15) were introduced in 1999 and then extended to another 41 areas in 2000. The money, a maximum of £30 per week, depended upon parental income, was paid to the young person directly. They had to be studying for at least 12 hours per week, and bonuses were also given for full attendance and for completion of the course of study. Essentially, it was intended to encourage those from low-income families to remain in further education (see Fletcher 2009). In October 2010, the UK government scrapped it as part of the budgetary cuts, replacing it with a bursary scheme for those on low incomes. Higher education funding changes and tuition fees are seen as a cause of youth politicisation but they are also a 'policy' and need to be examined in that light too. A survey carried out by the polling group Ipsos MORI for the Sutton Trust, an organisation which campaigns for easier access to university for people from disadvantaged backgrounds, found that whilst '86 per cent believe that attending university will help them "get on in life", 65 per cent have significant concerns about the financial implications' (Parr 2013: 8). Students from poorer backgrounds especially seem particularly averse to taking on a huge debt in comparison with those from wealthier backgrounds. The 2014 Student Academic Experience survey, conducted by the Higher Education Policy Institute (Hepi), found that 'a quarter (not an insubstantial amount) believe their degree is a "poor" or "very poor" return on their investment' (Baker 2014: 5). The higher education sector has to constantly convey its message regarding the value of a degree in order to counteract such negativity. Clearly, although over time there may be a sea change in how tuition fees are perceived by young people (with the notion of a tax possibly superseding the focus upon a substantial debt), currently this is not the case, and tuition fees, if not necessarily acting as a barrier to university entry, are certainly making some young people, and especially those from poorer backgrounds, think twice before they commit themselves.

National Citizen Service

One development that is worthy of mention is the introduction of a National Citizen Service in England, under David Cameron's leadership. Essentially, this entails a scheme aimed at encouraging young people, 16- and 17-year-olds, to learn new skills and to volunteer in their communities. It is seen as a non-military form of national service (compulsory national service ended in 1960 in the UK). Part of the plan is that young people will develop skills such as team building and communication skills. Young people, primarily those who had just finished their GCSEs, would attend a two-week residential, outdoor pursuits course, and then they would spend three to four weeks working on local community projects. First announced in 2010, a total of 12 pilot projects were launched in areas such as Cumbria, Devon, Cornwall and Teesside, which were then rolled out to the rest of England during 2011. MPs criticised the costs of the programme when youth services were being cut across the board and other critics[11] failed to see the purpose of the scheme. The anticipation was that up to 10,000 young people would take part in the scheme, which would eventually expand to 30,000 young people in 2012. In the event, more than 30,000 young people did sign up for it in 2012. By 2015, more than 130,000 young people were said to have participated. Upon completion of the scheme, the young people also have the opportunity to participate in a National Citizen Service graduation ceremony to celebrate and recognise their achievements. Despite its critics, the scheme is generally seen as a success, although the government does not plan to make it compulsory. The National Centre for Social Research has carried out an evaluation of the National Citizen Service. It affirms the aims of the initiative as being to build a 'more cohesive, responsible and engaged society'[12] and finds a range of positive impacts in relation to teamwork, communication, leadership and transition to adulthood but a smaller number of positive impacts and less consistency of impact in relation to social mixing and community involvement. The study recommends that more time should be allowed to recruit participants and staff, that there should be great flexibility of programme delivery and that more should be done to raise awareness of the scheme.[13] Andy Mycock and Jonathan Tonge have also assessed the National Citizen Service. They believe that it is 'an important plank of the Conservatives' promotion of the Big Society, but is representative of a broader lack of precision regarding motivations and perceived outcomes' (Mycock and Tonge 2011: 65). They also believe that it 'may need to link volunteering to democratic participation and citizenship more explicitly and connect to the state in addition to local communities' (Ibid.). Clearly, the National Citizen Service still exists, remains voluntary and focuses upon developing the personal and social skills of 16- and 17-year-olds. There is still work to be done, however, if the National Citizen Service is to achieve success on the terms outlined above.

BITE THE BALLOT

One relatively new campaigning organisation that encourages young people to participate in politics is entitled *Bite the Ballot*. Co-founded in 2010 by former teacher Michael Sani, *Bite the Ballot* aims to facilitate higher levels of youth participation in politics. Their quest, just as Rock the Vote did in America, is to encourage young people to have a greater understanding of politics and to register to vote. *Bite the Ballot* seeks to encourage young people to have a greater understanding of what is meant by politics and to comprehend the practicalities of how to register and how to actually cast their vote. As Managing Director Sani maintains, young people often have an interest in specific issues (e.g. transport) but they do not necessarily regard these as political (cf. Mason 2013). Young people need to make the link, therefore, between issues of concern to them and the world of politics. As *Bite the Ballot*'s website illuminates, it 'is a not for profit organisation that empowers young people to speak up and act, to make their votes and opinions count. We inspire young people to be counted and make informed decisions at the ballot box, encouraging them to take power and become the champions that will change the face of British politics. We are not affiliated to any political party—we think they all need to do more for the youth vote' (*Bite the Ballot*, http://bitetheballot.co.uk/). One innovation from *Bite the Ballot* has been the setting up of National Voter Registration Day; the first one took place in 2014. The date 5 February was chosen because this is the date of the 1832 Great Reform Act which introduced voter registration and extended the franchise, albeit to, as Sani points out, rich men. It will be interesting to assess whether this social enterprise, *Bite the Ballot*, can make a real difference to levels of youth political engagement and participation.

One other recent development instigated by *Bite the Ballot* and think-tank Demos, and, in part, financed by the Political Studies Association UK and by a number of universities including Newcastle, Royal Holloway and Lincoln, is the creation of a voter advice application called Verto (an anagram of voter). The App (more particularly a cross-device, cross-browser, mobile Web application) aims to encourage youth participation (the 5.6 million potential young voters) by providing the target demographic (16–24-year-olds) with a number of statements, where they swipe left or right if they agree or disagree with the statements. It then matches their responses with the political parties. The statements are grouped around policy categories such as health, education, crime and justice and the environment (see: http://bitetheballot.co.uk/verto/). Social media, including digital platforms, are potentially one way of re-engaging young people with politics. These are examined further in Chap. 4.

Other initiatives worthy of flagging up include a youth campaign group called MyLifeMySay (http://www.mylifemysay.org.uk), the organisation Democracy Matters (http://www.democracymatters.org.uk), the Politics Project's Clicktivism, (http://www.thepoliticsproject.org.uk), the group '45 for the 45th', the Hansard Society's Your Vote Matters, UK Youth's Youth Count! Democracy Challenge, the Rock Enrol® initiative developed by the Cabinet Office, the Student Room, Backbench—an online platform for young people to write about politics, the British Youth Council's Youth Vote and the Political Studies Association UK's Charter for Active Citizenship, all of which aim to encourage greater youth political participation.

FREE THE CHILDREN

The international campaigning and educational group, *Free the Children*, is another organisation that seeks to 'empower and enable youth to be agents of change' (Free the Children, http://www.freethechildren. com/). This group, started in 1995 by a 12-year-old Canadian boy, seeks to help young people to get involved with both local and global issues. It seeks to free children from poverty and exploitation. *Free the Children* provides resources for schools, a forum for debate and acts as a conduit to enable young people to bring about change on a global scale. Such organisations illustrate that young people are interested in issues and seek to bring about a changed world.

TO LOWER OR NOT TO LOWER...

In relation to this topic of youth political participation, a key issue is whether or not lowering the franchise to enable 16- and 17-year-olds to vote would have an impact upon levels of engagement? As illustrated in Chap. 5, where the focus is upon this vexed question of lowering the voting age, opinion is very much polarised. It does appear, however, that a certain momentum for change is gathering pace, not least because the Scottish referendum, held in September 2014, focused on the debate. The decision by Alex Salmond (Scottish politician who became Scotland's First Minister in 2007) to allow 16- and 17-year-olds to participate in this plebiscite led some to argue that this would eventually result in 16- and 17-year-olds voting in elections to the Westminster Parliament. Many see this as an inevitability and simply a matter of time before this becomes the reality. As noted at the time of writing, this is not going to happen in the referendum on continued European Union membership. When asked specifically about whether the voting age should be lowered to 16, Ben Kisby, interviewed as part of this research process, proceeds to explain his views, 'I think it is right that 16 and 17 year olds will be able to vote in the Scottish independence referendum. I think it is right they have a say in the future direction of the country. I think it is also something that should be seriously looked at for all elections in the United Kingdom and I reject the idea put forward by some that 16 and 17 year olds are necessarily insufficiently mature to reflect on political issues and cast their vote on the basis of these reflections'. He goes on to say that, 'One particular advantage I can see with lowering the voting age to 16 would be that it might force political parties to take young people's concerns more seriously than they do at present'. This point about young people's issues being taken on board by the political parties is examined in detail in Chap. 5. A rational assumption to make is that, if young people are less likely to vote in elections, politicians and policymakers would be better served by focusing their attention upon those sectors of society who are more likely to go out and cast their vote—namely, the older generations. Lowering the voting age is likely to ensure that young people's concerns make it on to the political agenda.

The Riots of August 2011

One area that has been cited as depicting the politicisation of young people is the riots of August 2011. Whilst many people regard what happened in the summer of 2011 as, essentially, wanton violence with little or no connection to political engagement or protest, others see the riots as the manifestation of disillusionment and despair. As Mycock and Tonge state, the riots 'brought the role of young people in society into sharp relief' (2012a: 138, b). There were opposing views as to what caused the riots, from the government's perspective, 'the riots were "pure criminality"'... underpinned by poor parenting, broken families and a lack of discipline in schools' (Ibid.). On the other hand, 'social inequality and rising youth unemployment, the impact of government spending cuts, particularly on youth services, increases in university tuition fees and the removal of the Educational Maintenance Allowance had created a "lost generation" with limited aspirations' (Ibid: 139). Andrew Mycock states that 'suggestions that these are the first post-political riots fail to acknowledge their multiple causes and broader issues concerning the segregation of young people from mainstream society' (Mycock 2011, www.opendemocracy.net). Some did not see the riots as political or even post-political protest; their interpretation was rather that the looting was due to greed and selfishness, and so it was not a political protest as such. Countervailing viewpoints prevail on this point but it remains the case that many of those who rioted, as Mycock and Tonge contend, constituted 'a "disempowered generation" who sought political recognition' (2012a: 139, b). In his polemical piece on the Open Democracy website, Mycock underlines government cuts that have disproportionately impacted the young people and that have 'hit youth services, closing youth clubs, and other support services that have often succeeded in connecting with those young people on the periphery of society' (Mycock 2011, www.opendemocracy.net). In his analysis of the riots, he goes on to say that this 'rapid rolling back of the remit of the state has diluted the link between young citizens and the state, leaving many disoriented and unsure of their place or worth in society'. He is not condoning the riots, rather seeking to explain their genesis; he continues 'Of course, young people and parents need to accept their responsibilities to society and to uphold the law. But there has been a gradual abrogation of the responsibilities of the state towards young people which is rarely acknowledged by politicians' (Ibid.). Research cited in the *Times Higher Education* reveals that most of the rioters were young, male and had previous convictions. As is stated, 'Among those with a record of offending, each individual had committed 14 previous offences on average. Almost 90 per cent of the rioters were male and half were under the age of 21'.[14] Political scientists and analysts need to be wary of dismissing the riots too easily as being purely down to consumerist greed and opportunism. Certainly, there were elements of that but there was also an underlying malaise that ought not to be ignored or even sidelined.

With regards to the riots, Kisby states, 'I think the August 2011 riots are one piece of evidence that supports the idea that significant numbers of young people are socially excluded and alienated, especially in the context of austerity and high unemployment'. Russell Brand, writing in his capacity as guest editor of the *New Statesman*, posits that the London riots of 2011 illustrate that 'young people have been accidently marketed to their whole lives without the economic means to participate in the carnival' (Brand, *Op. cit.* 26). Debate centres on whether the riots were political or not. Were they simply the manifestation of criminal behaviour or were the reasons behind the riots more deep-seated? Analysis differs, but certainly there are those who believe that some sectors of young people in Britain currently feel alienated by mainstream politics and feel that their views, wishes and beliefs are being sidelined, if not ignored. Alexander Hensby articulates how today's youth have been referred to as the 'jilted generation' (cf. Howker and Malik's work for further information), and unlike the baby boomer generation who grew up largely in an era of affluence, today's young people have come of age in an era of austerity. As cited earlier in this chapter, youth unemployment is of paramount concern here. David Lammy's[15] work, *Out of the Ashes*, provides an interesting and detailed analysis of the riots. As Lammy explains, 'The events of August 2011 clarified many of the things I was trying to get at. From the absence of boundaries and role models in children's lives, to the absence of work, dignity and opportunity on many of Britain's estates. From a "my rights" attitude in which people hesitate to think of others, to a consumerist culture driven by materialistic values. From community breakdown and social mistrust, to the pressure on the family in a low-wage economy. From racial polarisation and concerns about immigration to class divisions between those branded "chavs" and the rest' (Lammy 2011: 21). Clearly, the riots were multi-causal and it is hard to disentangle the reasons behind them. Lammy has, however, touched upon some of these reasons.

Another interviewee and leading academic who has written extensively on the topic of youth political engagement is James Sloam. In terms of whether or not 16- and 17-year-olds should be able to vote in the Scottish referendum, Sloam is of the view that,[16] there is 'no reason why 16–17 year olds should not vote. It's not just an issue of increasing youth turnout, it's an issue of extending the franchise. As a matter of principle, I believe it is important that 16–17 year olds have the vote. As the Youth Citizenship Commission suggested, if this is combined with good citizenship education it could actually increase interest in politics. Many teachers instinctively try to avoid discussing electoral politics (for fear of being seen as politically motivated), but if 16–17 year olds were included in the electorate, it would be impossible to avoid talking about electoral politics in schools. If a large number of 16–17 year olds do turn out for the referendum (though it is far from clear that they will), the move towards votes at 16 will become unstoppable'.

As to whether young people are interested in politics, Sloam believes that 'In general, young people are relatively uninterested in electoral politics (compared to older generations and previous generations of young people in the UK)—parties, voting etc.—but are very interested in "politics" (broadly defined) where it has relevance of their everyday lives. In most industrialised democracies, we have witnessed a proliferation of participation into different repertoires of engagement (including petitions, demonstrations, buycotts and boycotts etc.) and into new arenas of engagement (in particular, the internet and new social media). Therefore, in many countries youth participation is vibrant and diverse. However, the UK is in many ways an outlier. Unlike most other West European countries, there does seem to be a generational impact on the current cohort of young people, who are immediately put off by anything that is "tainted" by the word "politics", because our political system is so unrepresentative (in all senses of the word). This does not mean that they don't have strong civic values—indeed, levels of volunteering and charity work are strong. However, "interest" in politics remains strong, as illustrated by the massive expansion of politics/IR in HE in recent years'. The view espoused by Sloam, and articulated most comprehensively, is that young people are definitely interested in politics but we need to clarify exactly what is meant by politics.

When specifically questioned regarding his interpretation of the August 2011 'riots', Sloam proceeds to outline his viewpoint that the 'riots tell us how some young people have become marginalised from politics and by public policy. A significant number of young people feel that they have no political voice in society and are frequently victimised by public policy (e.g. tuition fees and EMA) and vilified by the media (despite crime levels having decreased, binge drinking having decreased, etc.). For better-educated young people (with better prospects) from more privileged backgrounds, this frustration has led to demonstrations (against student fees increases). For young people from less privileged backgrounds it has deepened the sense of social exclusion (I believe about two thirds of people arrested in the riots had special educational needs)[17]—if you feel you have no stake in society (especially in a consumer society) you are more likely to engage in violence, cause chaos, steel "trainers", etc.'.[18] This notion of not having a stake in society is particularly important. If we regard youth as the future, then it is particularly worrying if significant numbers feel that they, and their views, do not count. An alienated youth is a perennial theme with potentially disastrous consequences.

One only has to think of the cinematic portrayal of alienated youth such as of Marlon Brando in *The Wild One* in the early 1950s or James Dean also in the 1950s, or moving forward, films such as *Quadrophenia* (1979), *Trainspotting* (1996) and *The Inbetweeners* (2011) to see how this is a recurring theme. Perhaps this is a natural stage in life as one realises that one's lot in society may be less than one would otherwise wish. Angry young men, and it is has usually been males who are portrayed in this way, have attracted cinema-goers over the preceding few decades. Art has imitated real life in terms of how young people often feel this sense of alienation, isolation and a sense that the world does not understand them. Bill Osgerby expounds an interesting analysis of the media portrayal of young people, whereby the alienated youth is flagged up and where some might see young people in a negative light, possibly as posing a threat. On the contrary, there is also the notion of young people as 'fun', as representing hope and optimism (Osgerby in Briggs 2002: 371). Likewise, Russell Dalton's edited text *Engaging Youth in Politics: Debating Democracy's Future*, in part, examines this vexed question of whether youth are the problem or whether they are the solution (Dalton 2011: 15).

It is debatable as to whether young people have a lack of trust, apathy and no interest in politics as some might claim. Clearly, this is a generalisation but through researching young people and politics, it can be seen that many young people are extremely interested in politics—especially in the light of the increase in higher education tuition fees and youth unemployment levels. Many young people perceive that government policy is directly targeting their concerns and is likely to directly impact their future life chances.

One question worthy of contemplation is how low is too low? In relation to levels of turnout in elections, at what point does the lack of political participation by young people become a major issue—is there a point at which low levels of political participation endangers the democratic system? Virginie Muniglia et al. point out that the 'crisis of trust and confidence towards traditional forms of representation (as shown both by the growth of abstention but also by the change or even the disengagement from the classical forms of associative and union mobilisation), the growth of individualisation, the building of more varied and uncertain biographical trajectories, and the appearance of an unsettled and weakened sense of belonging to the national and local communities, are factors that encourage public authorities to rally specifically round the young generations' (Muniglia et al. 2012: 1). Clearly, the nature of political participation is changing, and possibly nowhere more so as in the case of young people. A case can be made that a certain level of apathy is a positive aspect. This is the idea, espoused by some, that a degree of apathy may imply that people are generally happy with their 'lot' in society. The idea being that if they were not happy or at least satisfied then they would be galvanised into action.

THE ARAB SPRING

The Arab Spring focused attention upon youth political participation on the world stage. Young people were at the forefront of this wave of protest and political action. Starting in Tunisia, on 17 December 2010, a street trader, Mohamed Bouazizi, set himself on fire in protest at how he had been treated by the police (they stopped him from selling fruit and vegetables without the requisite permits). This eventually triggered a wave of demonstrations that became known as the Arab Spring, taking place in early 2011. As David Matthews theorises, Bouazizi's death 'helped to inspire revolts across the region that deposed long-standing autocracies in Tunisia, Egypt, Yemen and Libya' (Matthews 2012: 39). Regime change in Tunisia took place the following January when the then President, Zine El Abidine Ben Ali, went into exile. These events were followed by a wave of protest, culminating in political and social changes across numerous Arab nations, including Egypt. What is interesting is the way that young people were at the forefront of these protest movements. In addition, what was also noteworthy is the way in which social networking sites such as *Facebook*™ and *Twitter*™, coupled with mobile phone technology, were utilised to convey the message to the wider world in a way that, given the absence of such technology, had not happened before. This instantaneous access to information enabled the sea of change to be conveyed to the wider world as it was happening. The immediacy of the new technology undoubtedly facilitated the speed of change.

Part of the Arab Spring legacy can be seen in European movements too. Mary Kaldor and Sabine Selchow have written about the 'bubbling up' of subterranean politics in Europe. They say this can be seen 'in the success of non-mainstream political parties from across the political spectrum—the Pirate Party in Germany and Sweden, Jobbik in Hungary, the True Finns in Finland, the 5 Star Movement in Italy, or Respect in Bradford, England' (Kaldor and Selchow 2013: 79). They say that this is 'causing ripples of discomfort in established institutions, challenging dominant ways of thinking and unsettling normal assumptions about how politics is done' (Ibid.). They advise a degree of caution, however, given that some of these movements contain 'xenophobic and populist movements as well as more emancipatory tendencies' (Ibid.). The Arab Spring, therefore, led to change in certain Arab nations but also indirectly contributed to change in European countries—change that, in large part, was orchestrated by young people.

Alternative Ways of Participating

As the Arab Spring, cited above, clearly showed, young people use a variety of methods of political participation, including petitions, *Facebook*, *Twitter* feeds and social networking sites. Alex Hensby, the researcher mentioned earlier, calls it, 'A smörgasbord of different participatory opportunities',[19] the general point being that of the 'students' range of participatory repertoires—petitions, demos, blogging, etc.'.[20] Examination, therefore, of the 'problem' of youth political participation leads to a questioning of whether there is indeed a problem. Is it simply that young people are participating in different ways, ways other than participating in mainstream politics? The concept of participation is examined in detail in Chap. 2. Differing theories of political participation are postulated to illustrate the contested nature of the concept. An assessment has to be made, for example, of when participation is 'real' participation. Could it be perhaps, as is often claimed, that certain participation is not genuine participation if those involved are being paid mere lip-service or given a metaphorical pat on the head? Does it count as participation if nothing ever happens or changes as a result of one's involvement?

STRUCTURE OF THE BOOK

This book is divided into eight chapters. After this, the introductory chapter, which looks at the concept of youth and extrapolates why young people and political participation has become a topic worthy of political enquiry, attention turns to Chap. 2 examining theories of political participation. The focus of Chap. 2 is upon political participation *per se*. The theoretical underpinnings in relation to political participation are examined in this chapter. What do we mean by political participation? How have political scientists and political philosophers attempted to define participation? Is there a difference between participation where one's aims are achieved and the participation through which benefits are gained which means that it does not necessarily matter if the goals are not attained? The Liberal politician and philosopher, John Stuart Mill, made reference to the benefits of participation beyond simply attaining one's specific aims; as will be explored in Chap. 2, this fits in with the Ancient Greeks and their notion of the 'good life'. Reference is also made to theoretical perspectives such as, Sherry Arnstein's 'Ladder of Participation', whereby there are gradations of participation, the higher-level rungs on the ladder involving greater degrees of participation than others. Lester Milbrath's seminal text (1965) on political participation and Geraint Parry, George Moyser and Neil Day's work are explored here. In addition, other works cited include Robert Putnam's *Bowling Alone* and work by Pippa Norris, amongst others. In this chapter, comparisons are also made with the wider society. The chapter analyses differing levels of political participation between different generations.

The focus of Chap. 3 is upon young people, and political participation on a pan-European basis is examined here. Utilising quantitative data gleaned from a variety of sources, this chapter provides a quantitative analysis of political participation levels in all 28 countries of the European Union. Comparisons are made between different types of political participation and also between differing levels of governance. It is interesting to investigate whether, for example, young people in Denmark are more willing to participate in politics than, say, the youth of Portugal. If so, why should this be the case? Why does the youth of one particular nation appear to be more galvanised and politically active than, say, the young people of another nation? Questions such as the proportion of young people being of the opinion that it is a citizen's duty to vote and whether this has altered over time are investigated, alongside other pertinent questions about young people and political participation/non-participation. Answers are sought to questions such as these.

The emphasis upon pan-European participation is followed by examination of new social media and its impact upon youth political participation in Chap. 4. This chapter examines new media and political participation and focuses upon political participation levels amongst young people, primarily in the UK, but using a comparative approach, where appropriate. Again, political participation is examined at differing levels of governance and, in addition, differing types of participation are compared. The usage of new technology, in particular Web 2.0 technology (such as, social networking sites like *Facebook*™, *Bebo*™ and *MySpace*™, and the use of microblogging sites such as *Twitter*™), is examined in order to ascertain the extent to which these new approaches facilitate and encourage greater political participation amongst young people.

Investigation turns, in Chap. 5, to the topical issue of whether or not the voting age should be lowered to 16. This chapter involves a detailed analysis of the key arguments for and against lowering the voting age to 16. The focus is upon a case study of Austria where the voting age was lowered to 16 (the first country out of the 28 members of the European Union to do so for national elections). In addition, detailed investigation is made of the situation closer to home in Jersey, Guernsey and the Isle of Man where the voting age has been lowered to 16. There is a vocal campaign in the UK to lower the voting age to 16 (cf. the *Votes at 16* Coalition), but many oppose this, and both sides of the discussion are subject to in-depth analysis in this chapter. Two more examples from mainland Europe are incorporated into the study. These are Germany and Bosnia. The reason this chapter investigates these two countries is that, firstly, with respect to Germany, it constitutes an interesting case study because there 16-year-olds can vote in some municipal elections in some states. Bosnia is chosen as the second country because there 16-year-olds can vote if they are employed. Chapter 5 investigates the way in which various bodies support lowering the voting age to 16. Equal consideration is given to the arguments espoused by those opposed to the idea of lowering the voting age. Analysis is provided as to why the majority of young people have not expressed support for this idea. Opinion tends to be polarised on this topic, and this is what makes it such an interesting issue and worthy of detailed examination. It is not intended that the book becomes a vehicle for arguing in favour of lowering the voting age but, rather, that it illuminates the key arguments across the board.

Youth political participation at the local level is the subject of Chap. 6. Comparative data will be used here but, in addition, a useful addendum to this chapter is a case study of Lincolnshire Youth Cabinet. On the basis of the qualitative methodology, namely in-depth interviews, the latter part of this chapter utilises a study of the members of Lincolnshire Youth Cabinet. In particular, Chap. 6 outlines why these young people participate in politics to a much greater extent than their peers. The chapter assesses the types of policy areas upon which young politicos prefer to focus. Investigation is also made of their motivations and whether the reality meets their original expectations. Assessment is also made of the career pathways that these young people hope to pursue in the future and the extent to which 'politics' features in their future career plans.

In Chap. 7, attention turns to the question of gender and youth political participation. Using focus groups, Chap. 7 examines the differing levels of political participation of young men and women. What accounts for this difference? Are young men more politically aware than young women? Do levels of political participation vary between the two groups? Young women have traditionally been the sector of the electorate least likely to cast their vote, and yet, if specific policy areas are investigated, there are many aspects that ought to be of primary concern to women. Child care provision, the increase in cases of sexually transmitted diseases, issues in relation to women in the workplace, such as the gender pay gap, are examples which ought to galvanise women to cast their vote. To reiterate, this chapter focuses upon gender differences in relation to political participation and non-participation. Some academics are not enamoured by focus groups but they do have a place in the research process. Authors such as David Morgan (*Focus Groups as Qualitative Research* (1997), *The Focus Group Guidebook* (1998)), Michael Bloor et al. (*Groups in Social Research* (2001)) and Pranee Liamputtong (Focus Group Methodology) would certainly testify to their value. The focus group material is used to supplement the quantitative data.

Chapter 8, the concluding chapter, draws all the key findings of the book together and summarises the lessons that have been learnt. This final chapter summarises the key findings of the investigation into young people and levels of political participation. It analyses the outcomes from this comprehensive investigation into young people and political participation. What can our politicians, policymakers and political scientists glean from this study? Should the voting age be lowered to 16 in line with other countries? Does participation at local level and at a younger age, such as via youth cabinet and youth parliament participation, lead to a long-term interest and involvement in politics? Can measures be taken in order to encourage more young women, in particular, to participate in the political process? In terms of policy transfer, are there lessons to be gleaned from other European countries in relation to young people and political participation?

CONCLUSION

As stated throughout this first chapter, youth political participation, for a plethora of reasons, is a topical issue and of key concern to politicians, policymakers, journalists and academics alike. If youth is the future, as given the cycle of life it inevitably must be, then their engagement or otherwise with politics and political issues is a topic that cannot, and must not, be ignored. A variety of issues including the national citizen service, youth unemployment and the increase in tuition fees has placed youth political participation clearly on to the political agenda. Allied to this, there is the ongoing question of whether or not the voting age should be lowered to 16 and 17 years. From the protests against the increase in tuition fees, to the Arab Spring of early 2011 and to the riots of August 2011, young people have been involved in protests on a worldwide scale and in relation to a myriad of differing issues. The extent to which this is overtly political protest remains the subject of debate. It does appear, however, that it is becoming increasingly difficult to label young people as apathetic.

Andrew Mycock exposes how governments often seek to 'expand avenues of engagement without addressing issues of youth empowerment', as he continues, '[the government] must also develop youth citizenship to ensure young people who feel disempowered and isolated from politics and society are valued and given a voice. We cannot fail the next generation' (Mycock 2011, www.opendemocracy.net). As will be investigated in subsequent chapters, they may not vote in mainstream elections in significant numbers or necessarily be interested in party politics or politics with a large 'P', but that does not mean to say that they are uninterested in politics with a small 'p'. It can be seen, therefore, that the focus upon young people and politics will remain of significant interest to many, and rightly so!

NOTES

1. The House of Lords Report Stage of the European Union Referendum Bill 2015–2016 took place on 18 November 2015. The Lords voted (293 to 211) to introduce an amendment to lower the voting age to 16 in the referendum. This was blocked by the Commons in early December 2015 (303 to 253 votes), in part based on perceived cost implications. On 14 December 2015, the Lords voted, by 263 votes to 246, to reject an amendment that challenged government figures on the cost of registering 16- and 17-year-olds, thereby leading to passage of the Bill.
2. *Source: The Independent*, 1 June 2013.
3. Eurostat, 29 April 2016.
4. Unpublished PhD manuscript, Alex Hensby, Edinburgh University, p.4.
5. Interview with author, 26 March 2013.
6. See the Connecting Young People in Lincolnshire website for details about issues of concern to young people www.c4yp.co.uk
7. Flett, K. (2010). If always broke, fix it. *Times Higher Education*, 25 November, p. 33.
8. See www.bbc.co.uk/news, 21 November 2012, accessed the same day.
9. See http://www.ukyouthparliament.org.uk/about/ for further details.
10. *Lincolnshire Echo*. (2011). Warning to stay away from protest. Tuesday, 18 January, p. 7.

11. For example, Dr Andy Mycock at the University of Huddersfield, see www.bbc.co.uk/news, 20 June 2011, accessed 5 July 2011.
12. See NatCen http://www.natcen.ac.uk/study/national-citizen-service-evaluation/our-findings-, accessed 2 June 2013.
13. Ibid.
14. *Times Higher Education*, 16 August 2012.
15. Lammy, D. (2011). *Out of the ashes: Britain after the riots*. London: Guardian Books.
16. Interview with author, 12 April 2013.
17. See Newburn (2012: 332).
18. Interview with author, 12 April 2013.
19. Presentation at the Political Studies Association UK Annual Conference, Cardiff, 27 March 2013.
20. Email correspondence with author, 3 June 2013.

BIBLIOGRAPHY

Baker, S. (2014). Don't let fees billy boil over. *Times Higher Education*, 22 May, p. 5.

Bloom, C. (2011). When the kids are united. *Times Higher Education*, 20 January, pp. 37–38.

Bloor, M., Frankland, J., Thomas, M., & Robson, K. (2001). *Focus groups in social research*. London: Sage.

Bolton, P. (2012). *Education: Historical statistics*. London: House of Commons Library. Retrieved May 29, 2013, from http://www.parliament.uk/briefing-papers/sn04252

Brand, R. (2013). We no longer have the luxury of tradition. *New Statesman*, 25–31 October, pp. 25–29.

Coughlan, S. (2015). Did £9,000 fees cut applications? *BBC News*, 14 January. Retrieved July 24, 2015, from http://www.bbc.co.uk/news/education-30684462

Dalton, R. (Ed.) (2011). *Engaging youth in politics: Debating democracy's future*. New York: International Debate Education Association.

Delebarre, J. (2015, September 16). *Youth unemployment statistics*. Briefing Paper 05871. House of Commons Library, London. Published 16 September. Retrieved September 27, 2015, from http://researchbriefings.parliament.uk/ResearchBriefing/Summary/SN05871#fullreport

Eulau, H. (1963). *The behavioral persuasion in politics*. New York: Random House.

Eulau, H. (1966). *Political behavior in America: New directions*. New York: Random House.

Fletcher, M. (2009). *Should we end the EMA?* Reading: Centre for British Teachers Education Trust.

Harris, A., Wyn, J., & Younes, S. (2010, February). Beyond apathetic or activist youth: 'Ordinary' young people and contemporary forms of participation. *Young, 18*(1), 9–32.

Hartley, M., & Huddleston, T. (2010). *School-community-university partnerships: Education for democratic citizenship in Europe and the United States of America.* Strasbourg: Council of Europe Publishing.

Hay, C. (2007). *Why we hate politics.* Cambridge: Polity Press.

Hensby, A. (2013). Seeking empowerment, making a difference?—Exploring participation and non-participation trends in the 2010/11 student protests against fees and cuts. Paper presented at the *Political Studies Association Annual International Conference*, City Hall, Cardiff, 25–27 March.

Higher Education Statistics Agency. (2015). First degree qualifiers by sex, mode of study and class of first degree. Retrieved September 30, 2015, from https://www.hesa.ac.uk/sfr210 table 12

Hudson, A. (2011). Defeated by violence and silence. *Times Higher Education*, 20 January, pp. 33–35.

Kaldor, M., & Selchow, S. (2013). The 'Bubbling up' of subterranean politics in Europe. *Journal of Civil Society, 9*(1), 78–99.

Lammy, D. (2011). *Out of the ashes: Britain after the riots.* London: Guardian Books.

Lasswell, H. (1958). *Politics: Who gets what, when, how.* New York: Meridian Books. First published 1936.

Lynch, R. (2013). Eurozone crisis: One in four youths is jobless. *The Independent*, 1 June.

Mason, R. (2013). Apathetic and disaffected: The generation who may never vote. *The Guardian*, 26 December. Retrieved January 14, 2014, from http://www.theguardian.com/politics/2013/dec/26/apathetic-disaffected-generation-may-never-vote

Matthews, D. (2012). Jobs for the boys. *Times Higher Education*, 26 April, pp. 39–41.

Milbrath, L. W. (1965). *Political participation: How and why do people get involved in politics?* Chicago: Rand McNally.

Morgan, D. L. (1997). *Focus groups as qualitative research* (2nd ed.). London: Sage.

Morgan, D. L., & Krueger, R. A. (Eds.) (1998). *The focus group guidebook.* London: Sage.

Morris, N. (2014b). Hereditary political affiliations now only a thing of the past. *i-newspaper*, 5 February, p. 5.

Muniglia, V., Cuconato, M., Loncle, P., & Walther, A. (2012). The analysis of youth participation in contemporary literature: A European perspective. In

P. Loncle, M. Cuconato, V. Muniglia, & A. Walther (Eds.), *Youth participation in Europe: Beyond discourses, practices and realities* (pp. 1–17). Bristol: The Policy Press.

Mycock, A. (2011). Riots in England: We must stay calm and plan for the future. *Open Democracy,* 10 August. Retrieved May 31, 2013, from www.opendemocracy.net/print/60806

Mycock, A., & Tonge, J. (2011, January–March). A big idea for the big society? The advent of national citizen service. *The Political Quarterly, 82*(1), 56–66.

Mycock, A., & Tonge, J. (2012a). The party politics of youth citizenship and democratic engagement. *Parliamentary Affairs, 65,* 138–161.

Mycock, A., & Tonge, J. (2012b). Alex Salmond's Bannock's bairns. *Open Democracy,* 20 February. Retrieved November 20, 2012, from http://opendemocracy.net

Newburn, T. (2012, July). Counterblast: Young people and the August 2011 riots. *The Howard Journal of Criminal Justice, 51*(3), 331–335.

Parr, C. (2013). Youth unsure of university cost-benefit analysis. *Times Higher Education,* 30 May, p. 8.

Savage, J. (2014). Time up for the teenager? *RSA Journal,* Issue 1, 16–19.

Simmons, R., Thompson, R., Tabrizi, G., & Nartey, A. (2014). *Engaging young people not in education, employment or training: The case for a youth resolution.* London: University and College Union.

Spannring, R. (2012). Participation and individualisation: The emergence of a new (political) consciousness? In P. Loncle, M. Cuconato, V. Muniglia, & A. Walther (Eds.), *Youth participation in Europe: Beyond discourses, practices and realities* (pp. 39–56). Bristol: The Policy Press.

Stoker, G. (2006). *Why politics matters: Making democracy work.* Basingstoke: Palgrave Macmillan.

Stoker, G. (2011). *Building a new politics?* London: The British Academy.

Topham, G. (2013). Young hit harder by bus cuts, say campaigners. *The Guardian,* 29 May, p. 11.

CHAPTER 2

Political Participation

The focus of Chap. 2 is upon the concept of political participation. The theoretical underpinnings in relation to political participation are examined in this chapter. What do we mean by political participation? How have political scientists and political philosophers attempted to define participation? Is there a difference between participation where one's aims are achieved and the participation through which benefits are gained which means that it does not necessarily matter if the goals are not attained?? John Stuart Mill, as mentioned in Chap. 1, made reference to the benefits of participation over and above merely achieving one's policy goals. As stated, this accords with the Ancient Greeks and their concept of the 'good life'. Reference is also made to theoretical perspectives such as, Sherry Arnstein's 'Ladder of Participation', whereby there are gradations of participation, the higher-level rungs on the ladder involving greater degrees of participation than others. Lester Milbrath's (1965) text on political participation and Geraint Parry, George Moyser and Neil Day's work are highlighted here. In addition, other works cited include Robert Putnam's *Bowling Alone* and work by Pippa Norris, amongst others. In this chapter, comparisons are also made with the wider society. Examination is made of differing levels of political participation between the different generations.

Sections of this chapter appeared in Briggs, J. E. (1998). *Strikes in politicisation.* Aldershot: Ashgate.

© The Author(s) 2017
J. Briggs, *Young People and Political Participation,*
DOI 10.1057/978-1-137-31385-0_2

WHAT IS POLITICS?

Before focusing explicitly upon the concept of political participation, it is necessary to take a step backwards and begin by briefly outlining what is meant by politics. It is fair to say that there exists both a narrow and a broad definition of politics (cf. Adrian Leftwich's *What Is Politics?* 2004, for a detailed summary). The narrow definition of politics refers to activity with respect to the state, to 'Politics and institutions', as Schwarzmantel states, 'politics deals with relations of power and that it is fundamentally concerned with one central political institution, the state' (1987: 2). The second definition refers to politics and conflict, and this relates more to political awareness as it is a much broader definition. Under this second definition, wherever a person has a dispute or conflict then politics comes into play, over the allocation of scarce resources, over whether, for example, more money should be spent upon defence or upon welfare. There may also be moral and religious disagreements, for example, over the issue of abortion. Disagreements may take place between groups in society, such as social class, race and gender divisions. Politics, therefore, involves disagreements and reconciliation of disagreements. The conflict which takes place may be about goals or it may concern methods of achieving those goals.

Under this second, much wider, definition, politics can be seen as encompassing all human activities. As Crick and Crick state, 'The activity of politics arises from the basic human problem of diversity' (1987: 6). Madgwick highlights the 'necessity of political activity: we simply cannot manage without it. Politics is about society's conflicts and disagreements, and it is hardly imaginable that these should not exist' (1984: 15). Using this broader definition, the personal becomes political. This includes, therefore, sexual politics, for example, the sexual division of labour. Millett, in her text, *Sexual Politics*, illuminates this much broader definition when she speaks of politics as being about power relationships, sexual 'power relationships' (1977: 24).

Millett sheds further light upon this debate when she asks the question, 'Can the relationship between the sexes be viewed in a political light at all?' (Ibid: 23). She continues, 'The answer depends on how one defines politics' (Ibid.). Millett 'does not define the political as that relatively narrow and exclusive world of meetings, chairmen and parties. The term "politics" shall refer to power-structured relationships, arrangements whereby one group of persons is controlled by another' (Ibid.). Obviously, Millett feels that it is pertinent to focus upon the broad definition of politics. Likewise, Siltanen and Stanworth argue that 'the private woman-public man conception misleads as to the relationship of the political to both private and public, and that it fosters misunderstanding of the character and genesis of the political potential of both women and men' (1984: 195). They continue, 'The private world—the world of personal relations and marriage, of friendships and family, of domestic routine and child-care—is, as feminists have persuasively demonstrated time and again, political as well as personal' (Ibid: 196).

Another political scientist who has emphasised this broader definition of politics is the aforementioned Schwarzmantel. He states that, 'Politics exists in any context where there is a structure of power and struggle for power in an attempt to gain or maintain leadership positions. In this sense one can speak about the politics of trade unions or about 'university politics'. One can discuss 'sexual politics', meaning the domination of men over women or the attempt to alter this relation. At the present time there is much controversy about race politics with reference to the power, or lack of it, of people of different colour or race in various countries' (*Op. Cit*: 2). This goes far beyond his earlier account of politics relating to 'state' activity.

The narrow definition of politics could be referred to as party politics or politics with a capital 'P', whereas the broader definition expands 'politics' to include activities on a number of different levels. Sexual politics and worker/employer relations, as illustrated, can be included within this definition. It is evident that many more young people are likely to be seen as having been politicised if the broader category is used than if the focus is purely upon those who entered the party political arena. In addition, it can be argued that the first definition excludes significant sectors of the population, for example, as this research shows in Chap. 7, women. It is worth stating that the gender dimension became very important to this research about young people. That is to say, at the outset it was appreciated that gender was likely to be a factor, but exactly *how* important was a surprising revelation.

POLITICAL PARTICIPATION

Political participation is one of those concepts with which political philosophers and political scientists have grappled for centuries. There are degrees of participation and it is sometimes difficult to determine exactly what is meant by participation. Paul Whiteley captures the importance of political participation as he says it is 'at the heart of democratic government and civil society, and without it there can be no effective democracy' (2012: 34). As Coxall, Robins and Leach say, political participation is 'citizen involvement in politics through for example, voting or pressure group and party activity aimed at influencing government and public policy' (2006: 54). For Ruedin (2007: 3), participation in politics is 'understood as an individual activity, albeit carried out in a specific context, and whilst interacting with others'. That specific context is identified by Ruedin as being the political institutions, and includes electoral rules and 'political activity in general' (2007: 3). In addition, as Booth says, with reference to America, but it does have wider applicability, 'political participation tends to be somewhat concentrated; individuals who perform the most difficult and time-consuming acts also often perform most of the easier ones' (1979: 38). He goes on to highlight how participation is unevenly distributed with 'many people taking part at fairly low levels, and far fewer engaging in large numbers of activities' (1979: 40). This is reflective of Milbrath's seminal work published in 1965 which describes a hierarchy of political participation, with a small group of the real activists at the top, a much larger section of those who do little more than vote in the middle and the relatively inactive at the bottom. People at the bottom tend to avoid reading or talking about politics; they included 34 per cent of non-voters in the 2015 General Election and a higher proportion of certain sectors of society, such as 18–24-year-olds (Milbrath 1965: 16–22). Much of the generic literature on political participation focuses upon the concept across society as a whole. It is true, however, that this literature and theoretical perspectives can be directly applicable to young people too. Indeed, analysis of youth political participation provides an interesting spotlight on many of the more generic issues.

One of the key theoretical concerns when focusing upon young people and politics is, of course, political participation. It is worthwhile clarifying at this particular stage that participation is not solely concerned with participation in *party* politics. It is broader than that; it is not simply concerned with formal aspects of politics such as voting, campaigning at election time or joining a political party. It includes, therefore, activities such as involvement in pressure groups, going on protest marches and demonstrations or joining support networks and informal groups, often based around a single issue with like-minded people. As Qvortrup states, 'Protest politics includes a number of activities of differing legality and legitimacy: demonstrations, physical obstruction, consumer boycotts, civil disobedience, petitions, riots and acts of terrorism' (2007: 59).

Numerous political scientists and political sociologists in particular have examined the intriguing question of why some people participate in politics whereas others do not. Rush (1992) has identified a number of pertinent issues which are crucial to this debate. He highlights the fact that there are problems involved in trying to define political activity and also that there are problems in trying to explain *why* individuals get involved in politics. He emphasises that there are a number of factors which influence whether or not individuals get involved in politics. These include knowledge, values, attitudes, experience and personality.

Political participation is linked to the notion of democracy. The extent to which citizens participate in the political process is the major indicator of the extent to which democracy prevails. The two 'types' of democracy are direct and indirect (or representative democracy). Direct democracy flourished mainly in Ancient Greece, though even in Athens women and slaves could not vote! With respect to direct democracy, however, Parry et al. believe that new technology has the potential to allow 'a "voting machine" to be installed in every home', a futuristic occurrence they term 'this brave new democratic world' (1992: 4)—not so futuristic nowadays when consideration is given to the all-pervading nature of the World Wide Web and ownership levels of personal computers. This aside, the usual form of participation constitutes indirect democracy given that, for the mass of the populace, involvement often terminates after they have cast their vote in periodic elections (if indeed they choose to do this) (cf. Moodie 1971; Rose 1989, for further detail regarding low levels of political participation). Low levels of participation were highlighted by Gabriel Almond and Sidney Verba as far back as the early 1960s (1963). In their comparative study of five nations, they discovered that a substantial majority of Britons were not even passive members of a political grouping and, although they published more than 50 years ago, many of their findings appear to be still applicable given that they flagged up the general lack of participation.

Other pertinent issues surrounding political participation include discussion of the purpose of participation. Why should anyone want to participate? One theory states that people participate in order to protect their own interests, be that property or other resources. This is borne out by the increase (if instances cited in the media are indicative) in the numbers of the so-called NIMBY's, the 'Not In My Backyard' brigade, who campaign and participate only when it is an issue which directly concerns them.

Examination of the population as a whole reveals that even though levels of participation are low, recent decades have witnessed some degree of increase. Another potential explanation of increased levels of participation, and central to the theme of this text, is the growth of youth culture (Beer 1982). The emergence and expanding numbers of teenagers, fuelled in the 1960s by the 'coming of age' of the baby boomers, led to substantial numbers of young people who, motivated by a social and political conscience, protested and participated in political activity against or in support of a wide range of issues. These included campaigns against the Vietnam War, protests over nuclear armament and marches to draw attention to the issue of sexual equality. The 1960s, in particular, constituted an era when there was a feeling in the air that ordinary citizens could change the *status quo* and tackle the establishment. The emergent pop culture was also part of this phenomenon. As Jon Savage articulates, 'In the 1960s, the first wave of a truly international British pop culture coexisted with and informed a sequence of liberal legislation, including increased rights for gay men, and women in terms of abortion and divorce. This pop culture had been informed by the increased opportunities afforded by the 1944 Education Act' (Savage 2014: 18). Certainly, increasing numbers of students entering higher education played a part in this phenomenon. It is necessary to consider whether a youth culture is, as the name implies, a transient stage to be attributed to the folly of youth perhaps, something which a person 'grows out of', or whether it lasts into middle and later life. What has happened to the 1960s radicals? Are young people at present just as willing to participate and get involved in political activity? Certainly, the youth culture thesis has much to offer and appears, in part at least, to explain increasing levels of participation.

It has been argued that a great deal of participatory activity tends to be reactive in that pressure groups, for example, are often formed to oppose some aspect of government activity (such as opposition to the location of the then proposed third London airport) rather than striving to obtain something which they do not already possess. Parry et al. believe that under indirect or representative democracy, the citizens are '"controllers" rather than "participants"' (*Op. Cit*: 5). Although perhaps even this is debatable given the extensive room for manoeuvre that many political actors have once in office and the difficulties, some would say impossibility, involved in attempting to remove an incumbent politician from elected office. Is it the case that participants always get what they want and that any decisions taken are 'better' decisions? It might seem reasonable to claim that the more people that are consulted before a particular decision is taken by those in positions of power, the greater the likelihood that the course of action chosen will be a true reflection of the 'wishes of the people'. A further issue revolves around whether or not the participants are simply articulate minorities and, therefore, unrepresentative of the population at large. Surely, too, one cannot be sure that the 'most worthy' causes will have the most articulate advocates.

It is worthwhile contemplating whether there are more intrinsic values attached to participation. What about self-fulfilment or some kind of internal satisfaction? Again, Parry et al. have alluded to this aspect. They highlight the 'self-development or political education' (Ibid: 432) which may derive from participation. This is where participation is regarded as more than simply a means to an end (with the end being 'better' decisions emerging). It is regarded as an end in itself. Using this interpretation, it does not matter so much if a person does not achieve his or her goals as, merely by having participated, an individual will benefit. Higgins and Richardson cite John Stuart Mill's 'preference for being a human being dissatisfied rather than a pig satisfied' (1976: 9). Surely, however, this point about the self-fulfilling, life-enhancing nature of participation depends upon how society regards participation as a *value*? It is necessary for participation, in itself, to be held in high esteem.

Carole Pateman's work on the politicising role of participative democracy is worthy of mention at this particular juncture (1970). Pateman's study constitutes a critique of revisionism. She believes that the revisionists have turned democratic theory on its head and that the revisionists' view of democracy is really an élite rule. Pateman puts forward a convincing case for the retention of a participatory theory of democracy and tries to bring together two themes; these themes are a sense of personal efficacy which draws upon the work of Rousseau, John Stuart Mill and G.D.H. Cole and also an emphasis upon workplace democracy. Together these constitute her theory of participatory democracy. It is worthwhile to have an in-depth look at Pateman's work in order to shed further light upon the process of politicisation.

Pateman is critical of contemporary theory. As she states, 'in the contemporary theory of democracy it is the participation of the minority elite that is crucial and the non-participation of the apathetic, ordinary man lacking in the feeling of political efficacy, that is regarded as the main bulwark against instability' (Ibid: 104). Pateman believes that this is a misconception and that real benefits are to be gained through having a fully participatory society. She is of the opinion that 'the evidence supports the arguments of Rousseau, Mill and Cole that we do learn to participate by participating and that feelings of political efficacy are more likely to be developed in a participatory environment' (Ibid: 105). She is keen to emphasise the links between democratic participation and individual characteristics, 'the experience of participation itself will develop and foster the "democratic" personality, i.e. qualities needed for the successful operation of the democratic system' (Ibid: 64). She believes that there are psychological traits which can be cultivated through having a participatory society. She explains that 'socialisation, or "social training", for democracy must take place in other spheres in order that the necessary individual attitudes and psychological qualities can be developed. This development takes place through the process of participation itself. The major function of participation in the theory of participatory democracy is therefore an educative one, educative in the very widest sense, including both the psychological aspect and the gaining of practice in democratic skills and procedures' (Ibid: 42). Pateman dismisses the notion that a participatory society would lead to a loss of political stability, 'there is no special problem about the stability of a participatory system; it is self-sustaining through the educative impact of the participatory process. Participation develops and fosters the very qualities necessary for it; the more individuals participate the better able they become to do so. Subsidiary hypotheses about participation are that it has an integrative effect and that it aids the acceptance of collective decisions' (Ibid: 42–43).

Pateman employs a wide definition of the term 'political' and thus does not confine her theory to the national or local government spheres. She regards industry as a most important area in which participation should be increased and where benefits will accrue. She believes that greater participation in industry is crucial. Building upon Cole's work regarding self-government in the workshop and his emphasis upon guild socialism, Pateman's belief is that 'individuals and their institutions cannot be considered in isolation from one another' (Ibid: 42). Participation in areas such as industry, higher education and local government would, according to Pateman, 'enable the individual better to appreciate the connection between the public and private spheres' (Ibid: 110). Pateman thus puts forward a powerful critique of the revisionists' arguments and offers her thesis relating to the participatory theory of democracy and the benefits to be gained through a participatory society. The main justification for her theory 'rests primarily on the human results that accrue from the participatory process' (Ibid: 43). As she says, 'One might characterise the participatory model as one where maximum input (participation) is required and where output includes not just policies (decisions) but also the development of the social and political capacities of each individual, so that there is "feedback" from output to input' (Ibid.).

Having presented Pateman's case and highlighted the positive aspects of participation, it is worthwhile considering the arguments against greater political participation. It is beneficial to look at why it might not be regarded as a good idea. One argument could be that democracy can, to a certain extent, be a painful process. That is to say that the more the 'people' are consulted, the longer it takes. Also greater consultation is likely to mean increased costs. In addition, it might be argued that a relatively acquiescent population leads to greater political stability. Surely, too, it is necessary to distinguish between participation and influence? What is the point of participation if nothing is achieved? In terms of the policy-making process, perhaps it is also important *when* participation takes place. That is to say it might be easier to effect change at certain stages in the procedure rather than at others, for example, at policy germination stage rather than at policy implementation stage (cf. Forman 1985; Dorey 2005 for further details on the policy-making process). Another, possibly negative, aspect is the difference of opinion of those in positions of power compared with the population at large. An oft-cited example concerns capital punishment, where opinion polls have consistently indicated that public opinion favours its reintroduction, whereas MPs continue to vote against it. Does it matter that élite opinion appears to be 'out of sync' with the views of those they are elected to serve? One possible scenario is that greater political participation will lead to the articulation of extremist views (cf. Rummens and Abts for detailed discussion of political extremism).

Voting, standing for office, trade union activity, membership of a political party, attendance at party meetings, school governorships and activism in general are all, more or less, relatively easy to measure, as Parry, Moyser and Day clearly show. Apart from more overtly ascertainable aspects like, for example, voting in a general election, Parry et al. believe that what they term the 'less episodic forms of participation' (*Op. Cit.* 3), such as complaining to the council, can also be assessed. Part of the debate surrounding political participation entails contemplating what makes people interested in politics and, consequently, why are some people more interested in politics than others. Coxall and Robins highlight the fact that there are a number of factors which predispose some people to be more interested in politics than others. As they state, 'The most influential agencies are the family, education, peer groups, the mass media and important political events or experiences'. They go on to say that 'every individual stands in the middle of a network of social influences' (1989: 31). Obviously, as Coxall and Robins suggest, there are a whole host of influences which affect people's political views and their political behaviour, but this research expounds the view that certain 'political events and experiences' can have an important influence upon the propensity to participate politically. There are a number of examples of historical 'events' which may have had a positive or negative influence upon political opinions and behaviour, such as the Second World War, the 1978/9 'Winter of Discontent', the 'Falklands Factor' (the surge in support for the Conservatives after the defeat of the Argentinean invasion of the Falkland Islands in April 1982), the community charge or poll tax (the widely unpopular local tax brought in by the Conservatives in 1989 in Scotland and 1990 in England and Wales), the Iraq War and the introduction and subsequent raising of higher education tuition fees. In terms of specific manifestations of participation, for example, attendance at party political meetings, this is factually ascertainable but it does not reveal anything about the state of mind of that particular activist. It does not convey, for example, the reasoning behind the attendance. The participants may have ulterior motives for attending political meetings. By way of example, it is often said that many members of the Conservative Party join the organisation in order to enhance their social life as opposed to being deeply committed to the goals and aspirations of the Party. The coffee mornings and jumble sales may provide the so-called blue-rinse brigade with more of an incentive for activism than any exposé of the basic tenets of conservatism could ever hope to achieve.

APATHY: SHOULD WE EMBRACE IT?

A further debate concerns whether or not apathy is, in fact, a political act. The distinction between positive and negative abstention is clearly important here. If the focus is purely upon voting behaviour, then positive abstention is, for example, where all the alternatives are examined and the voter does not like what is on offer so he or she makes a conscious decision not to bother to vote. Negative abstention includes the voter simply not being bothered to vote or being deterred by the fact that it rains on polling day. Michael Rush has examined this notion of lack of political involvement. He states that 'Non-involvement in politics has been variously ascribed to apathy, cynicism, alienation and anomie'. He proceeds to further distinguish between these categories, 'apathy is a lack of interest, cynicism is an attitude of distaste and disenchantment, while alienation and anomie both involve a feeling of estrangement or divorce from society, but where alienation is characterised by hostility, anomie is characterised by bewilderment' (Rush 1992: 126–127). It could be suggested that a certain degree of apathy is an essential ingredient of any realistic theory of democracy. The former Tory Cabinet Minister Sir Ian Gilmour was quoted as saying that 'Political apathy is to some extent rather a good sign. It means that people aren't all that worried; they are reasonably contented' (Browne 1986: 4). Apathy may indeed indicate contentment (Eulau 1963, 1966), and when the situation deteriorates, or if people feel they can make a difference, they vote. There were echoes of this approach when Margaret Beckett, a Minister in the Blair Government, talked of the 'politics of contentment' to explain voters not turning out to vote. This point is explored in greater depth later in this chapter. There is also debate as to whether or not people are actually apathetic. The Power Inquiry, an independent inquiry into political participation (cf. White 2006), found that 'Contrary to much of the public debate around political disengagement, the British public are not apathetic. There is now a great deal of research evidence to show that very large numbers of citizens are engaged in community and charity work outside of politics. There is also clear evidence that involvement in pressure politics—such as signing petitions, supporting consumer boycotts, joining campaign groups—has been growing significantly for many years. In addition, research shows that interest in "political issues" is high. The area of decline is in formal politics' (Power Inquiry 2006: 2). It is evident, therefore, that people may not necessarily be participating in terms of party politics but in a myriad of other ways.

It is pertinent to examine different types of political participation. Again, youth political participation often provides a focal point. Psephological inquiry is relevant at this point. Voting could be described as the minimum form of political participation but, for most people, it is also the maximum. Figures relating to electoral turnout provide interesting, possibly dismal, reading. Paul Whiteley highlights key reasons that have been postulated to explain why voting has declined, the first of these, 'is derived from sociological theories and argues that changes in society have detached citizens

from the political process. The second derives from the cognitive engagement model and suggests that individuals have lost interest in the political
process and in elections. The third relates to the general incentives model
and argues that citizens face declining incentives to get involved in politics
and to vote, and this has reduced their rates of participation' (*Op. Cit*:
47). The decline in youth turnout illustrates these differing perspectives.
In addition to the debate as to why voting has declined, questions such
as why, in the past, has the working class tended to vote Labour and what
accounts for working class Conservatism are also relevant to the debate
surrounding the concept of political participation. The study of voting
behaviour constitutes a fascinating area of political science. Political scientists differ, however, in terms of their explanations as to why people vote
the way they do. There are many different theories and models about voting behaviour. Some studies concentrate upon the social backgrounds of
individual electors, others concentrate upon party identification (attach-
ment to a specific political party) and the third most oft-cited model
stems from rational choice theory (cf. Sanders 1991, for detailed analysis
of the main theories underpinning voting behaviour). These models and
their intrinsic components change over time, for example, religion is less
important nowadays as a determinant than it perhaps was at one stage.
Psephology can never be an exact science, especially considering the secret
ballot but, nevertheless, we can make a number of assumptions regarding
the factors which influence the way that people vote. Despite class dealignment (cf. Butler and Stokes 1974), social class was traditionally held by
many political scientists to be a major, if not the major, factor which influenced the way people voted. The impact of class has certainly declined
since Peter Pulzer's now infamous claim that 'Class is the basis of British
party politics: all else is embellishment and detail' (Pulzer 1975), but the
importance of social class as a determining factor should not be totally
sidelined (cf. Heath et al. 1985). It is generally held that there are both
objective and subjective factors which can be utilised in order to pigeon-
hole electors into specific social classes. Objective factors include the socio-
economic characteristics such as occupation and wealth, and the subjective
aspect is the way that the voter regards himself or herself. There may be
contradictions here too, for example, objectively, a voter might be termed
working class but, subjectively, he or she may think that he or she is middle
class and vote accordingly. This was used, in part, to explain working class
Conservatism—although deference has, in the past, also been proposed
as a theory to explain why a certain proportion of the working class votes

Conservative, that is, they regard the Conservatives as the 'natural party of government', the born leaders. It is worth noting that there is a contradiction only if it is expected that people who are 'objectively' working class will behave politically in a certain way, that is, to vote Labour. There is clearly evidence that deference has declined in importance (cf. Butler and Stokes 1974; Denver and Hands 1992: 64–65; Denver et al. 2012) and that 'secular' or pragmatic explanations have become more important. Another explanation, therefore, proposes that members of the working class vote Conservative for secular reasons, that is, on the basis of specific policies, they are attracted to the Conservative Party. The sale of council houses, which the Conservatives first offered to the electorate in 1979 and which was enacted under the 1980 Housing Act, is claimed to be a case in point. It is worth emphasising that without substantial working class support, the Conservatives would never have won a general election (Cocker 1986: 65). Middle-class Labourism is partly explained with reference to working class origins, sticking to their 'roots' and by the fact that these deviants tend to work in what are deemed to be caring professions, such as health workers or teachers (Coxall and Robins 1989: 269).

Apart from social class, other factors have been postulated in an attempt to explain voting behaviour. These factors include, for example, age, gender, ethnicity, region, trade union membership and family (Ibid: 264–282). These cleavages are said to have an effect upon the way people vote. It is unnecessary to go into a great deal of detail regarding the various aspects, but it is worthwhile noting that psephologists differ as to how much weight they attach to these criteria. The 1980s and 1990s, in particular, witnessed a great deal of partisan dealignment. That is to say, there was a weakening of voters' loyalty to specific parties and a subsequent increase in electoral volatility. Nowadays, voters are more willing to change the way that they vote rather than to provide consistent support for a political party irrespective of the particular policies which that party embodies. There is also evidence that secular voting is on the increase. Voters are voting for parties which they feel will best serve their interests. It is generally held that electors 'shop around' more. There is also the view that sectoral cleavages are more important than class alignment—the public/private sector cleavage being one. The theory behind this notion of consumption cleavages is that the voters' choice is influenced by their pattern of consumption. The basic premise is that those who use private health care are more likely to vote Conservative and those who, for example, use state schools are more likely to vote Labour. Dunleavy and Husbands emphasised sectoral cleavages as an influence upon voting behaviour; they noted that the post-war period witnessed 'the increasing importance of sectoral cleavages' (1985: 24) and that this had a marked effect upon voting behaviour.

The analysis of voting behaviour may, superficially, appear to be an easy task. One can point to the existence of quantifiable data, statistics and so forth. As evidenced above, however, psephological inquiry constitutes a very contentious area of investigation, and political scientists differ as to the importance they attach to the various explanations. Indeed, the truth may be akin to the insight offered by Sanders that 'Many activists, on both sides of the party political divide have long been convinced of what they regard as a simple truth of electoral politics: that the incumbent government stands an extremely good chance of getting re-elected if enough people believe that "I'm alright, Jack"' (1991: 6). The rise in the electoral fortunes of the UK Independence Party (UKIP) also points to changing habits of revoting behaviour. It will be interesting to see whether these changes, evidenced in the 2013 and 2014 local election results, and the 2014 European election results, constitute a protest vote or whether they signify a more significant switch in voting habits. At the 2015 General Election, UKIP did not live up to electoral expectations (attaining 12.6 per cent of the vote and only one MP), but it remains a relatively powerful voice in British politics. Thus, it can be seen that discussion of theories of party choice is relevant to a central debate about political participation. It helps to explain and understand the rationale behind how and why people participate as they do in mainstream politics.

Other forms of political participation include pressure group activity (cf. Wyn Grant's extensive body of work on pressure groups for further details) and a wide variety of campaigns which involve collective action. The extent of involvement varies, as Dowse and Hughes state, 'people participate in politics in many different ways, with different degrees of emotional involvement and at different levels of the system' (1972: 289). Nevertheless, involvement in pressure groups is, relatively speaking, a major way in which people participate in politics. Trade union activity, as an example of protective pressure groups, provides opportunities for involvement but, setting aside sporadic strike action, levels of participation, on a day-to-day basis, are usually low.

There is a growing body of literature which specifically relates this to changes which have occurred in women in terms of levels of political participation. Tolleson-Rinehart, in her text on *Gender Consciousness and Politics*, recalls that she has 'spoken not merely of political participation but of political *engagement*[her italics]to indicate the spectrum of politi-cization, from internal feelings of confidence and interest, the connection to the political system and the commitment to acquire political informa-tion, to the performance of actual participatory acts' (1992: 128). This continuum is relevant to the discussion in this chapter. Female political participation underwent an increase effectively from 1997 when we saw a doubling of the number of female MPs (up from 60 in 1992 to 120 in 1997, including 101 Labour female MPs). In part, this was due to the strategy of employing all-women shortlists, prior to being subject to a legal challenge in the 1996 case of Jepson and Dyas-Elliott versus the Labour Party. Female political participation, both in terms of standing for election and voting, has been the subject of a great deal of investigation (cf. Bochel and Briggs 2000; Briggs 2008) and is examined in more detail in Chap. 7.

It is fascinating to ascertain why some people participate in politics and others do not. They have to see the benefits of participation, that is, to see they can make a difference or a difference will be made to them through having participated. It is the case that those who hold strong or extrem-ist views are said to have a greater propensity to participate politically. Those holding more moderate views tend to be less likely to participate. In addition, there is a school of thought that regards a certain amount of apathy or lack of participation as a positive factor, indicating that people are perhaps relatively happy with their 'lot' in life. Both John Prescott and, as mentioned previously, Margaret Beckett, the former Labour Deputy Prime Minister and the former Labour Minister/Labour's Campaign Coordinator, respectively, for example, referred to the 'politics of con-tentment' when describing previous Labour supporters not turning up at the polls (1999 local elections). Labour feared that an 'armchair revolt' would impact their chances of electoral success and the argument was that people were generally happy and, therefore, were not galvanised enough to actually go out and vote! Cynics dismissed this theory as blinkered and failing to recognise that Labour's core supporters were turning away from them. On the contrary, in addition to recognising the benefits accrued through political participation, there is a case to be made that some people participate from a sense of civic duty. Many women, for example, voted and were mindful of the actions of the suffragettes in helping to secure the vote for women. The vote, therefore, in this situation is regarded as hav-ing been won after a lengthy and bitter struggle. The central issue here is to remember those who fought for the vote. It seems to be the case that this sense of civic duty is in decline. It is rare these days to see people walking to vote and sporting a rosette in their party colours, proudly going to exercise their civic duty, voting for 'their' party no matter what. Almond and Verba, in their study of five political systems (1963), found that the UK was highly participatory. As they say, the 'participant role is highly developed. Exposure to politics, interest, involvement and a sense of competence are relatively high' (1963: 455). It does appear, however, that the extent of this participatory culture has changed over the past 50 years. Levels of trust with regards to politicians and government have declined significantly, not least due to the MPs' expenses scandal that erupted in 2009. Partisan dealignment has taken place and people's loyalty to one particular political party or another is no longer as strong as it used to be. Voters are more willing to switch and move their support from one particular political party to another. As Denver states, 'The dominance of the two major parties has been much reduced and the bases on which voters support them have altered. The clear class and partisan alignments that existed in the 1950s have given way to a dealigned electorate: electoral stability has been replaced by volatility, national uniformity by variability and habitual voting by a more judgemental approach' (Denver 1997: 142; also cf. Denver 2007: 72–93). The introduction of compulsory voting, as occurs, for example, in Belgium and in Australia, has also been mooted (see Chap. 5 for more detail) as a way of forcing people to fulfil their civic duty. At the moment, however, participation via voting is voluntary.

There are many ways and varying degrees of participating politically. Political participation is an activity that a majority of the population undertake but, for most, their level of participation remains minimal, usually at the level of voting. For a significant sector of society too, they do not even do that. Turnout levels at local, European and general elections have proved a cause for concern. Although turnout at the UK general election in 2015 increased slightly (see Table 2.1) to 66.1 per cent (up slightly on the 2010 General Election's figure of 65.1 per cent), it is still a

Table 2.1   Electoral turnout in UK general elections

- 1992–77.7 per cent
- 1997–71.5 per cent, lowest since 1935
- 2001–59.4 per cent, lowest since 1918
- 2005–61.3 per cent
- 2010–65.1 per cent
- 2015–66.1 per cent

cause for concern to political scientists, psephologists and politicians alike. Essentially, this means that 33.9 per cent of the electorate, for whatever reason, did not vote in 2015. As well as those voting, there is a small minority of people who are labelled the activists. These are people who are committed to participating politically. These may or may not vote; indeed, some may feel that activism is a more productive way of achieving one's aims and may feel that voting does not necessarily help in the quest to bring about change. Such activities may include demonstrations and marches, boycotts and, more recently, 'buycotts' whereby ethical goods and services are encouraged (cf. Young 2010: 1081), writing to one's MP or local councillor, gaining publicity for their 'cause' via the media and, in the more extreme cases, resorting to direct action, and possibly, even violence.

Studies of political participation have often focused upon voting behaviour but, as well as conventional means of political participation, it does also include more unconventional means, such as, direct action, protest and even violence. One of the questions to address when examining political participation is at what point does real participation occur and when is it merely lip-service that is being paid as opposed to genuinely taking on board what someone is saying or doing? Can we make a case for the life-enhancing value of participation *per se*? This is to say, is there an intrinsic value in political participation even if one's aims are not achieved? Does this equate with what the Greeks labelled the 'good life'? To reiterate John Stuart Mill's famous observation, 'It is better to be a human being dissatisfied, than a pig satisfied; better to be Socrates dissatisfied than a fool satisfied' (Mill 1863, cited in Acton 1972: 9). Are participation and representation necessarily incompatible? Do direct action and participation lead to the speedy formulation and alteration of policy, that is, do people make a difference? How important is it for our representative bodies and legislatures to be a microcosm of society at large, to be a mirror image of the social composition of the nation as a whole? Is there more direct action nowadays than perhaps there was previously? Is it possible, practicable or feasible to create a system of direct, as opposed to indirect or representative, democracy? Currently, the system that operates is one of indirect or representative democracy whereby we vote for parties and candidates to act on our behalf. In mass industrialised countries, indirect democracy appears to be the more feasible option. Having said this, technological advancements may mean that the population at large is able to vote on a wide range of issues and we witness a shift to a more direct form of democracy.

History of Participation

Certainly, over the past four or five decades, we have witnessed increasing levels of political participation from the population at large. The growth and development of new social movements is testimony to this phenomenon. Indeed, there is an expanding literature in this field that charts this development (cf. Dalton and Keuchler; della Porta and Diani; Jenkins and Klandermans; Dobson; and Garner). From the setting up of the Campaign for Nuclear Disarmament in 1958, through to other groups such as the Child Poverty Action Group, set up in 1965 or the campaign against homelessness, Shelter, set up in 1966, we have witnessed the growth and proliferation of new social movements. Many such groups and movements of social protest emerged in the late 1950s and 1960s. Why should this be the case? Many reasons have been postulated as to why this came about at this particular time. Studies point to such phenomena as declining deferential attitudes and an increase in people being more willing to resort to protest and political participation in order to try and achieve their goals. It used to be the case that people in the UK were extremely deferential to those in positions of power and authority. Indeed, it was said that in some communities, for example, the local doctor was usually a God-like figure because he held the knowledge. It was usually a 'he' too being a given that the majority of doctors were male. Gradually, from the late 1950s, people began to be more questioning of those in positions of power rather than simply accepting, unchallenged, the views of those at the higher echelons. As mentioned earlier, deference is one of the theories used to explain working class Conservatism in that a proportion of the working classes, roughly 30 per cent, traditionally voted Conservative and, for many of these, the rationale behind this apparent 'deviant' behaviour was that they deferred to the Conservatives as being the natural party of government, the born leaders in society. Again, this is a phenomenon that started to change from the late 1950s.

From the 1950s and 1960s then, people become more questioning of those who hold power. Alongside this, there is also the growth and development of the concept of a teenager or 'youth' in general. Prior to this era, it was very much held that a person was either an adult or a child. The notion of an 'in-between' stage did not really exist. What happens during this time in question is that there is a definite period, the pre-adult stage, that is labelled a teenager. This is a stage in one's life when free time and disposable income are clearly discernible. Abrams (1961), for example, has undertaken research that shows how young people in the late 1950s/ early 1960s had significantly greater amounts of spare cash (more than double the spending power in 1959 than they had possessed in 1939), and thereby purchasing power, than previously. Real wages had increased, and full employment was in place. Young people could now spend this money as they pleased—quite often in a frivolous manner, on products such as records, fashion and cosmetics. Companies and entrepreneurs were starting to realise the importance of this sector of society. Abrams' research is said to have 'contributed to an extraordinary flowering of youth culture: the music, fashion and attitude that brought London, and Britain, to the attention of the world from the 1960s through to the 1990s' (Savage 2014: 18). These young people had time and they had cash. As Jon Savage attests, 'Abrams observed the first effects of the postwar boom. By mid-1958, there were more than 6.4 million people aged between 15 and 25 in Britain. In this period, unemployment was low and the young could command good wages' (Savage 2014: 16). Savage elucidates further, 'This change that Abrams described was already occurring, but he gave it a name, a focus and a price. In doing so, he also ratified the definition of youth that had arisen 15 years before, when the word "teenage" passed into general currency within the US' (Ibid.). This all contributed to the creation of a separate and quite distinctive youth culture. No longer were young people regarded as 'mini-adults'. They were very different indeed. They had their own 'styles' in terms of fashion, music, films and literature. Films aimed primarily at young people received mass audiences and rave reviews (cf. *The Wild One* 1953; *Rebel Without a Cause* 1955; *Rock Around the Clock* 1956; *Jailhouse Rock* 1957; *Look Back in Anger* 1958; *Saturday Night and Sunday Morning* (1960); *A Taste of Honey* 1961—coincidentally, based on a play written by the then 18-year-old Shelagh Delaney; *The Young Ones* 1961; *A Kind of Loving* 1962; *Summer Holiday* 1963; *A Hard Day's Night* 1964; *To Sir, with Love* 1967; *Easy Rider* 1969). The difference was, for these 'teenpics' and grittier so-called kitchen-sink films, so great that some of this was unfathomable, almost an alien culture, to the adult world. Witness, for example, the furore surrounding Elvis when he first burst on to the cultural scene, in the mid-1950s, with his swivelling hips and gyrating pelvis (cf: People's Century DVD). Alongside these cultural phenomena, there was the growth and development of the expansion of the higher education sector. More and more young people were delaying entry into the world of work and going on to study further. The effect of this was twofold; on the one hand, they had time to participate politically, time that they would not have had had they proceeded immediately into the world of work after finishing full-time education; on the other hand, they were 'expanding their minds', becoming susceptible to new ideas and ways of thinking critically. Again, this contributed to a more critical population, challenging the accepted order and traditional ways of operating.

The world was changing rapidly during this period too. The development of the atomic bomb meant that Armageddon was, for many, not just fiction but now a distinct reality—the examples of Nagasaki and Hiroshima sharply demonstrated the horrors of this total warfare. This led to people protesting and participating politically as a way of stemming the march towards mutually assured destruction during the Cold War era. The setting up of the aforementioned Campaign for Nuclear Disarmament was one way to try to halt this development.

Societal changes were occurring in other ways; the rise of feminism, for example, led to a number of unprecedented developments. The growth of the women's liberation movement and the impact of major (and some might say life changing) works, such as *The Feminine Mystique* (1963) by the American liberal feminist Betty Friedan and *The Female Eunuch* (1970) by the Australian academic and feminist writer Germaine Greer, made women (and some men) question how they lived their lives. Alongside this, the scientific advances that led to the development and mass availability of the contraceptive pill meant that, for the first time in history, women could properly control their own fertility levels and decide whether and how many children they would have. Other changes, such as the increase in the number of divorces and the rise in the number of women in the workplace, impacted the kind of society that emerged from the era of change and upheaval of the 1950s and 1960s.

In addition to all the points made above, another key if not central reason postulated for the emergence and development of new social movements is the so-called post-affluence thesis. Predominantly associated with the work of the American academic, Ronald Inglehart (1977a, b), the argument here is that as people became better off financially, they could turn their attention away from basic economic survival and then they might be interested in animal rights or environmentalism. The converse is also argued as being true, that is to say if, for example, an individual is worrying about where their next meal is coming from, they are hardly likely to display much concern for the plight of a rare species of bat or other endangered creature. The 1950s and 1960s are generally regarded as an era when people's living standards rose. Full employment, rising wages in real terms, meant more disposable income. People had access to more consumer durables and labour-saving devices that freed them up from the drudgery of some of the worst aspects of work and household chores. The wider availability of these new inventions and the relative ease of access via higher purchase payments meant that people had more spare time, more money and were able to turn their attention away from basic economic survival and thereby take an interest in these issues of wider, possibly, more altruistic concerns. Whilst not forgotten, the dire living conditions and circumstances endured by many during the economic downturn and great depression of the 1930s, and the harsh reality of the Second World War, were confined to the annals of history. Again, this served to contribute to feelings of optimism and empowerment that many say they felt in the 1950s and 1960s.

In political terms, this era is also important in terms of it being dubbed the age of consensus and the age of affluence. The era, roughly speaking, from 1945 to 1970, is often regarded as the era of consensus. In diagrammatic terms, the two major political parties, Labour and Conservative, were travelling along a parallel path. There was general agreement about 'how to' do things, if not on 'what to' do, and they agreed to the 'rules of the game'. There was broad policy agreement, and yet disagreement on the specifics. After the success of wartime planning, the post-war recovery and with the ascendancy of Keynesianism, they agreed, for example, on the parliamentary system of government, on the mixed economy, welfare state, full employment and a key role for the state. As Adelman states, 'This "consensus" approach involved the maintenance of the Welfare State, the pursuit of the goal of full employment, state management of the economy and a foreign policy based on a close relationship with the United States both in and outside NATO' (Adelman 1991: 124). This is not to say, however, that there was no disagreement. Some issues did become so-called political footballs, kicked from one side to the other, steel nationalisation being a case in point. Indeed, some observers felt that the extent of the consensus had been exaggerated (see Pimlott 1988), possibly that we look at the past through rose-tinted spectacles and that there always seems more consensus in the past than was the reality. Nonetheless, there was a remarkable degree of similarity and agreement between the two majors parties during the 1950s and 1960s, so much so that the term

'Butskellism' was coined,[1] a conjunction of the surnames of the Labour and Conservative Chancellors of the Exchequer, Hugh Gaitskell and R.A. Butler (see Pearce and Stewart 1992: 467). This word graphically illustrated the similarities between the two major political parties. These similarities and synergy undoubtedly contributed to a period of stability. In addition, the 13 years of continuous Conservative Government, between 1951 and 1964, has been labelled the 'age of affluence'. The Conservatives increased their majority over Labour from 17 in 1951, to 67 in 1955 and to 107 in 1959. Identity cards were abolished in February 1952 and rationing finally came to an end in 1954. There was talk of a new Elizabethan era, with the young Queen Elizabeth II ascending to the throne in February 1952. The subsequent Coronation in June 1953, the conquest of Everest by Edmund Hillary in 1953 and the running of the four-minute mile by a Briton, Roger Bannister, in 1954 were all said to have contributed to the buoyant mood of the nation, a mood of optimism and renewal. As mentioned earlier, this was a time when living standards rose considerably, and two key quotes that are often used to depict the era are Harold Macmillan's comments that 'We are all middle class now' and you've 'never had it so good', highlighting the fact that, poverty still existed but generally people were better fed, had better housing and were better educated than they had ever been before.

It is within this political framework that we witnessed the growth and development of new social movements; this is one manifestation of this more questioning and less deferential society that emerged at the end of the 1950s and during the 1960s. New social movements are identifiable by a number of key characteristics (cf. Scott 1990)—they are located in the civil as opposed to the political sphere of life. They tend to stand apart from mainstream politics and from politicians and political parties. The focus, therefore, is upon people power and notions of power and direction emanating from the grass-roots upwards. They tend to be non-hierarchical and shy away from traditional concepts of leadership; groups will, therefore, either not have a leader or will have a rotating chair or a perceived sharing of power. The green movement, for example, has traditionally been keen to avoid placing too much emphasis upon a leader or figurehead. New social movements are also concerned with lifestyles and values. Rather than simply being engaged in a seemingly never-ending quest to acquire more money and material goods, new social movements wanted to transcend this and look for a deeper meaning of life. There is resonance here with the political emphasis shown by former President

Sarkozy and also by Prime Minister Cameron of the UK, whereby they believe that the happiness quotient should also be examined when looking at the wealth of a nation, and this is not simply measurable by GDP but that there might be other 'feel-good' factors that contribute significantly to a nation's health and well-being (cf. Helliwell et al. 2012, for further information about world happiness levels). On an individual level, money does not necessarily equate with happiness and perhaps this is also applicable to the nation-state. In addition, given that new social movements are concerned with lifestyles and values, is participation an end in itself, if it culminates in those participating questioning their beliefs and priorities? An example to illustrate this focus upon lifestyles and values is the women's movement whose mantra the 'personal is political' quite clearly evokes this emphasis upon consciousness-raising and a focus upon lifestyles and values and the fact that perhaps it 'doesn't have to be this way'. It does appear that, as mentioned earlier, there is a growing literature on new social movements, but there is a comparative lack of research that assesses the impact of new social movement activity. Bearing this in mind, is participation futile if groups fail to achieve their objectives? This ties in with earlier points about the merit of participation as a value in itself, or whether this loses its attraction if goals are not met. Byrne believes that it is difficult to accurately define new social movements, as he puts it, 'Social movements, then, are amorphous entities which resist neat classification' (Byrne 1997: 11). Accepting this difficulty, Garnett and Lynch define new social movements as follows: firstly, having a diverse membership, cutting across old class boundaries; secondly, having broad ideological objectives as opposed to focusing upon specific issues; thirdly, wanting to win publicity via the media as opposed to lobbying in Parliament and fourthly, building up coalitions of interests rather than having a settled hierarchy or formal membership (2009: 16).

New social movements do provide a vehicle for people to participate politically and especially for those who might be disillusioned with mainstream politics. The animal rights, the gay rights, the peace, the environmental, women's liberation and student movements are all classic examples of new social movements. They have adapted and changed over recent years, and we have also witnessed the growth of, as some see it, countermovements. For example, the Fuel Protest Movement that emerged in the autumn of 2000 is regarded by some as being in direct opposition to the gains won by the environmental movement with motorists believing that they are losing out. Similar arguments are also applied to Fathers for

Justice group *vis-à-vis* the women's liberation movements and to the Pro-Hunting and Blood Sports groups in relation to the animal rights movement (cf. Garnett and Lynch 2009: 518). As groups make gains, those opposed to their ideas and beliefs struggle and fight to air their views too.

LADDER OF PARTICIPATION

Sherry Arnstein devised a ladder of participation. The eight rungs on the ladder represent degrees of participation. The higher up the ladder, the greater the extent of the real participation that takes place. In ascending order, the rungs are manipulation, therapy, informing, consultation, placation, partnership, delegated power and citizen control. The bottom two rungs are essentially non-participation, the middle three rungs represent a degree of tokenism and the top three rungs constitute a degree of citizen power. Essentially, Arnstein's ladder illustrates that not all participation is the same. There may be occasions when we feel we are participating, but perhaps others are simply paying lip-service to what we say or that the participation itself constitutes some sort of therapeutic exercise. We may feel better through having had some involvement but have we made a difference? Has anyone taken any real notice of us? Do our endeavours count for anything?

Arnstein's ladder was taken on board by Hart (1992) and adapted to apply specifically to children and young people's participation. Clearly then, this notion of a ladder or 'degrees/differing levels of participation' is an extremely useful tool of analysis. As Hart puts it, 'there should be gradually increasing opportunities for children to participate in any aspiring democracy, and particularly in those nations already convinced that they are democratic' (Hart 1992: 4). Although he does proceed to say that, 'Regrettably, while children's and youths' participation does occur in different degrees around the world, it is often exploitative or frivolous' (Ibid). Hart defines participation as 'the process of sharing decisions which affect one's life and the life of the community in which one lives' (Hart 1992: 5). He also sees it as 'the fundamental right of citizenship' (Ibid). Borrowing from Arnstein's ladder, Hart's ladder (1992: 8) also has eight rungs, but this time the categories are, in ascending order: manipulation; decoration; tokenism; assigned but informed; consulted and informed; adult-initiated, shared decisions with children; child-initiated and directed; child-initiated, shared decisions with adults. The bottom three rungs constitute non-participation, whereas the top five rungs represent varying degrees of participation. Again, as with Arnstein's diagrammatic representation, the higher up the ladder one ascends, the greater degree of independence and control. Hart writes that many in society are fearful of a loss of control that they perceive goes alongside greater participation from certain groups, such as children and young people. For Hart, 'Productive collaboration between young and old should be the core of any democratic society wishing to improve itself, while providing continuity between the past, present, and the future' (Hart 1992: 37). So, the notion coming from Hart is that children's participation should be genuine participation and not simply for the sake decoration or tokenism. He appreciates the fears of some of the reversion to a state of nature depicted in William Golding's *Lord of the Flies* (1962) and flags up the continued role of the adult in this participatory process. (See also Davis et al. 2014: 11 on 'meaningful participation'.)

NEW TECHNOLOGY AND POLITICAL PARTICIPATION

As stated earlier, in large industrialised states, indirect or representative democracy is the most viable option. It is simply not feasible or practical to have everyone voting on every issue. Having said this, given technological advancements in computer, mobile and related technology, it is increasingly likely that more people will find it easier to participate in politics. Already, we witnessed the former Coalition Government's usage of e-petitions as a way of consulting the population at large. These online petitions require at least 100,000 signatures before they are considered and even then there are additional 'filters' and gate-keepers who determine whether or not the topic will gain Parliamentary time and be debated. Nonetheless, it is a step in the direction of greater political participation from the masses at large. As reported in the *Guardian*, 'there have been debates on an in/out EU referendum, prisoner voting rights, drugs policy, circus animals, fisheries policies, fuel prices, ending benefits for London rioters, disclosure of Cabinet Office minutes covering the Hillsborough football stadium disaster, and on contaminated blood' (Wintour 2011). E-petitions might be a step in the direction of actual voting on issues but how much clout will be given to the people's voice? Traditionally, there has been a mismatch between so-called élite opinion and ordinary opinion, to reiterate the example mentioned earlier, and between votes and opinion poll surveys with regards to the reintroduction of capital punishment. Élite opinion and public opinion are consistently out of alignment.

Is it the case, therefore, that élite opinion may act as a potential 'brake' upon possible extremist views? Should we be wary of the potential dangers of submitting too many issues and questions to the public vote?

Online polling is used by many groups and organisations, from television talent and reality shows, such as ITV1's *The X Factor* and Channel Five's *Big Brother*, where the audience is asked to vote for the winning contestant, through to online surveys and opinion polls. The technology exists, therefore, for people's opinions, views and beliefs to be canvassed to a much greater extent than they are currently. People can vote quickly and easily from the relative comfort of their own homes. Conversely, mobile phone technology means that many people are constantly contactable via their iPhone™, iPad™ and equivalent and so could, in theory, vote on the move. New technology, therefore, facilitates the physical act of casting one's vote but there are a couple of issues with this—the potential for error, or even fraudulent activity, exists. One American computer studies professor is purported as saying that as every first-year computer studies undergraduate knows, there are ways of making what is on the screen record differently in the database. In addition, although there are many ways of facilitating the physical act of casting one's vote, the crucial issue is the re-engagement of people with the political process. Even if one were to physically carry voters to the polling station, this will not necessarily get them to reconnect with politics and political issues. It is not, therefore, addressing the crux of the problem *vis-à-vis* political participation, namely, political engagement and interest in the issues.

AUDIT OF ENGAGEMENT

There are degrees of participation and, relatively recently, there has been debate as to the relative lack of political participation from the population *per se*. The Hansard Society's annual audit of political engagement highlights levels of political engagement in the public at large. The 2013 survey (*Audit of Political Engagement 10*) found high levels of disenchantment with just 41 per cent saying they were certain to vote in a general election (compared with 48 per cent in 2012 and 58 per cent in 2011). More worryingly perhaps, only 12 per cent of 18–24-year-olds said they were certain to vote (compared with 22 per cent in 2012 and 30 per cent in 2011). By 2015 (*Audit of Political Engagement 12*), levels were up slightly, with 49 per cent certain to vote, and 16 per cent of – 24-year-olds certain to vote. The Hansard Society survey also tests people's knowledge of politics. Here too, levels were very low, for example, in 2013, only 22 per cent could name their MP, only 23 per cent were satisfied with the way MPs generally do their job and, interestingly enough for this research, 29 per cent (nearly three of ten) thought that the minimum age for voting was 16 years—as is outlined in Chap. 5, perhaps the voting age should be lowered, especially given this figure of 29 per cent who thought that it already was set at 16! In the 2015 survey, 28 per cent of respondents could not name the party to which their MP belonged. Those expressing satisfaction with the system of governing declined to 26 per cent in the 2015 audit. Numerous reasons have been postulated for this lack of political engagement and participation, including apathy, disillusionment and lack of trust, especially in the aftermath of the MPs expenses scandal that first emerged in 2009. Public regard for politicians is currently at an all-time low. The Power Inquiry found that people 'do not feel that the processes of formal democracy offer them enough influence over political decisions—this includes party members who feel they have no say in policy-making and are increasingly disaffected' (2006: 3). Allied to this, people feel that 'the main political parties are too similar ... the electoral system is widely perceived as leading to unequal and wasted votes ... [that] they lack information or knowledge about formal politics [and that] voting procedures are regarded by some as inconvenient and unattractive' (Ibid.). Having said this, a certain amount of apathy might be regarded as a positive aspect. As Ben Saunders states, it is possible for 'low turnout to be democratically "innocent"—it may simply be that the people in question are content with things as they are or choose to abstain because they are not affected by the decision' (Saunders 2012: 318). It may indicate that people are generally happy with their lot if they have not been galvanised into political action. The student demonstrations against the rise in higher education tuition fees and the abolition of the EMA for those entitled to it in further education may mean that the tide has in fact turned and people, especially young people, are starting to participate politically to a much greater extent than hitherto.

CONCLUSION

Varying theories of political participation are espoused by political scientists and politicians alike. After discussion of the nature of politics, Chap. 2 examined the reasons behind participation and non-participation and linked this directly to youth political participation. The chapter also looked at participation for its own sake and whether there is merit in participating even if one's aims are not realised. Differing forms of political participation were cited. The concept of a 'ladder', or degrees of participation, was raised before moving on to look at the opportunities for participation facilitated by new technology. The following chapters will examine specific aspects of youth political participation in greater depth.

NOTE

1. The term was first used in an article in the *Economist* on 13 February 1954.

BIBLIOGRAPHY

Abrams, M. (1961). *Teenage consumer spending in 1959*. London: Press Exchange.

Acton, H. B. (Ed.) (1972). *J. S. Mill utilitarianism, on liberty and considerations on representative government*. London: Everyman's Library.

Adelman, D. (1991). *Signs of the times*. London: Hodder and Stoughton.

Almond, G., & Verba, S. (1963). *The civic culture: Political attitudes and democracy in five nations*. Princeton, NJ: Princeton University Press (Chapter 14).

Beer, S. (1982). *Britain against itself*. London: Faber.

Bochel, C., & Briggs, J. E. (2000, May). Do women make a difference? *Politics, 20*(2), 63–68.

Booth, J. A. (1979). Political participation in Latin America: Levels, structure, context, concentration and rationality. *Latin American Research Review, 14*(3), 29–60.

Briggs, J. E. (2008, December). Young women and politics: An Oxymoron? *Journal of Youth Studies, 11*(6), 579–592.

Browne, S. (Ed.) (1986). *Is democracy working?* Newcastle: Tyne Tees Television.

Butler, D., & Stokes, J. (1974). *Political change in Britain* (2nd ed.). London: Macmillan.

Byrne, P. (1997). *Social movements in Britain*. London: Routledge.

Cocker, P. G. (1986). *Government and politics*. London: Edward Arnold.

Coxall, B., & Robins, L. (1989). *Contemporary British politics*. London: Macmillan.

Coxall, B., Robins, L., & Leach, R. (2006). *British politics*. Basingstoke: Palgrave Macmillan.

Crick, B., & Crick, T. (1987). *What is politics?* London: Edward Arnold.

Davis, A., de la Harpe Bergh, G., & Lundy, A. (2014). *Young people's engagement in strengthening accountability for the post-2015 agenda*. London: Overseas Development Institute.

Denver, D. (1997). Elections and voting behaviour. In L. Robins & B. Jones (Eds.), *Half a century of British politics* (pp. 128–143). Manchester: Manchester University Press.

Denver, D. (2007). *Elections and voters in Britain* (2nd ed.). Basingstoke: Palgrave Macmillan.

Denver, D., Carman, C., & Johns, R. (2012). *Elections and voters in Britain* (3rd ed.). Basingstoke: Palgrave Macmillan.

Denver, D., & Hands, G. (1992). *Issues and controversies in British electoral behaviour*. Hemel Hempstead: Harvester Wheatsheaf.

Dorey, P. (2005). *Policy making in Britain: An introduction*. London: Sage.

Dowse, R. E., & Hughes, J. A. (1972). *Political sociology*. London: John Wiley.

Dunleavy, P., & Husbands, C. T. (1985). *British democracy at the crossroads*. London: Allen and Unwin.

Eulau, H. (1963). *The behavioral persuasion in politics*. New York: Random House.

Eulau, H. (1966). *Political behavior in America: New directions*. New York: Random House.

Forman, F. N. (1985). *Mastering British politics*. London: Macmillan (Chapter 13).

Friedan, B. (1963). *The feminine mystique*. London: Gollancz.

Garnett, M., & Lynch, P. (2009). *Exploring British politics* (2nd ed.). Harlow: Pearson Education.

Greer, G. (1970). *The female eunuch*. London: MacGibbon and Kee.

Hart, R. A. (1992). Children's participation from tokenism to citizenship. In *United Nations Children's Fund, Innocenti Essays Number 4* (pp. 1–41). Florence: UNICEF.

Heath, A., Jowell, R., & Curtice, J. (1985). *How Britain votes*. Oxford: Oxford University Press.

Helliwell, J., Layard, R., & Sachs, J. (2012). *World happiness report*. New York: The Earth Institute Columbia University.

Higgins, G. M., & Richardson, J. J. (1976). *Political participation*. London: Politics Association.

Inglehart, R. (1977a). *The silent revolution: Changing values and political styles among Western publics*. Princeton, NJ: Princeton University Press.

Inglehart, R. (1977b). *Modernization and post-modernization: Cultural, economic and political change in 43 countries*. Princeton, NJ: Princeton University Press.

Leftwich, A. (Ed.) (2004). *What is politics?* Cambridge: Polity Press.

Madgwick, P. J. (1984). *Introduction to politics* (3rd ed.). London: Hutchinson.

Milbrath, L. W. (1965). *Political participation: How and why do people get involved in politics?* Chicago: Rand McNally.

Millett, K. (1977). *Sexual politics*. London: Virago.

Moodie, G. C. (1971). *The government of great Britain* (3rd ed.). London: Methuen.

Parry, G., Moyser, G., & Day, N. (1992). *Political participation in Britain.* Cambridge: Cambridge University Press.

Pateman, C. (1970). *Participation and democratic theory.* Cambridge: Cambridge University Press.

Pearce, M. L., & Stewart, G. (1992). *British political history, 1867–1990.* London: Routledge.

Pimlott, B. (1988). The myth of consensus. In L. M. Smith (Ed.), *The making of Britain: Echoes of greatness* (pp. 129–142). Basingstoke: Macmillan.

Power Inquiry. (2006). *Executive summary and recommendations of the report of power: An independent inquiry into Britain's democracy.* York: Joseph Rowntree Trust.

Pulzer, P. (1975). *Political representation and elections in Britain* (2nd ed.). London: Allen and Unwin.

Qvortrup, M. (2007). *The politics of participation: From Athens to e-democracy.* Manchester: Manchester University Press.

Rose, R. (1989). *Politics in England* (5th ed.). London: Macmillan (especially Chapter 6).

Ruedin, D. (2007, December). Testing Milbrath's 1965 framework of political participation: Institutions and social capital. *Contemporary Issues and Ideas in Social Sciences, 3*(3), 1–46.

Rush, M. (1992). *Politics and society.* London: Prentice Hall.

Sanders, D. (1991). Voting behaviour in Britain. *Contemporary Record*, February, pp. 2–6.

Saunders, B. (2012). The democratic turnout 'problem'. *Political Studies, 60,* 306–320.

Savage, J. (2014). Time up for the teenager? *RSA Journal*, Issue 1, 16–19.

Schwarzmantel, J. (1987). *Structures of power.* London: Wheatsheaf.

Scott, A. (1990). *Ideology and the new social movements.* London: Unwin Hyman.

Siltanen, J., & Stanworth, M. (1984). *Women and the public sphere.* London: Hutchin.

Tolleson Rhinehart, S. (1992). *Gender consciousness and politics.* London: Routledge.

White, I. (2006). *Power to the people: The report of power, an independent inquiry into Britain's democracy.* London: Parliament and Constitution Centre. SN/PC/3948.

Whiteley, P. (2012). *Political participation in Britain: The decline and revival of civic culture.* Basingstoke: Palgrave Macmillan.

Wintour, P. (2011). E-petitions need to be rethought urgently, says Labour MP. *The Guardian*, 16 November. Retrieved August 16, 2012, from http://www.guardian.co.uk/politics/2011/nov/15/epetitions-rethought-urgently-labour-mp

Young, M. B. (2010). To buy or not to buy: Who are political consumers? What do they think and how do they participate? *Political Studies, 58,* 1065–1086.

CHAPTER 3

Young People and Participation in Europe

Attention turns, at this juncture, to the topic of young people and political participation on a pan-European basis. Utilising quantitative data gleaned from a variety of sources but, predominantly, the European Social Survey, this chapter provides a quantitative analysis of political participation levels in all 28 countries of the European Union. Comparisons are made between different types of political participation and also between differing levels of governance. It is interesting to investigate whether, for example, young people in Denmark are more willing to participate in politics than, say, the youth of Portugal. If so, why should this be the case? Why does the youth of one particular nation appear to be more galvanised and politically active than, say, the young people of another nation? Questions such as the proportion of young people being of the opinion that it is a citizen's duty to vote ('and whether this has altered over time') are investigated, alongside other pertinent questions about young people and political participation/non-participation. Answers are sought to questions such as these.

PARTICIPATION IN DIFFERENT EUROPEAN COUNTRIES

Youth participation is an issue in all 28 countries of the European Union. Participation varies throughout the 28 countries—especially where they have compulsory voting, such as in Belgium (where it has existed since 1893). On the whole though, the issue of low levels of political participation amongst young people does appear to be a pan-European phenomenon. Research reveals the remarkable parallels amongst young people in all

© The Author(s) 2017
J. Briggs, *Young People and Political Participation*,
DOI 10.1057/978-1-137-31385-0_3

European countries. By comparison with their older counterparts, young people seem less inclined to participate in mainstream politics and also more likely to participate in single-issue campaigns. They are interested in 'issues' but not necessarily in the political system *per se*.

Research undertaken by Edward Fieldhouse, Mark Tranmer and Andrew Russell reveals that turnout is in decline in elections across Europe and that young people are less likely to vote than older people. Using data from the European Social Survey, they looked at national elections in 22 European countries between 1999 and 2002 and found that the average overall turnout rate was 70 per cent compared with 51 per cent for electors aged 18–24. Clearly, this 19 percentage point gap is a significant difference between young voters and voters in general (2007: 797). The authors explain that the highest levels of turnout are where there is a degree of compulsion to vote, including, 'Belgium, Greece, Italy, Luxembourg and the Nordic countries' (Ibid: 801).

Examination of some of the countries analysed by Fieldhouse et al. (2007) reveals interesting comparisons in terms of youth political participation.

Extracted and adapted from Fieldhouse et al. (2007: 804), Table 3.1 illustrates the differential turnout between younger voters and the rest

Table 3.1   Age differentials and turnout by country

Country	Year of national election	Official turnout percentage	European social survey (estimate)		Difference
			Percentage 18–24-year-olds	Percentage 25+	
Austria	2002	80.49	61.5	83.2	−21.7
Belgium	1999	90.58	87.6	91.0	−3.4
Switzerland	1999	43.22	19.1	47.5	−28.4
Germany	2002	79.08	65.5	80.4	−14.9
Spain	2000	68.71	37.7	73.9	−36.2
Finland	2000	76.80	44.9	67.9	−23.0
France	2002	60.30	39.9	67.7	−27.8
UK	2001	59.38	31.6	62.5	−30.9
Greece	2000	74.97	48.1	79.0	−30.9
Ireland	2002	62.57	30.9	68.5	−37.6
Italy	2001	81.44	80.8	81.5	−0.7
Luxembourg	1999	86.51	99.5 (21–24-year-olds)	85.5	14.0
Netherlands	2002	79.06	65.0	80.4	−15.4
Norway	2001	74.95	46.3	78.6	−32.3
Poland	2001	46.18	32.4	49.2	−16.8
Sweden	2002	80.11	71.4	81.1	−9.7
Slovenia	2000	70.36	38.8	75.3	−36.5

of the eligible voting population in a number of European countries. The only country here where turnout amongst young people was higher than amongst older people was in Luxembourg (14.0 percentage points higher); for all the other countries the turnout was lower amongst young people and, in some cases, significantly lower, for example, Ireland where it was 37.6 percentage points lower, Slovenia 36.5, Spain 36.2, Norway 32.3 and the UK and Greece both 30.9 percentage points lower. Clearly, the issue of lower turnout amongst younger voters is a European-wide phenomenon and not exclusive to one particular country or group of countries. The differential between older and younger voters does decline significantly where compulsory voting is in operation, as in Belgium, for example. Generally speaking, however, younger voters across Europe are less likely to turnout and cast their vote than their older counterparts.

Fieldhouse et al. accentuate research that 'support the notion that the youngest sections of society are de-coupling from central aspects of political life in many countries' (Ibid:814), proceeding to cite Wattenberg (2002) who notes widespread 'apathy' among the youngest voters in the USA to the 2000 presidential election and refers to the 'know nothing' generation. Park (2000) reports that at the turn of the twenty-first century, 'only a tenth of 18–25-year-olds were 'interested' (or 'very interested') in politics in Britain—less than half of the corresponding proportion from the cohort of 18–25-year-olds a decade earlier' (Ibid.). Fieldhouse et al. found that a number of factors influence the propensity of young people to cast their vote, and these include: 'young electors from ethnic minorities and with dependent children were less likely to vote', that 'level of political interest, years of education and economic satisfaction all play a part', as do 'religious belonging and group membership' which also had a 'significant effect on the voting habits of young people' (Ibid: 816). Essentially, what Fieldhouse et al. are saying is that 'the character of young voters is important in deciding who votes and who does not regardless of the prevailing level of turnout in the countries in which they live' (Ibid: 817). They do proceed to add, however, that the country is still important in terms of playing 'a significant part in explaining why some young people vote and others do not' (Ibid.). As they say, 'certain features of the state of European democracies, such as the level of political interest and civic duty, do have an influence on who votes and who does not, but this does not explain in full the extent to which young people vary in their participation across countries' (Ibid: 819). It is interesting, therefore, to examine young people and political participation within countries just as much as between countries to ascertain the answer to the vexed question why some young people participate and engage politically and why others do not.

Continuing this theme, a further investigation into young people and political participation in Europe is the study 'Participatory Citizenship in the European Union' which examined levels of political engagement across Europe, collecting data from the then 27 member states of the European Union.[1] Bryony Hoskins et al. investigate participatory citizenship levels in the European Union. The authors examine the concept of citizenship and focus upon participatory or active citizenship. By adding the focus upon action, 'the agency of citizens as actors in relation to policy and the state is emphasized' (2012: 9). They support the thesis that older people vote more (Ibid: 28) and that 'when it comes to alternative ways of political participation, youngsters tend to be more active than older generations' (Ibid: 28). Citing data from the 2007 Flash Eurobarometer on 15–30-year-olds, the authors state 'one in four respondents reported having signed a petition, while one in five respondents said they joined a demonstration in the last year [numbers which] are considerably higher than comparable figures for older adults' (Ibid: 28). Clearly, then evidence reveals that young people are more likely to participate politically in ways other than voting. In terms of involvement in a political party and involvement in formal political activities, again, Hoskins et al.'s research demonstrates that there is a 'lower participation rate for younger people' (Ibid: 29). However, they do emphasise that the latest Eurobarometer figures (spring 2011) show that 57 per cent of all EU citizens express a moderate or strong interest in politics, but they go on to say perhaps we should be concerned 'that 43 per cent of the population in Europe is not interested in politics' (Ibid: 29). This is a substantial minority of European citizens who profess to not having an interest in politics. Again, in terms of young people, the study shows that young people in Eastern and Southern Europe have 'positive attitudes towards participation and citizenship values are higher than in western Europe' (Ibid: 30); likewise, 'social justice attitudes such as gender equality and knowledge and skills on democracy tend to be higher in Western Europe' (Ibid: 30–31). In terms of political civil society activities, the authors reveal research, namely, the International Citizenship and Civic Education Study (ICCS), illustrating that many students in Europe want to protest in legal activities, 'like writing a letter to a newspaper, wearing a badge or t-shirt expressing their opinion, collecting signatures for a petition, and so on. Only a minority of students expected that they would want to participate in illegal protest' (Ibid: 33).

Given that 2013 was the European Year of Citizens, in recognition of the twentieth anniversary of European Union Citizenship (set up under the terms of the 1993 Maastricht Treaty), it remains apposite to focus upon getting young people in Europe to engage and participate more in politics at both macro and micro levels. Hoskins and Kerr put forward a number of policy suggestions in relation to participatory citizenship. These include, moves to 'provide education and training materials for all citizens, including young people in schools who are future voters' and to 'use social media and networking to engage people with the European elections and with key issues that are dominating European politics, such as … youth unemployment' (Ibid: 29). They also cite other key issues to which all EU citizens will need to respond, namely, climate change, the ageing population (the demographic time-bomb as some commentators have referred to it), EU enlargement and the global economy (Ibid: 31). Certainly, the youth of Europe will need to address all of these vital issues at some stage in the future.

Aaron J. Martin's (2012) *Young People and Politics: Political engagement in the Anglo-American democracies* also examines youth political participation. However, the book does not focus upon Europe but rather upon the extent to which young people are engaging with the political process in the Anglo-American democracies, namely, the USA, Britain, Canada and Australia. There are, however, clear parallels with the European scenario. Martin examines voter turnout, political attitudes (levels of trust and interest), participation beyond voting and what can be done/suggestions for the future. Taking the perception that young people don't vote or participate as his starting point, Martin examines the extent to which this lack of interest and involvement is true. Essentially, Martin flags up the changing nature of youth political participation and how, in terms of behaviour and attitudes, young people have become more volatile and unpredictable. The key findings are that 'Voter turnout amongst young people is not in secular decline but rather is much more volatile'. In part this appears to be driven by 'low levels of civic duty' amongst the young. Likewise, 'political trust is quite volatile' amongst young people as well as amongst older people. Political interest is 'not in secular decline among the young' but Martin does point out that gaps between the young and old on this issue have opened up over time (Martin 2012: 16). He proceeds to proclaim that 'electoral engagement is declining amongst the young (this is especially true of party identification and party membership)', that young people are more likely than older people to be 'engaged in non-electoral forms of political participation such as signing a petition and attending a demonstration' and that young people are 'more engaged than older people in politics on the Internet' (Ibid: 17). Martin provides us with a clear distinction between generational and lifestyle effects. Lifestyle effects centring on the idea that 'young people eventually become more politically engaged as they age, [being] linked to the responsibilities of adulthood' (Ibid: 3). The idea being, as people age, they change their political attitudes and behaviour. Conversely, the generational effect means that, 'experiences during adolescence and early adulthood make a lasting imprint on young people's attitudes and behaviour' (Ibid.). If we adhere to the generational effects thesis, then we will see the electorate changing significantly over time. If young people are disengaged and not voting, this will stay with them as they age. Martin's work is also interesting not just in terms of its analysis of various forms of political participation, such as via the Internet, but also because he argues that, rather than seeing young people as non-voters it is better to view them as 'volatile voters' (Ibid: 21). This enables the participatory potential of young people to remain at the forefront of any debate. Clearly, there are examples of extremely low levels of young voter turnout, such as the 2000 US Election and the 2005 UK General Election, but to say that young people are habitual non-voters is to neglect their potential power and influence. It appears to be the case that young people have lower levels of civic duty than their older counterparts, but that does not mean that their non-voting is a foregone conclusion. As Martin says, 'Voting, it seems, is attractive to young people at times and at others it is not' (Ibid: 35). This is crucial to bear in mind when examining young people and political participation on a pan-European basis. They may not be voting in particularly high numbers, but their potential to vote, participate and protest should be neither forgotten nor ignored. If politicians and policymakers neglect young voters, they do so at their peril. To ignore the wishes and interests of a significant sector of society, perhaps more importantly, the future of society, is political foolishness.

James Sloam provides an interesting analysis of youth political participation on a pan-European basis. He believes that 'youth participation is strongly related to a country's civic culture. In countries where certain forms of engagement are relatively high for all ages—for example, demonstrations in Spain and petitions in the UK—this is usually the case for young people too' (Sloam 2013c). He proceeds to illustrate how, across Europe, politicians may be choosing to ignore the views and wishes of young people, asserting that the 'ageing of European populations means that 18 to 24 year olds are a shrinking group in European electorates. If only a small proportion of this shrinking group votes, politicians will pay little heed to young people's interests, leading to further disillusionment'. Sloam emphasises that a 'further symptom of this malaise is the lack of contact between young Europeans and the people who make the decisions that affect their lives. In the EU15, contact between young people and politicians or officials is about half the rate of the population as a whole' (Ibid.). For Sloam, this means that 'politicians and public officials have much work to do if they are to engage effectively with today's young Europeans. Efforts to interact with young people on issues of concern, including youth unemployment, might be a starting point' (Ibid.). James Sloam's table shows the proportion of people who undertook five main types of political activity across the old EU15 countries (Table 3.2).

Table 3.2 The proportion of people who undertook five main types of political engagement across the EU15 countries *(bold numbers are for the overall population, non-bold for young people aged 15 to 24 years)*

Per cent who	Young people	College degree	Less than lower secondary education or no qualifications	Top two household income brackets	Bottom two household income brackets	Overall
Voted in last national parliamentary election (per cent of eligible citizens)	59	**88** 71	**79** 26	**85** 56	**75** 52	82.1
Displayed a badge or sticker (in the last year)	11.6	**11** 12	**4** 9	**9** 12	**6** 16	7.9
Signed a petition (in the last year)	26.9	**39** 37	**11** 16	**35** 35	**· 16** 24	25.9
Joined a boycott (in the last year)	15	**30** 19	**7** 9	**25** 16	**10** 19	18.1
Participated in demonstration (in the last year)	13.7	**11** 17	**4** 11	**7** 11	**6** 16	7.8
Numbers of respondents	13,409	*25,707* 1314	*22,399* 1344	*1766* 205	*1827* 199	*107,322*

Source: European social survey cumulative data (waves 1 to 4, 2000–2008); Sloam (2013c)

James Sloam provides a second table, reproduced below, that depicts youth participation rates as a percentage of the participation rates for all citizens in each of the old EU15 countries. It provides an interesting comparison for participation rates across eight different activities, and it can be seen that the UK is at the lower end of the scale. Belgium has very high rates of political participation, but it is worth remembering that voting is compulsory in Belgium and has been so since 1893, presumably therefore deeply ingrained in the national psyche through an awareness of the legal imperative (Table 3.3).

Using data available from the European Social Survey (2010, 2012, 2014), the following charts were compiled to illustrate differing aspects of youth political participation. The first chart compares levels of political interest amongst 18–24-year-olds across the European Union nations. The subsequent charts examine and enable a comparison to be made of five specific countries. The selected countries are Belgium, Denmark,

Table 3.3 Youth participation rates as a percentage of the participation rates for all citizens in each of the EU15 countries

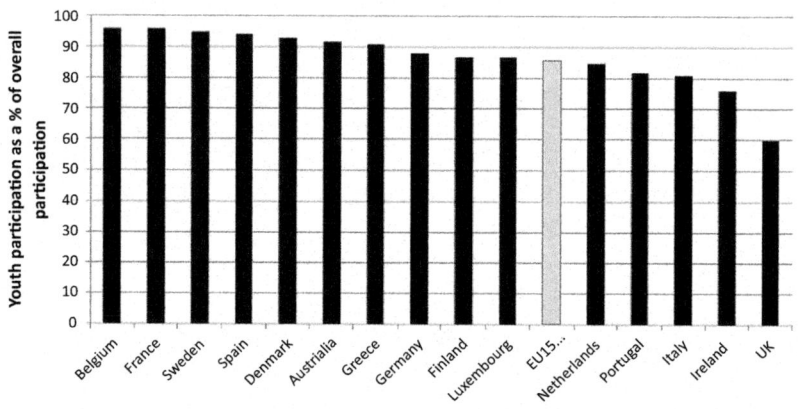

Note: Eight activities were included in calculating total participation rates: 'voting in last national election', 'working for a party or action group', 'working for another [political] group association', 'displaying a badge or sticker', 'signing a petition', 'joining a boycott', 'participating in a demonstration'
Source: European Social Survey cumulative data (waves 1 to 4, 2000–2008); Sloam (2013c)

Greece, Portugal and the UK. The five countries are compared in terms of levels of political interest amongst young people, levels of political trust in their country's parliament, levels of trust in their country's politicians and levels of satisfaction with democracy. The five countries were chosen to provide a geographical spread across the European Union, with a balance in terms of northern and southern countries, and relatively affluent and much poorer nations.

Table 3.4 depicts level of political interest amongst young people on a pan-European basis. Some bar charts below suggest that whilst young people may have to vote because of some aspect of compulsion, they may not necessarily express an interest in politics. Belgium, Denmark, Greece, Portugal and the UK were selected. This is, in part, due to Fieldhouse et al. (2007) citing compulsory voting as having an effect, and mention Belgium, Greece and the Nordic countries. Portugal provides a compara-

Table 3.4 Comparative political interest amongst 18–24-year-olds on a pan-European basis

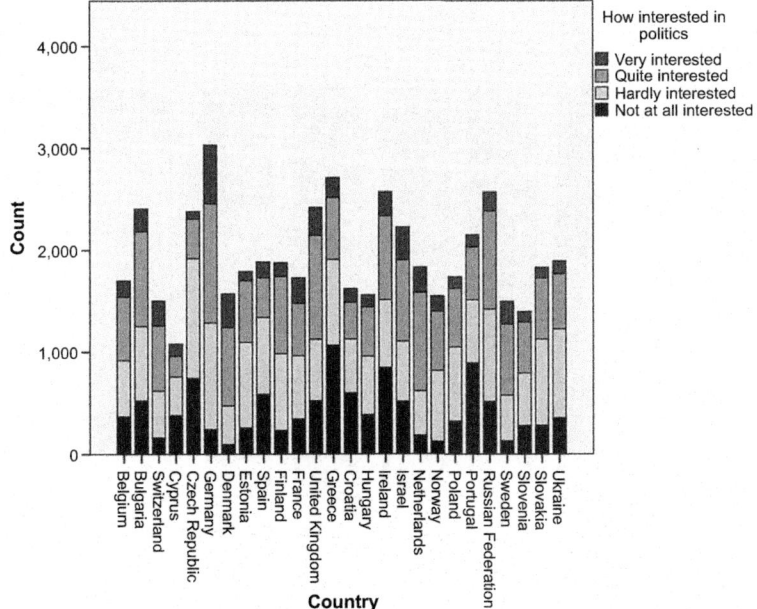

Source: Tables 3.4–3.8 are based upon cumulative data obtained from the European Social Surveys (2010, 2012, 2014), ESS5, ESS6 and ESS7

tive perspective. The UK was possibly self-selecting but young people, perhaps surprisingly, do express more interest than some other nations.

A cross-national comparison of levels of political interest amongst young people reveals the following data across the five countries:

[NB: The latest available data is included for each country—hence differing years] (Table 3.5).

It is interesting that even though Belgium has compulsory voting, there are surprisingly high numbers of young people who state that they hardly have any interest in politics whatsoever. There may be many reasons behind this phenomenon. It could be that the coercive political system leaves them feeling alienated or resentful. Likewise, Denmark has high levels of young people expressing hardly any or no interest in politics.

Table 3.5 Levels of political interest amongst young people in Belgium (ESS 2014), Denmark (ESS 2014), Greece (ESS 2010), Portugal (ESS 2012) and the UK (ESS 2012)

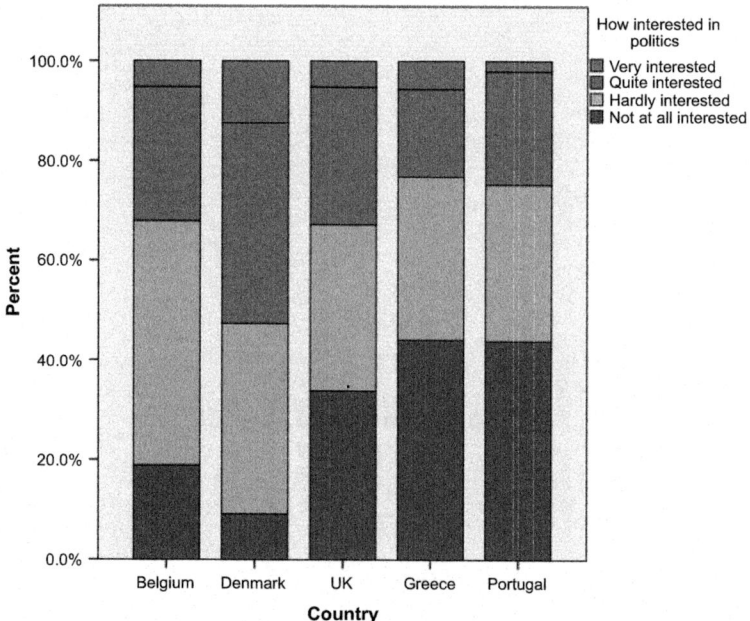

Note: All bars for each country rounded up to 100 per cent

Similarly, Greece has relatively high numbers expressing little or no interest in politics. It can be seen that levels of interest in politics amongst young people vary from country to country.

If examination is made of levels of political trust in their country's parliament, an interesting picture is revealed (Table 3.6).

In terms of trust in the country's Parliament, young people in Belgium are mainly centred on the mid-point of the scale. For a more detailed analysis of levels of political trust in Belgium, see Marc Hooghe et al. (2015). Denmark appears to have relatively high levels of trust in the country's parliament. Greece, perhaps not surprisingly given the way in which it has suffered during the current economic crisis, has extremely low levels

Table 3.6 Levels of political trust in their parliament by young people in Belgium (ESS 2014), Denmark (ESS 2014), Greece (ESS 2010), Portugal (ESS 2012) and the UK (ESS 2012)

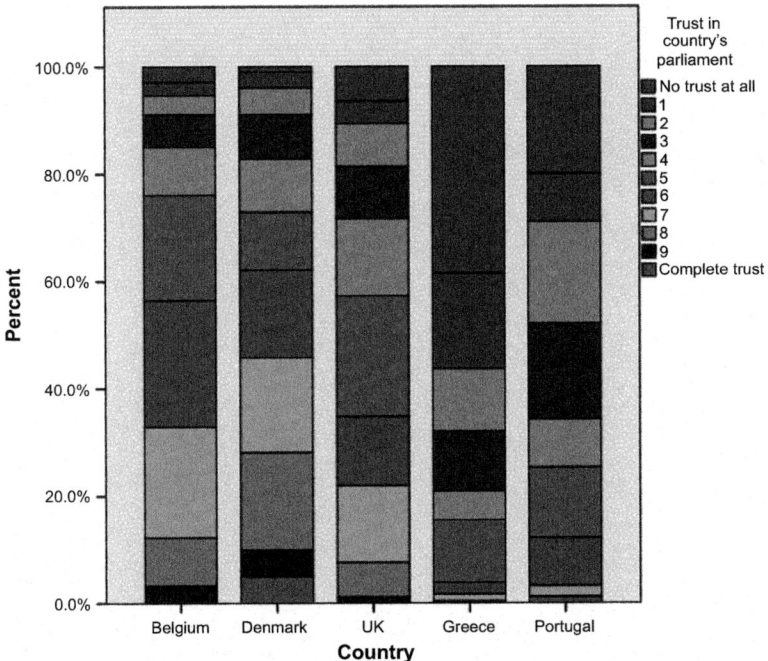

Note: All bars for each country rounded up to 100 per cent

of trust expressed in the country's parliament. In Portugal, there are significant numbers stating they have no trust in the country's parliament, but there are also significant numbers across the spectrum who do claim to have trust. The picture in the UK is fairly evenly spread across the spectrum.

In terms of the next criterion, namely, trust in politicians, it is worthwhile comparing the same five countries (Table 3.7).

In Belgium, whilst there are significant numbers expressing no trust in politicians at all, the rest of the responses are fairly evenly spread across the spectrum. There are significant levels of trust in politicians in Denmark. There is a lack of trust in politicians amongst young people in Greece. In

Table 3.7   Trust in politicians amongst young people in Belgium (ESS 2014), Denmark (ESS 2014), Greece (ESS 2010), Portugal (ESS 2012) and the UK (ESS 2012)

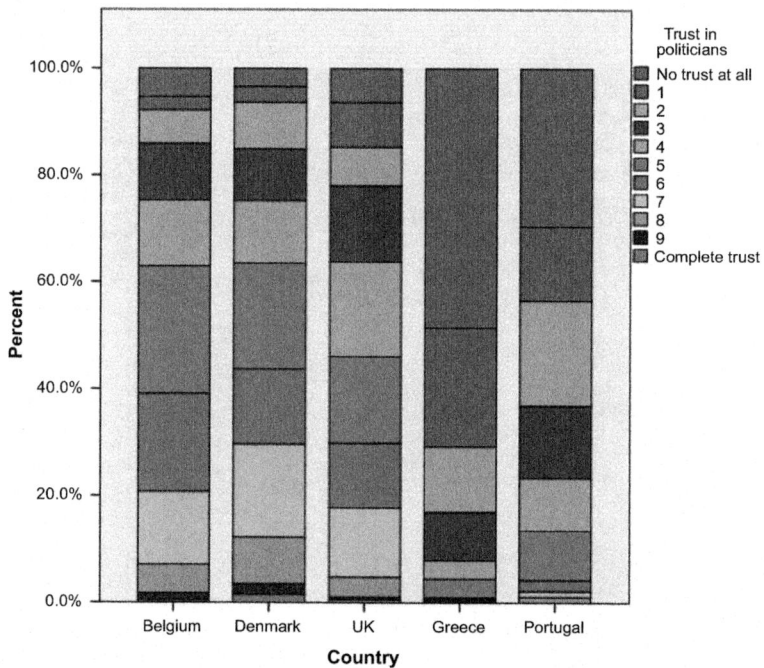

Note: All bars for each country rounded up to 100 per cent

Portugal, there are high numbers of young people claiming that they do not trust politicians. In the UK, although significant numbers of young people express a lack of trust in politicians, the results for levels of trust in politicians are fairly evenly spread across the spectrum.

In terms of satisfaction with levels of democracy in their country, the five key comparisons revealed the data given in Table 3.8.

Denmark has high levels of satisfaction with democracy. In Greece, there are significant numbers of young people claiming that they are dissatisfied with the way democracy works.

If we examine youth political participation in detail in a couple of specific countries, interesting parallels are revealed.

Table 3.8 Levels of satisfaction with democracy in Belgium (ESS 2014), Denmark (ESS 2014), Greece (ESS 2010), Portugal (ESS 2012) and the UK (ESS 2012)

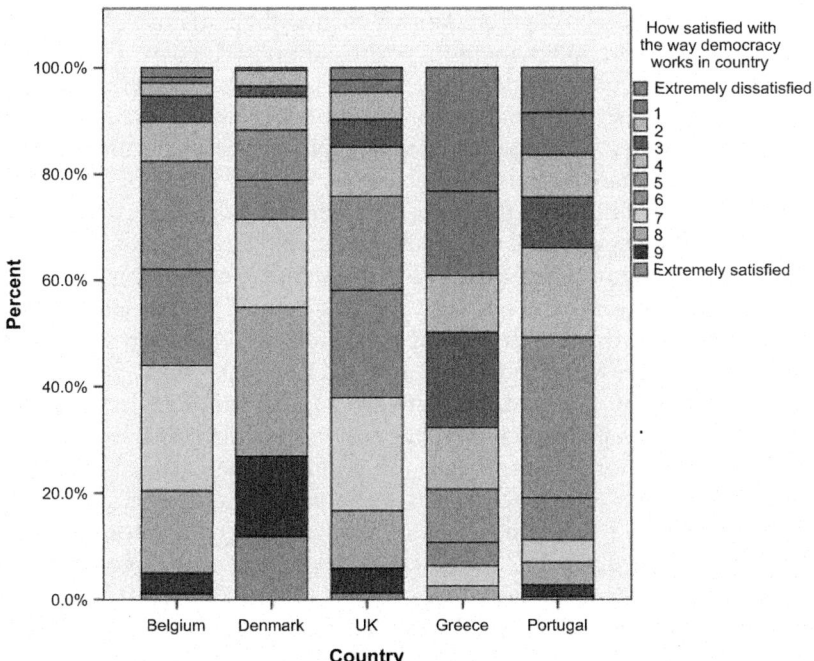

Note: All bars for each country rounded up to 100 per cent

GERMANY

In terms of Germany, Ursula Hoffmann-Lange and Franziska Wächter have undertaken research and sought answers to questions such as whether young Germans have enough time to be able to participate politically, given that they are seeking jobs or the demands that are imposed upon them at school or university, and also whether girls and young women participate to the same extent as boys and young men. They spotlight the usage of the AID, a survey aimed at answering questions such as these. In conjunction with survey data from three Youth Surveys undertaken by the German Youth Institute (in 1992, 1997 and 2003), the data look at 18–30-years-olds and, combined with the AID data, covers a period of almost two decades. As Hoffmann-Lange and Wächter state, 'The social and political involvement of young people is quite pronounced, and since 2002 it has even increased. In 2009, 39 percent of the 12- to 25-year olds devoted some of their free time for social or political purposes, up from 34 percent in 2002' (2011: 11). They go on to say that while 'girls and young women are considerably less often members in formal organisations than are boys and young men, participation in the new social movements shows no similar gender bias', whereas there is a difference in terms of education in that the 'higher the educational level is, the higher the involvement in civic and political affairs' (Ibid.). There has also been, in Germany, an increase in those expressing an interest in politics, 'in 2003 only 22 percent of the 18- to 29-year-olds were strongly interested in politics, in 2009 34 percent indicated a strong interest' (Ibid.). Protest activity, for example, going on a demonstration or signing a petition was also up by 2009, '80 percent of the 18- to 29-year-olds claimed to have participated in social protest activities, 90 percent even indicated that they had already considered such participation' (Ibid: 12). Back in 2003, these figures were 65 per cent and 80 per cent, respectively. In addition, Hoffmann-Lange and Wächter flag up the fact that there is a decreasing difference in the levels of participation of young men and young women. They believe that this illustrates that efforts to increases the participation levels of young women have reaped dividends. They say that voter turnout amongst young people has declined, 'in 1972 this was 84.6 percent in the age cohort of 18 to 20, and 84.4 in the next older cohort (21 to 25 years)' (Ibid: 12). These respective figures were 63.0 per cent and 59.1 per cent by 2009. Yet, although voting has decreased (and this runs contrary to what some young people are saying in response to survey questions about voting), there has been an increase in direct political action, with protests against a large-scale urban development project, Stuttgart 21, and a protest against a storage site for atomic waste, in Gorleben, being cited as examples of such protest. Hoffmann-Lange and Wächter articulate these opposing trends—a decrease in voting behaviour and an increase or greater propensity to engage in protest action amongst young people in Germany. They say this is indicative of a 'communication problem between the political establishment and members of the young generation' (Ibid: 12); a solution to this issue, which is partly caused by young people not having their political interest sparked and cultivated at the family level, is to ensure that they have 'personal contact with politicians' and they receive some sort of 'political education inside and outside of school' (Ibid.).

Wolfgang Gaiser, Martina Gille and Johann de Rijke depict the problems faced by young Germans in relation to the labour market and especially given the current economic climate. As they state, 'the young generation is facing special problems in joining the working world' (2011: 19). They assert how young people have had to become much more adaptable and flexible in terms of the world of work and how they have been increasingly affected by the impact of globalisation. They analyse attitudinal survey data from the 2009 Youth Survey and find that amongst 18–29-year-olds, '71 percent judge their own living standard to be "fair" in comparison to others, 10 percent as very much more than "fair"' (Ibid: 20). Levels of satisfaction with their 'lot' in life remain, therefore, relatively high. Of the 20 per cent expressing dissatisfaction, it seems that education is an important factor, 'Youth from educationally deprived households more often regard themselves as relatively deprived' (Ibid: 20). Hardly surprising perhaps, but low socio-economic background and other factors, such as unemployment, also lead to greater levels of dissatisfaction. There is also a difference between those from the former East German states and those from the West, with those from the West having higher levels of satisfaction, although this difference is narrowing with the passage of time. Generally, the youth 'who regard themselves as relatively deprived also tend to feel insecure' (Ibid: 21). This insecurity manifests itself in feeling that they have a lack of self-determination. As the authors state, feelings of social disorientation have increased, and life experiences such as 'problems in the immediate social surroundings, long-term unemployment or serious money problems in the family, prove themselves to be significant for the sense of justice and the degree of social disorientation' (Ibid: 22). Clearly, if one feels one has been dealt a raw deal, it is hardly surprising that this impacts one's perceptions of justice and equality. Gaiser, Gille and de Rijke believe that the way forward is to focus upon education and the various civic groups and services that are available to young people, thereby strengthening young people's 'cultural and social capital' (2011: 22).

Ursula Hoffmann-Lange states that regarding lowering the voting age in Germany, 'So far, the voting age has been lowered to 16 years for state elections (not federal elections) in two German states (Brandenberg, Bremen). In Lower Saxony, the voting age has been lowered to 16 for local elections. While the general public including young people are only marginally interested in lowering the voting age, the SPD, Green Party, Left Party and parts of the FDP favour to lower the voting age in other states as well. There are also some public interest groups sponsoring initiatives for a general lowering of the voting age, and even initiatives to lower it to 14. The most radical groups even demand to abolish the voting age altogether and allowing parents to vote on behalf of their children until the children ask for voting themselves'.[2] When asked whether she thinks young people are interested in politics, Hoffmann-Lange states, 'There is a lot of empirical evidence indicating that the political interest of young people is lower than the political interest of adults. Controlling for the higher educational level of young people, their interest in politics has even declined in recent years. At the same time, the difference between those with tertiary and basic education has dramatically increased among the younger generation. But even the political interest among young people with higher educational levels is lower than it used to be at times when only a small proportion of young people attended institutions of higher education'. In Germany then, young people appear to have declining levels of political interest. Perhaps their quest to lower the voting age is seen by some as a way to counteract this decline. When asked whether young people are interested in mainstream politics or whether they are more interested in political issues, Hoffmann-Lange states, 'Interest in mainstream politics has declined, while interest in specific issues may be high, for example, opposition against the use of nuclear energy or against building new highways/railways/construction of runways of airports, etc. The protest potential is high, but the level of information is mostly rather low'. There are parallels here with young people in other countries whereby they are more likely to express an interest in political issues as opposed to mainstream politics and the political parties *per se*. When asked what can be done in an attempt to encourage more young people to take more

interest in politics, Hoffmann-Lange responds by saying, 'Civic education is certainly a major instrument to achieve this. Even more important is micro-mobilisation in the family and peer groups. Political parties
could do a lot more to actively mobilise young people'. Again, the links
with other countries is marked; civic education in the UK, for example,
is often mooted as a way to engage young people with politics (cf. the
work of Kisby, or Tonge and Mycock on the issue of citizenship education). In terms of why young people are less likely to vote than older
people, Hoffmann-Lange states, 'Because they feel that elections don't
make much of a difference. The decline in turnout is also pronounced
among adults, simply because our democracies function well and political conflicts between democratic parties are no longer ideological, but
rather about specifics in which most voters are not interested (Carmines:
Stimson: hard issues versus easy issues). However, if the mobilisation
potential of an election is high, for example, 2008 in the US presidential
elections, the age differential tends to diminish'. So, Hoffmann-Lange is
signalling the participatory potential of young people and that they may
not vote in elections when they feel there are no deep divisions between
the major political parties on key issues but that they can be galvanised
into action when they feel that there is a distinct difference between the
political choices open to them. This ties in with Fieldhouse et al.'s analysis
of factors affecting turnout, whereby they stress factors that 'affect the
level of turnout in a country include the closeness of the major parties in
the polls, the responsiveness of the executive, party polarisation, and the
electoral system and rules in operation' (2007: 798). When asked whether
new technology might be a way of facilitating the participation of young
people in politics, Hoffmann-Lange is quite dismissive, 'I don't think so.
Politics has always been the turf of a small minority. The great majority
of young people use the internet for gaming and entertainment and not
for discussing political issues'. This is an interesting observation and one
which will be re-examined in Chap. 4 where the participatory potential of
new technology *vis-à-vis* young people will be examined in detail. Suffice
to say at this juncture, perhaps Hoffmann-Lange is right to be dismissive
given the usage made of new technology and social media in particular
by young people. Certainly, they do use it, but the extent to which they
use for the purposes of engaging and participating in politics is minimal.
In terms of whether she has a view on lowering the voting age to 16,
Hoffmann-Lange's final point is that she 'is not opposed to doing it, but
I don't expect that this would have any significant impact'.

According to Martina Gille,[3] one of these German academics, who have written extensively about young people and political participation in Germany, 'In Germany, the political interest of young people is less strong than of older people. The gap between young people and adults is more or less constant since 1990. Also, the gender difference—boys are more interested in politics than girls—is an unchanging phenomenon'. Gille states that 'in Germany, national voting is only allowed for persons who are 18 years old or older. Voting for people up to [from] 16 years is only allowed for some local elections (community level). And only in one "Länd"—Bremen—voting on Länder level is allowed for young people up to [from] 16 years. Beyond that, national and Länder elections are only allowed for persons with German nationality'. Klaus Hurrelmann, a German academic, likewise professes that 'we stimulated a debate on lowering the minimum age of vote to 16 in several federal states. In Austria, the lowering has become law last year or so for the whole country and all voting entities and levels'.[4]

Martina Gille goes on to state, 'Interest in politics and the level achieved are closely connected: interest in politics is strongest among adolescents and young adults with a higher level of education and weakest among those with a lower level of education'. Expanding upon this point, Gille states, 'Though in the public discussion, youth is described as not interested in politics and a withdrawal from the political sphere is claimed'. Gille proceeds to state that, 'However, the results of our youth surveys show that the social and political involvement of young people is not decreasing, in the contrary it is increasing'. Gille's work and observations reveal a similarity with youth in the UK. It is interesting to note and to flag up these cross-national similarities. There is a belief in some quarters that young people are not interested and involved in politics and, yet, survey results reveal the reality to be slightly different.

BOSNIA AND HERZEGOVINA

Research has been undertaken, in other European countries, regarding youth political participation. Aleksandar Vranjes,[5] for example, an academic at the University of Banja Luka, Bosnia and Herzegovina, has investigated the issue. A group of Vranjes' students participated in a research project at the end of 2011 (November 2011). His comments refer to that research which may not be entirely representative but which does provide us with a snapshot of youth political participation in Bosnia-Herzegovina and is a useful indicator. Vranjes outlines article 1.4 of the Election Law of Bosnia and Herzegovina which states that 'Each citizen of Bosnia and Herzegovina who has attained eighteen (18) years of age shall have the right to vote and to be elected (hereinafter: right to vote) pursuant to provisions of this law'.[6] Vranjes states, 'Therefore, this Law is still valid and lowering the right of vote to 16 years of age is not actual right now'. Article 1.4 of the Election Law of Bosnia and Herzegovina also states that, 'To exercise his or her right to vote, a citizen must be registered as a voter, pursuant to this law' and that a 'person can be registered in the Central Voters Register for only one municipality'. As far as Vranjes knows, 'employment is not a condition for having a right of vote',[7] and checking the Election Law documentation of Bosnia and Herzegovina reveals Vranjes to be correct. Vranjes proceeds to explain the research in which his students took part. Altogether, 387 students took part in the research, 235 (60.7 per cent) female and 152 (39.3 per cent) male. In terms of the age of the respondents, 10.3 per cent were aged 17, 64.9 per cent aged 18, 4.4 per cent aged 19 and 20.4 per cent 'other'. Most of the participants were high school students from Nevesinje (23.5 per cent), Derventa (15 per cent), Banja Luka (40.8 per cent) and other places (20.7 per cent). The majority of the interviewees, 95.6 per cent, are Serbs.

In terms of the questions, the answers were as follows: In response to the question, '*Are you interested in politics?*' 12.4 per cent were strongly interested, 34.9 per cent were interested, 37.7 per cent were uninterested and 15 per cent were strongly uninterested. So, 47.3 per cent expressed some level of interest compared with 52.7 per cent who claimed to have some level of lack of interest—a slight majority towards being uninterested but not a massive difference; young people in Bosnia-Herzegovina seem to be fairly evenly split on this issue.

With regard to the question, '*Are you informed about politics?*' 11.6 per cent claimed to be very informed, 49.4 per cent said they were informed, 32.8 per cent stated they were insufficiently informed and 6.2 per cent claimed to be uninformed. This works out that 61 per cent claim to have some level of information, whereas 39 per cent claim to have a lack of information or no information whatsoever. In response to the question, '*Who do you trust the most?*' the results were: Family: 82.9 per cent, Church: 12.7 per cent, Police: 0.8 per cent, Politicians: 0.8 per cent, Court of Justice: 0.2 per cent, Don't Know: 2.6 per cent. Clearly, there are high levels of trust in relation to the family but, apart from the Church, levels of trust in other institutions are minimal to say the least. The question, '*What do you think about Bosnia-Herzegovina?'* elicited the following responses: 10.6 per cent regarded it as a 'normal' country, 34.9 per cent view it as an artificial creation, 44.4 per cent see it as a country which will disintegrate, 2.3 per cent see it as a future member of the European Union and 7.8 per cent have no view on this question. In terms of the question, *'Whether Bosnia should become a member of the European Union?'*, the following responses were received: Yes: 31 per cent, No: 55.6 per cent, Don't Know: 13.4 per cent. In answer to, *'Should Bosnia be a member of NATO?'* Yes: 16 per cent, No: 70 per cent, Don't Know: 14 per cent. Clearly, there is a resounding opposition to NATO membership. Finally, regarding the question, *'If there were elections tomorrow, would you vote?'* the responses were as follows: Yes: 52.2 per cent, No: 33.3 per cent, Don't Know: 14.5 per cent. A slight majority are, therefore, expressing a certainty to vote.

So, from the research unveiled by Vranjes,[8] it can be seen that in terms of whether or not young people are interested in politics, 52.7 per cent of the interviewees said that they are not interested in politics. However, as Vranjes goes on to say, the majority 'of the participants have built their attitudes about some political processes. If they are not directly interested, they might have learned about it either from primary or secondary social groups, or from [the] media. Based on what we can conclude that most of the participants in research are interested in politics, even [if] some of them are not aware of that'. So, they claim to not be interested in politics but their answers to some of the other questions would belie this response. In terms of whether young people are interested in mainstream politics or whether they are more interested in political issues, Vranjes states 'I got the impression that they are mainly interested in the mainstream politics, which means that they do not pay attention about the specific political problems. From there, we can find a cause of their inactivity, lack of participation, etc. because they are not interested about specific political issues'. In response to a question about what can be done to encourage young people to take more of an interest in politics, Vranjes says 'From the answers in the research, I noticed that most of them have a "holes" in education about politics. Most of their political knowledge had been obtained from the media, which is not enough to understand all the political processes which primarily affect them. So my answer would be that we need to improve the education of young people about politics, which would produce ... political participation'. Political education, as in other countries, does seem to be a crucial vehicle in terms of encouraging young people to participate in politics and equipping them with the necessary skills and tools needed to participate politically.

In terms of why young people are less likely to vote in elections than their older counterparts, Vranjes believes, 'Because most of them are not aware that the results of the election affect them as well. Young people have built the picture that for all important matters, older people should be asked, and at the same time they complain that they are neglected as a group. Once again, proper education about ... politics is [the] only key of this problem'. Again, the link here with proper, political education is undeniable. Young people appear to see the political world as having greater links with and relevance to their older counterparts. If the political world is deemed to be out with their experiences and lacking in relevance to their daily lives, then it is quite natural that they will see this as primarily being the realm of the older generations. With regards to whether new technology could provide us with an answer, Vranjes is of the opinion that, 'Thanks to the so-called "Facebook™ revolutions" in Egypt and Tunis, we learned that new information and communication technology can awake political abstainers, and most of them are young people. I certainly agree that with new technology we can increase the political participation of young people, because Web 2.0 services primarily attracting their attention, and that is a good channel to facilitate the participation of young people in politics'. In terms of whether the voting age should be lowered to 16, Vranjes believes that 'If we accept the thesis that young people are not sufficiently educated about politics (which is [the] cause of their decreased participation, lack of interest, etc.), then I think that in Bosnia and Herzegovina the vote should not be lowered to 16 years of age'. This is very much a catch-22 situation here—if young people are not educated then they are less likely to profess an interest in politics, but they are unlikely to reveal greater levels of political interest until they have higher levels of political knowledge and awareness. The two concepts appear to be intricately related.

Another academic who has conducted research into young people and political participation in Bosnia, Azra Hromadzic from Syracuse University, states when asked whether she thinks young people are interested in politics, 'This is a difficult question, and I hesitate to generalize. I have a whole chapter/article in preparation where I try to complicate the dominant idea that young people in Bosnia and Herzegovina are passive and uninterested in the political process and politics in general. I focus on practices that are often not even seen as "political"—such as cheating in exams or using connections to get into desired universities, to show how in this way youth do engage in a critique of the state (via education) ... even though this is not a typical way of doing politics, I find these actions to be political, in the anthropological sense of the word. I also think that young people displace their political future, thus potential, into the (imagined) spaces and times beyond Bosnia and now'.[9] When asked whether young people are interested in mainstream politics or are they more interested in political issues, Hromadzic replied, 'Political issues, I would say. Again, what counts as political is debatable and never fixed. Some are interested in mainstream politics, however'. She goes on to say, 'I was surprised to see how many youth turn to politics as a career choice. But their visibility and power are often contested. While in Bosnia [in summer 2012], I heard people comment, sarcastically: "They said that we (older people) should let the youth take over. We did that (in this town, the cantonal governor and mayor are both under 35), and look at what they did. Chaos. Inexperience. Greed. Corruption"'. Clearly then, some observers are critical of youth involvement in politics. When asked what can be done to encourage young people to take more interest in politics, Hromadzic responds by saying, 'Rescue it from ethnopolitics and focus upon citizenship-related issues', a factor of specific concern to Bosnia and Herzegovina when one examines their recent history. In terms of why young people are less likely to vote than older people, her response is, 'Because their political impulses and desires are often dislocated—projected into another space/"Europe" and future'. Hromadzic is more optimistic than some commentators in terms of the potential of new technology and social media to engage young people in politics and political participation, stating, 'I can see that potential. It needs to be tested, but it has proven to be a powerful tool elsewhere, no?'. In relation to whether she has a view about the voting age being lowered to 16, Hromadzic states, 'Not really. I would need to think much harder about this one. My immediate, gut reaction is "it should not" but I need to study/support my reaction somehow with a solid argument and I do not have one right now!'. In line with many other observers, she remains to be convinced about lowering the voting age to 16 years (this issue is addressed in further detail in Chap. 5).

CONCLUSION

It can be seen that, using both qualitative and quantitative data from a number of European countries, young people are less likely to vote and participate in formal politics than older people. This difference operates on a pan-European basis. Older people are more likely to turn out and cast their vote in elections. This could mean that politicians are able to effectively ignore, or at least sideline, the views of younger people if they are unlikely to vote. The pragmatic politician would surely focus his or her attention upon the views and policy concerns of older people if they are the ones who are more likely to vote. Yet, when examination is made of levels of political interest and a concern for political issues, young people are not uninterested in politics. They are concerned about issues like animal rights and the environment. Politicians would be well served to focus their attentions upon trying to re-engage with young people via these specific issues. In addition, given that younger people, leaving aside the concept of the 'silver surfer', are more likely than older people to utilise new technology and, in particular, social networking sites, politicians might consider how they themselves can make better use of social networking sites, such as *Facebook*™, *MySpace*™ and *Bebo*™ and micro-blogging sites such as *Twitter*™ in order to re-engage with the youth of today. Attention now turns, in the next chapter, to this issue of how young people can and are using new technology to participate politically.

NOTES

1. See http://ec.europa.eu/citizenship/news-events/news/29052012_en.htm accessed 8 November 2012.
2. Email interview with Ursula Hoffmann-Lange, Professor of Political Science at Bamberg University, Germany, 2 October 2012.
3. Email interview with Martina Gille, Zentrum für Dauerbeobachtung und Methoden Deutsches Jugendinstitut (Research Associate in the German Youth Institute's Social Monitoring and Methodology Department), e. V., 3 September 2012.
4. Email interview with Professor Klaus Hurrelmann, Professor of Public Health and Education at the Hertie School of Governance in Berlin, 3 September 2012.
5. Email interview with Aleksandar Vranjes, academic in Bosnia and Herzegovina, 3 September 2012.
6. See www.oscebih.org The Organisation for Security and Co-operation in Europe Mission to Bosnia and Herzegovina.
7. Further email contact with Aleksandar Vranjes, 29 October 2012.
8. Email interview with Aleksandar Vranjes, 3 September 2012.
9. Email interview with Dr Azra Hromadzic 15 September 2012.

BIBLIOGRAPHY

ESS Round 5: European Social Survey Round 5 Data. (2010). Data file edition 3.2. Norwegian Social Science Data Services, Norway—Data archive and distributor of ESS data.

ESS Round 6: European Social Survey Round 6 Data. (2012). Data file edition 2.1. Norwegian Social Science Data Services, Norway—Data archive and distributor of ESS data.

ESS Round 7: European Social Survey Round 7 Data. (2014). Data file edition 1.0. Norwegian Social Science Data Services, Norway—Data archive and distributor of ESS data.

Fieldhouse, E., Tranmer, M., & Russell, A. (2007). Something about young people or something about elections? Electoral participation of young people in Europe: Evidence from a multilevel analysis of the European Social Survey. *European Journal of Political Research, 46*, 797–822.

Gaiser, W., Gille, M., & de Rijke, J. (2011). Youth caught between uncertainty and confidence. In The German Youth Institute (Ed.), *Growing up in Germany* (pp. 19–22). *Impulse*, Bulletin of the German Youth Institute.

Hoffmann-Lange, U., & Wächter, F. (2011). Between participation and protest. In The German Youth Institute (Ed.), *Growing up in Germany* (pp. 10–12). *Impulse*, Bulletin of the German Youth Institute.

Hooghe, M., Dassonneville, R., & Marien, S. (2015). The impact of education on the development of political trust: Results from a five-year panel study among late adolescents and young adults in Belgium. *Political Studies, 63*, 123–141.

Hoskins, B., Abs, H., Han, C., Kerr, D., & Veugelers, W. (2012). *Contextual analysis report: Participatory citizenship in the European Union*. Brussels: European Commission.

Martin, A. J. (2012). *Young people and politics: Political engagement in the Anglo-American democracies*. London: Routledge.

Park, A. (2000). The generation game. In R. Jowell, J. Curtice, A. Park, K. Thomson, L. Jarvis, C. Bromley, & N. Startford (Eds.), *British social attitudes* (Vol. 17). Aldershot: Ashgate.

Sloam, J. (2013c). Young people are less likely to vote than older citizens, but they are also more diverse in how they choose to participate in politics. *London School of Economics and Political Science* Blog, London. Retrieved November 7, 2013, from http://blogs.lse.ac.uk/europpblog/2013/07/19/young-people-are-less-likely-to-vote-than-older-citizens-but-they-are-also-more-diverse-in-how-they-choose-to-participate-in-politics/

Wattenberg, M. (2002). *Where have all the voters gone?* Cambridge, MA: Harvard University Press.

CHAPTER 4

New Media and Political Participation

This chapter examines the usage of new forms of media to enhance and facilitate political participation. It assesses political participation levels amongst young people, primarily in the UK but with references to other countries, where appropriate. Again, political participation is examined at differing levels of governance, and, in addition, differing types of participation are compared. The usage of new technology, in particular Web 2.0 technology (such as, social networking sites like *Facebook*™, *Bebo*™ and *MySpace*™, and the use of micro-blogging sites such as *Twitter*™), is analysed in order to ascertain the extent to which these new approaches facilitate and encourage greater political participation amongst young people.

What Is New Media?

In this digital age, it is worth investigating whether new technology provides or potentially provides a vehicle for young people to participate politically. As Birdwell and Bani (2014: 69) inform, young people today 'are "digital natives", and unlike older generations do not think there is a hard and fast distinction between the "online" and the "offline" world'. New media, in this instance, are primarily centred on the Internet and the possibilities that it permits for participating in politics (cf. for example, Moss and Coleman 2014, on deliberative e-democracy). As Paul Webb states, 'Novel forms of digital democracy carry potential to enhance citizens' political knowledge and their capacity to interact in new ways with elected representatives' (2015: 41). Since its inception, the Internet has

© The Author(s) 2017
J. Briggs, *Young People and Political Participation*,
DOI 10.1057/978-1-137-31385-0_4

revolutionised communication and information conveyance. To quote Nina Eliasoph, 'The internet has become more than a means of communication; it has become a site of activism itself' (2013: 147). The last 20 years have seen a veritable transformation in terms of how we access information and how we communicate with each other. The information superhighway has impacted our working lives and how we operate in our private lives too. From emailing work colleagues, to gaming and shopping online, societal change has been monumental. The possibilities are wide-ranging and, as is all too clear, can be used for both positive and negative purposes. The dark side of this new technology is manifested in the proliferation of Internet porn, Internet crime, including fraud and other criminal activity, and the nastier side of human interaction such as bullying via so-called Internet 'trolls' on sites such as *Twitter*™ and *Facebook*™ (witness, for example, the abuse aimed at the Cambridge classicist with a media profile, Professor Mary Beard, or the abuse suffered by journalist and activist, Caroline Criado-Perez, as she campaigned to have a woman—Jane Austen was selected—depicted on the £10 note). This new media, therefore, have opened up alternative ways of working and of living our lives, in general, but they have also led to problems that require new ways of policing and pose new questions with which our judicial system has to deal. What is perhaps surprising too is the speed at which this change has occurred. Within the space of two decades, the workplace in particular, for many people, has changed completely. So much so, that a return to the workplace of, say, 1990, would be almost unrecognisable. The paper-based world where business operated at a much slower pace and was, possibly, more manageable, is consigned to the past. The weighty, clunky computers of the past have generally been superseded by the hi-tech, slick models of the present day.

Possibly the greatest change for many people is the proliferation of emails, providing instantaneous communication on a global scale. The 'real time' method of contacting people has opened up a world of possibilities. As well as facilitating the process of working, it does, however, have a negative side. There is talk of the 'tyranny of emails' that are seemingly endless, many of which appear to necessitate an instantaneous response. Studies unmask rising stress levels suffered by many employees in a futile quest to deal with the incessant flow of emails and e-communication in general. Indeed, it might be questioned how many of these emails are necessary. Is it a case that the medium has almost become the message? In some instances, there is mention of an addiction to emails, in the same way as one might become addicted to gambling or to substance abuse. Many workers feel obliged to constantly check emails, including outside of office hours, at any time of the day or night. The smart phone has facilitated this approach, and the mobile handheld device means constant contact with the reality. This culture of a 24-hour level of availability inevitably has an impact upon levels of stress amongst the workforce. Many people, for example, speak of feeling obliged to check emails whilst on holiday or on sick leave. Are we, as a society, storing up problems for the future? It is noteworthy how many employers are now investigating the implications of this, and attempts are often made to encourage employees to examine their work–life balance. Rising levels of stress must, in part, be blamed upon this culture of being ever-present—even if this is often on a virtual basis. In short, new media have transformed the way we work and have opened up an endless array of possibilities in both the world of work and in our private lives, but there is often a heavy price to be paid for this. The negative aspects of this new world should not be underestimated. The seedier, pornographic and criminal aspects are certainly with us, as is the downside to the world of work where there is often pressure to be on tap on a 24-hour basis.

Mobile technology has facilitated and added to these issues. The advancements in technology mean that we can now work and play on the move. Being able to access the Internet on devices such as laptops, net-books and tablet technology—including the ubiquitous *iPad*™ and similar devices—and via mobile phones, including the so-called Android and smart phones, means that the working environment can literally be anywhere. The notion of the paperless office is, in some respects, becoming a reality. We are able to work in transit; we receive information and play on the move, and in many respects location is no longer an issue. For many commuters, for example, the working day is extended as they continue *en route* and answer emails or write reports on the train journey to and from work. The daily commute becomes integral to the working day.

A walk through any busy city centre reveals a significant proportion of people using their mobile phones. Clearly, they are not all using these for work-related purposes. Indeed, the assumption is that most will be using it for recreational usage, but such a straw poll does signify the proliferation of such technology in what is, in the grand scheme, a relatively short period. Indeed, it is estimated that, globally, 75 per cent of the world's population now own a mobile phone (World Bank Report, July 2012).

This constitutes a staggering figure by anyone's imagination and is illustrative of how pervasive and extensive that change has been.

WEB 2.0 TECHNOLOGY

The technological revolution has progressed in a series of stages and the terminology refers to Web 2.0 technology. This is, as mentioned above, a movement beyond its initial usage towards a greater emphasis upon such aspects as social networking sites and more interaction between the users of such technology. As Darren Lilleker and Nigel Jackson elucidate, 'Emerging in 2005, Web 2.0 ushered in a networked, participatory culture to be observed online with tools facilitating asynchronous or symmetrical conversations to take place within a variety of online environments' (2010: 69) and possesses a reach 'beyond national borders and cultures' (Ibid.). Over recent years, the growth and development of sites such as *Facebook*™ and *Twitter*™ have transformed our working and social lives. Earlier sites, such as *Friends Reunited*™, opened up a world of possibilities, enabling people to reconnect with those from their past. Prior to the development of new technology, it would not have been feasible to rediscover such lost contacts and acquaintances, or at least it would have been much more difficult, time-consuming and with a greater chance of failure. Granted, this development is not always seen in a positive light, as those who have lost spouses and partners to some childhood sweetheart from the past will surely be quick to testify. The uses to which this technology has been put are many and varied but certainly the potential should not be underestimated.

The technological advances that continued apace throughout the 1980s and 1990s led eventually to the proliferation of sites aimed at facilitating social interaction. These included *MySpace*™, *Bebo*™ and *Facebook*™. The first two of these took off initially, and primarily in the USA, but they were soon to be superseded by *Facebook*™. More latterly, this appears to have been foreshadowed by usage of the micro-blogging site, *Twitter*™, which permits a slightly different, and possibly easier, form of social interaction.

Created by American Jack Dorsey in 2006, who was inspired by the desire to find out what his friends were doing, *Twitter* started in San Francisco, California. It was initiated in March 2006, initially funded by a creative company called *Obvious*; it was launched in August 2006 and set up officially as *Twitter* Incorporated in May 2007. Within a short space of time it grew exponentially, and by early 2009 there were 7 million

Twitter users and rising rapidly. Nowadays, on a worldwide basis, there are 140 million users, with 10 million of those being based in the UK in May 2012.[1] Twitter celebrated its sixth year on 21 March 2012, announcing that it had 140 million users and 340 million tweets being sent on average each day.[2] *Facebook* revealed in February 2013 that they had 845 million users on their books.[3] With its identifiable signature bird logo, essentially, *Twitter* provides a real-time, short-messaging service that can be used over a variety of networks. From breaking news to updates from friends, colleagues and acquaintances, people are able to follow what is happening on a global scale. Short messages, called 'Tweets', are posted online. These are limited to a maximum of 140 characters and so authors have, by necessity, to be concise and focused. This brevity appears to be part of its appeal. Highly publicised events that generated widespread interest, such as the death of the pop superstar Michael Jackson on 25 June 2009 or the 2010 FIFA World Cup, led to a deluge of tweets. Celebrity tweeters, such as Demi Moore, Lady Gaga and Justin Bieber, command huge followings on the micro-blogging site. In the UK, Stephen Fry, Jessie J, Lily Cooper (née Allen) and John Prescott, amongst others, are at the forefront of high-profile tweeting. This notion of 'in a nutshell'/bite-sized pieces of information appears to be what makes the micro-blogging site so attractive to its users. Perhaps this is symptomatic of society today? Critics might argue it constitutes a dumbing-down or a reduction in information to such an extent that it becomes virtually meaningless. Others see it as direct, targeted data in an information-rich, possibly drenched, society. Certainly, it has its keen advocates but also its vocal detractors. Essentially, it asks one simple question which is 'What are you doing?' It has, however, been used for a myriad of differing uses, from getting news out quickly to advising people of forthcoming events. Many conferences, for example, now use Twitter as a way of relaying details about papers, panels and speakers. They often have live Twitter 'feeds', which is a constant stream of information updates in terms of what is happening. Academics, and others, are beginning to see the potential of Twitter as a method of sharing information and of maintaining contact. Twitter accepts messages from a variety of sources including via SMS text messages, from the Web and from mobile technology. Advocates expose the fact that, given that responses to the question 'What are you doing?' are largely rhetorical and do not necessarily require a response, immediate or otherwise, it does not lead to information overload. It's an update; it's not necessarily a two-way process. Recipients do not necessarily need to respond to these updates; it is their choice.

As with most aspects of modern life, there is a downside and Twitter users need to beware that they are not exempt from the usual rules and regulations of social engagement and interaction. Specific court cases, sometimes resulting in imprisonment, reveal the perils of abusing social networking sites. The laws of defamation may be invoked when such abuse occurs. Users need to heed the legal framework within which they operate; threatening or offensive tweets have resulted in court action being taken. Racist and homophobic abuse has been challenged and prosecuted. Such offensive cases include the person who tweeted offensive messages about footballer Fabrice Muamba (he recovered after suffering a cardiac arrest on the football pitch), the man who threatened former Conservative MP, Louise Mensch, and the man arrested in Kent for posting a picture of a burning poppy. Celebrities such as Katherine Jenkins and Tom Daley have been the victims of such abuse. The prosecutions come under section 127 of the Communications Act 2003—which relates to sending 'grossly offensive' messages over the telecoms networks. In 2011, a total of 1286 people were prosecuted under Section 127.[4] In addition to the Communications Act 2003, there is also the Malicious Communications Act 1988, which includes electronic communications. A key court case involved Paul Chambers who, in January 2010, tweeted a joke about bombing Doncaster Airport. In July 2012, Chambers won an appeal at the High Court against his conviction. The presiding judge, Justice Igor Judge, said that the law should not prevent 'satirical or iconoclastic or rude comment, the expression of unpopular or unfashionable opinion about serious or trivial matters, banter or humour, even if distasteful to some or painful to those subjected to it'.[5] This decision may possibly lead to less of a knee-jerk reaction to satirical or 'off the cuff' comment, the prize being freedom of speech.[6] On the contrary, it may mean critics feel that it is easier for nasty, threatening, sexist and violent comment to go unchallenged.

It could be that people feel cocooned from prosecution when they write such comments, possibly in the sanctity of their own bedrooms. This is not to defend but rather to understand such behaviour, for is it too easy to fire off an offensive message without pausing for thought in relation to the potential repercussions of such action? In the heat of the moment, a 140-character tweet may seem relatively innocuous. Yet, it should be borne in mind that sending an offensive, or even illegal, tweet can lead to the loss of one's good name, one's employment and, in the final instance, even the loss of one's liberty. This represents a substantial price to pay for, what some commentators might regard as, a moment of madness.

As stated, academics have begun to see the potential of *Twitter*™, as have politicians and policymakers alike. The 2012 US presidential election, for example, culminated in a victorious tweet from Barack Obama that simply stated 'Four more years'. The 2011 Arab Spring uprising was renowned for the way in which tweets kept the wider world informed in relation to what was happening in Egypt, Tunisia and elsewhere. Ordinary people were able to relay their message to the wider world and get 'their' story out to the public at large in a way that would have been unfeasible only a relatively short time previously. More negatively, although it was later disputed, some blamed *Twitter*™ for inciting and perpetuating the UK riots in August 2011.

New Sites

Two relatively new social media sites that are increasingly used by young people are *Instagram*™ and *Snapchat*™. Created by Kevin Systrom and Mike Krieger and launched in 2010, *Instagram* is a free, online mobile photo-sharing, video-sharing and social networking service. *Snapchat* is a free, mobile messaging application and can be used to share photos, videos, texts and drawings. It is said to be particularly popular with young people. Created by Evan Spiegel, Bobby Murphy and Reggie Brown when they were students at Stanford University, *Snapchat* was launched in 2011. In a survey conducted in 2013, 22 per cent of 16–24-year-olds used *Snapchat*, compared with 4 per cent aged 25–34, 2 per cent aged 35–44, 1 per cent aged 45–54 and 3 per cent aged 55 and more.[7] In terms of *Instagram* usage, it had 14 million users in the UK in July 2015, and a younger profile than Facebook, with 39 per cent of *Instagram* users aged 16–24. In addition, 64 per cent of *Instagram* users are female.[8] Since 2014, *Facebook* has seen a 7 per cent drop in active usage in the UK, whereas *Instagram* has had an 18 per cent increase. In addition, 16–24-year-olds make up 16 per cent of *Facebook*'s UK users.[9] In terms of social media usage in the USA, 28 per cent of adult Internet users use *Instagram*. This breaks down as 55 per cent aged 18–29, 28 per cent aged 30–49, 11 per cent aged 50–64 and 4 per cent aged 65 and more.[10] Other sites include *Tumblr*, which is a cross between a social networking site and a blog, and *Flickr*, which is a photo-sharing site.

Does It Aid Greater Participation?

In terms of whether or not it aids greater participation, new technology certainly facilitates involvement and inclusion. It makes it easier for one to participate and, potentially, for one to participate politically (cf. Raoof et al. 2013; Gibson and McAllister 2015). At the touch of a button or a screen people have the ability to air their views and/or cast their vote. Witness the popularity of popular television programmes that permit audience participation such as *The X Factor, I'm a Celebrity Get Me Out of Here* or *Big Brother*. The ease of being able to vote online, via SMS text messaging or over the telephone, results in huge numbers of people, potentially, having their say. Certainly, the existence of the redial button permitting repeat voting means that the total numbers of votes does not equate to the total number of voters but, certainly, the popularity of such programmes evidences the extent to which huge numbers of people *are* prepared to participate. If they care about an issue, a topic or an individual then people can be galvanised into taking action. The potential certainly exists for this to be transferred to the political arena. If people are interested then they will participate. Politicians and policymakers should take note! Andy Furlong and Fred Cartmel illuminate how UK politics is traditionally 'rooted in class-based cleavages underpinned by collectivism' (2012: 26) but that in the contemporary scenario 'class consciousness finds weak expression and young people are forced [to] negotiate complex transitions, individualised rather than collective solutions may be sought by young people whose top priority is to get by and attempt to juggle complex lives lived out in multiple institutional sites' (Ibid.). This may, in fact, be part of the issue. Young people are not uninterested in politics but because of the way modern life operates and the pace at which it takes place, they participate in different ways. Engagement via new social media might be one way of bridging that gap, enabling individualised/ atomised young people to participate in politics on their terms. As Simon Tormey points out, 'many experts have noted, young people are particularly unreceptive to electoral or mainstream politics' (2015: 3). To quote the fictitious Jean Louise (Scout) Finch in Harper Lee's sequel *Go Set a Watchman*, 'Politics bores me to distraction' (2015: 78). This is probably the mantra of many young people. Tormey proceeds to ask whether the answer to youth apathy is citizenship classes and/or compulsory voting, as in Belgium and in Australia, continuing 'one of the persistent themes of work on the topic of the crisis of representation is the "boredom" or "apathy" of young people; code for the reluctance of the young to vote for or mandate a representative to act on their behalf' (Tormey, *op. cit*: 7). It could be that new social media provide an antidote to this reluctance.

There have been moves in this direction, with online voting piloted as a way of rectifying low voter turnout at local level in some areas. Part of the issue, however, is that it may be relatively easy to facilitate the actual act of casting one's vote, but the problem lies deeper. The question is how do we re-engage a potentially disengaged electorate? The November 2012 elections for the new Police and Crime Commissioners, held in 41 areas in England and Wales, are a case in point. Some commentators excused the low turnout by saying that these were first-time elections, that people need to get used to them and that they would have had a higher turnout had they been held in May (as the next set will be in 2016). Nonetheless, a turnout figure of 14 per cent is shocking by anyone's standards and raises clear questions about what this means for democracy and for political participation *per se*. The question is whether electronic voting would have significantly altered the turnout figure. Some academics and commentators suspect not, especially given the apparent lack of interest with which the general public greeted the prospect of elected Police Commissioners. It is not just about having a 'way' to participate, it is about having the 'will' to do so too. New technology may facilitate the physical act of casting one's vote but, if people are not engaged with the political system, no matter how easy it is made, they will still not participate. The concept of political participation was examined in detail in Chap. 2 with Sherry Arnstein's *Ladder of Political Participation*, later adapted by David Hart, providing a graphic illustration that there are varying degrees of participation and not all participation is as it seems.

E-participation, however, is not just about voting, and includes discussion, engagement and other forms of activism (cf. Ward and de Vreese 2011, on political consumerism). It could, for example, be a way for people to garner information about political events and happenings. Luis Hestres illuminates how the 'Internet has also become a critical conduit of freedom of expression, particularly in democratic societies. Many scholars have found a positive relationship between Internet use and political engagement. ...This relationship seems to hold across nationalities ... and seems especially strong among young people' (Hestres 2013: 1266). Many young people, for example, now claim to receive most of the political news and information from online sources. It is a way for them to share ideas with like-minded people and to question those in positions of political power. This aside, there is the existence of the phenomenon of so-called silver surfers; for example, 31 per cent of the UK's Web users include people over the age of 50.[11] As the *Telegraph* stated in June 2010, 'Nearly 39 million Britons use the internet regularly and people over 50 now make up more than a quarter of those users'.[12] More than 12 million people aged 50 and above now use the Internet on a regular basis. Older people appear to be becoming more *au fait* with the Internet and, in addition, many sites are specially targeting older people, the so-called grey pound being attractive to those with business acumen. These people are said to regularly use the Internet and online access. On the contrary, the 'older-old' tend to be least likely to use the Internet. The charity Age UK estimates that 70 per cent of those aged more than 65 years have never used the Internet and could fall victim to 'digital exclusion',[13] left behind in terms of information and, possibly, Internet deals. The majority of people who make regular use of the Internet are still, however, said to be young people. Given that they have grown up with computers, this is hardly surprising. For young people, computers have been part of their lives since infancy. They will not remember a time before the all-pervasive home computer. Even for middle-aged people growing up in the 1970s and 1980s, they can remember a time pre-Internet whereby information was gleaned primarily from books, television and newspapers. Where computers did exist, such as the Amstrad or the Sinclair Spectrum, they were rudimentary, extremely slow to work and prone to crashing. They were, therefore, a world away from the superfast broadband which exists today, with search engines that can answer most questions in an instant and e-books that make paper-based sources if not a thing of the past, certainly an acquired taste. Mobile technology has facilitated this information revolution even further; the size and speed of such devices mean that information, as well as being available at the touch of a button in the home environment, is now accessible on the move. Location is no longer a hindrance to information. Protest movements and extremists have been able to utilise the speed and immediacy of the Internet and mobile devices to further their cause. As Emily Bell states, 'The language of protest and shock have adapted themselves more quickly to the new technology platforms than any filtering mechanism or official media can keep up with. Whether it is the relatively benign topless ambushes of the Femen group of feminists, the handmade signs of Occupy Wall Street, or the hacking of Twitter accounts of the Syrian Electronic Army, protest can aggregate an international audience before the news anchor has brushed her hair.

Terror has adopted the same path as we witnessed with the Boston bombings and now the butchering of a man in broad daylight on a London street' (Bell 2013:10). Bell's latter example is a reference to British soldier Lee Rigby who was brutally murdered on a London street in May 2013. The technology can be used to spread the message about a cause—be that a cause with which the majority would agree or a cause or action that they would find abhorrent.

For younger people, therefore, new technology has facilitated participation in politics (cf. Bakker and de Vreese 2011; Loader et al. 2016). Most young people own or possess a mobile phone. If this is compared with landline usage, it can be seen that there is a clear generational difference. Many young people say that they never use a landline but rely totally upon their mobile phone for communicating with others. As Morena Cuconato and Natalia Waechter state, 'New Internet-based communication offers both the tools to facilitate a pervasive diffusion of youth culture and an arena in which young people can find free space to renegotiate and as a result reinvent their individual and collective identity as independent social, cultural and political actors' (2012: 143). New technology, therefore, has the potential to facilitate greater political participation by young people. The notion of providing the 'tools' or vehicle with which to do this and a 'space' or political arena within which to discuss and participate is worthy of flagging up. Cuconato and Waechter go on to say that the 'recent Arab revolution shows that new technology has brought an extension of the aims of participation, broadening their territorial spectrum and enabling co-ordination and political influence on a transnational scale' (Ibid: 150). They illuminate the extent to which media hype over-emphasises the power of social media, in that 'even if social media did play a leading role in driving the uprising in Tunisia and especially in Egypt, the idea of a "Twitter revolution" or "Facebook revolt" as spread through the media worldwide sounds hyperbolic' (Ibid: 151). People are still needed to take action even if the technology does facilitate the communication of ideas and any 'message'. Having said this, if the press and usual channels of communication are suppressed then it is not surprising that 'Twitter, Facebook, YouTube and other local social media sites become essential in getting news out of the country, and mainstream media has come to depend on citizens reporting for their own coverage' (Ibid: 152). One only has to look at television news today to see the number of occasions whereby news reports rely on citizen journalists to provide footage caught instantaneously on mobile phone cameras. This illustrates that it has become increasingly difficult for journalists to keep up with the pace of events. Gone are the days when journalists would be immediately dispatched to an incident or happening to find that they were the first on the scene recording events. Nowadays, it is increasingly likely that a member of the public will have already captured the key moments, and it is that initial footage which has caught the event on camera and is used by news agencies worldwide. Given all this, Cuconato and Waechter believe that we should not exaggerate the potential power of new social media for engaging young people in politics and political activity. In their view, it should be seen for what it is—a tool, vehicle, conduit or similar—and that the real power is the young people themselves. Some of the issues explored in Chap. 1, such as youth unemployment and increasing higher education tuition fees, might galvanise these young people into becoming increasingly politicised and politically active. Granted, they may use new social media to discuss, debate, plan and organise, but it is the young people themselves who are the driving force behind this activity. Andrés Scherman et al. in their study of youth protests in Chile differentiate between so-called cyberoptimists, who see social media as reducing 'the costs of communication, association and participation' (2015: 153) and cyberpessimists who 'argue that the use of the Internet drives people away from politics, public affairs and social life' (Ibid.) before proceeding to identify a more 'nuanced reality ... [whereby] the effects of online technologies on the political behaviour of young people are mediated by specific uses (e.g. information versus entertainment) and moderated by predispositions' (Ibid.). Likewise, Donatella della Porta accords that 'opinions on the advantages and disadvantages of the Internet are split' (2013: 88). As with most aspects of life, there are both positive and negatives associated with the usage of social media.

Shakuntala Banaji and David Buckingham divulge 'long-term reductions in voting rates, declining levels of trust in politicians and waning interest in civic affairs' (2012: 159) and so seek to question whether the Internet can, in fact, deliver in terms of 're-engaging young people in the public sphere, and of creating new forms of political and civic culture among young people?' (Ibid: 161). They also looked at whether 'participation online result[s] in greater participation offline?' (Ibid.) and whether some young people are more likely than others to do this. In a study panning seven European countries (namely, Hungary, the Netherlands, Slovenia, Spain, Sweden, Turkey and the UK), they examined levels of civic potential provided by the Internet, examining 'approximately fifty civic/political websites and thirty youth specific sites in each country, making a total of 560 sites' (Ibid.). They found that 'interest in civic and political websites appeared to be stronger among older respondents (19–25-year-olds rather than 15–18-year-olds), those not living with their parents, those who identified themselves as religious, and girls and young women' (Ibid: 163). This gender dimension is interesting and is examined in greater depth in Chap. 7 where the focus is upon gender and youth political participation. In addition, the Internet was 'an important tool for young people who were already engaged in civic or political activities offline' (Ibid.). According to Banaji and Buckingham's study, despite the existence of 'interactive applications such as blogs, wikis, message boards, forums, video uploading, podcasts and so on, static websites composed primarily of written text and a few visual images still appear to be the norm' (Ibid: 164). It is worth pointing out, therefore, that despite this myriad of interactive applications and differing vehicles for conveying information, young people appear to be relatively conservative in terms of the usage that they are making of these new(er) forms of communication. Perhaps young people are not quite so impressed by the whizz-bang approach to political participation as might at first be thought. Yes, they are using the new technology but beyond that they are relatively conventional in terms of how they use it.

Young People, New Media and Political Participation

There is a fledgling but expanding literature on new social media and youth political participation (cf. Theocharis 2010, 2012; White and McAllister 2014). Therese O'Toole, for example, has specifically investigated political participation amongst young members of the ethnic minorities. She outlines how new media have facilitated their political participation by flagging up, 'research suggesting that globalised forms of communication and networking have made internet based political action increasingly significant, and, facilitated by new technologies, contemporary forms of action are increasingly concerned with global issues. An important aspect of this development is the enhanced scope for networking, consciousness-raising and DIY activism' (O'Toole 2014: 29). In the study 'activists' use of Information and Communications Technology (ICT) was important in facilitating more direct forms of engagement with global and international issues, and these captured the imagination of many activists—in ways which found little equivalence at the level of national politics' (Ibid.). The international dimension and global reach of new social media is clearly an aspect that appeals to young people, in this specific scenario of young people from ethnic minority backgrounds.

Cross-national research, focusing upon Spain, the Netherlands and Italy, carried out by Davide Calenda and Albert Meijer, centres on young people's political participation and the Internet. Their online survey, completed by 2224 students, reveals 'that political participation in the digital world both reproduces and challenges existing forms of political participation' (2009: 881). Perhaps, not surprisingly, young people 'who read about politics in newspapers will read about it online, the ones that read about sports will not suddenly decide to visit websites providing political information' (Ibid: 882). Calenda and Meijer find that 'the extent of online political participation is influenced both by the level of internet use and the extent of offline political participation [...] participation is influenced by the technology that provides support for the idea that young people take practices of participation from different domains (MySpace, YouTube) into their political behaviour' (Ibid: 893–894). Scherman et al. (2015: *Op. cit*: 167) see a positive correlation between 'the use of both Facebook and Twitter and participation in student demonstrations and street marches against the construction of a power plant in Patagonia. Controlling for ideology, political interest, social capital and traditional media, people with an active account in these online media are more likely to protest'. Online political participation is, therefore, certainly undertaken by young people, but it does depend upon how much they participate politically offline. Presumably, if a young person is uninterested in politics, it is unlikely that social media, regardless of the interaction that they potentially facilitate, will cultivate that interest by itself.

Research conducted by Mark Shephard et al. also reveals the prevalence of social media as a way for young people to participate politically. As the authors state, 'Opportunities range from the capacity to receive and share information, but also to interact with a global audience. But challenges are also widespread, and include selective consumption/interaction, inadequate representation of viewpoints, limitations in the space available to communicate, and knowing the degree to which online information is actually valid' (Shephard et al. 2014: 37). Clearly, the opportunities for political participation and engagement are many and varied, but there are also limitations and pitfalls with regards to social media. Their research looks at social media platforms in relation to the Scottish independence referendum and analyses more than 5300 comments on the BBC's *Have*

Your Say discussion threads. They believe that citizens, especially young citizens, 'would benefit from knowing more about these channels and the way they operate, which would then allow citizens to cast a critical eye over what they read, see and hear via social media' (Ibid: 40). Shephard et al. expose some of the pitfalls of social media usage and advocate 'Statutory provision in citizenship education programmes in schools, colleges and universities across the UK of training for young people to use social media in critical participative ways' (Ibid: 40). Social media is a valuable conduit for political participation but it does have drawbacks. The suggestion put forward by Shephard et al., namely, that young people need to be educated in its usage, is an important precursor to engagement in the political process.

Another platform or vehicle permitting political participation is the e-petition. The usage of the traditional petition system in politics has a long history, as evidenced by the petitions bag for paper-based petitions located behind the Speaker's Chair in the House of Commons. The e-petition, therefore, constitutes a relatively recent phenomenon. The collation of signatures in support of a specific proposal or issue has existed for centuries and, indeed, is one of the basic tenets of the democratic system facilitating the expression of public opinion. It is a classic example of direct democracy in action. Witness, for example, the petitions in support of votes for women. The first petition asking for the vote for women was presented to Parliament in 1832 by Henry Hunt, MP. Another one of the petitions in support of the extension of the franchise to women was presented to Parliament by the philosopher and politician John Stuart Mill in 1866. It contained around 1500 signatures and can, coincidentally, still on occasion be seen on display in the confines of the Palace of Westminster. The petition is a useful device for enabling politicians and those in positions of political power to gauge the strength of public opinion on any given issue. Debate centres on how much importance politicians attach to petitions and whether they take them seriously. Given that women did not get the vote until 1918 at the age of 30, and 1928 at the age of 21, on the same terms as men, it is debatable as to the impact that a petition has upon the political process. They can, however, help to raise awareness of an issue and to keep up the pressure for change even if they don't necessarily result in immediate action.

More recently, traditional, paper-based petitions have given way to electronic or e-petitions. As Rushanara Ali MP states, 'Online campaigning platforms such as Avaaz and 38 Degrees often gain hundreds of thousands—and sometimes millions—of signatories for their petitions. Mass participation is not dead, even if it is often little more than the click of a mouse' (Ali 2014: 45). The Coalition Government's e-petition website (epetititons.direct.gov.uk) was launched in August 2011. This was preceded by the Labour Government's petition initiative, 'The 10 Downing Street e-petitions system, introduced in November 2006, also demonstrated the public appetite for an online system; it received 5.5 million signatures on 29,000 petitions in its first year of operation alone. In July 2007 the government's Governance of Britain Green Paper welcomed the proposal for an e-petitions system' (Hansard Society 2012: 11). New technology facilitates the opportunity for ordinary citizens to participate in the political process. At the touch of a button, people can vote on the issues of the day or can, given certain provisos, set up a petition themselves. It is relatively easy, once people have access to the appropriate computer equipment and technology, for citizens to express their viewpoint on a whole host of topics. Some might argue that it is, potentially, almost too easy to participate and that the e-petitions require a degree of political education to have taken place to ensure that people are voting in an informed and educated manner. The e-petition is not simply something that is started by politicians in order for them to ascertain public opinion on any given issue; it is also an opportunity for the ordinary people to instigate the political process and for them to try to get topics and issues on to the political agenda. A whole host of e-petitions have been initiated by numerous individuals and campaigning groups and it is now easier than ever before for people to start the political ball rolling. The government has also decreed that once a petition attains at least 100,000 signatures, then it *may* gain time for it to be discussed in Parliament. The emphasis is upon the word 'may', as reaching the magical figure of 100,000 signatories does not automatically guarantee that the topic will be discussed. There is still a filtering system, or gatekeeper role, in operation. This has led to frustration amongst some people, particularly members of the public who perhaps assumed, wrongly, that crossing the threshold of the 100,000 signatures meant that the topic was guaranteed time for discussion in Parliament. Reconnecting this back to the ladder of participation, mentioned earlier, people will stop participating if they feel that no action is being taken, and thus it may end up having a negative effect. According to a Hansard Society report on e-petitions, 'the public is generally more likely to sign a petition than they are to engage in most other forms of democratic activity apart from voting' (Hansard Society 2012: 5). They do point out, however, that 'it is not, in its current form, a means to empower them through greater engagement in the political and specifically parliamentary process and it affords only limited opportunity for deliberation on the issues raised' (Ibid: 9). It is worth, at this juncture, reiterating the theories of political participation, outlined in Chap. 2, and recognising that there are degrees of political participation. Given that young people are more likely to use new technology than their older counterparts, it is probable that they are more likely to use the e-petition system in order to air their views and participate in politics.

As can be seen, young people are using new social media in order to discuss, debate and organise politically, but social scientists and other commentators need to be wary of attaching too much importance to this, relatively, new technology. It is the medium but it should not and has not become the message. Having said this, Jon Savage, for one, expresses a positive note, 'Today's teenagers will find solutions to the pressing problems that vex adults. They are already familiar with ideas of sustainability at the same time as they swim in a media revolution that is still ill-understood by adults' (Savage 2014: 19). Savage is acutely aware that young people appear more at ease with new technology than the majority of adults who have not grown up in the era of new technology. Young people have usually been immersed in new technology throughout their formative years. They often display a familiarity, a confidence and a competency far beyond that of most adults, who, whilst not exactly technophobic, have had to learn these new skills in adulthood.

It is still relatively early days with regards to new media and how they impact the political system and provide opportunities for people to participate politically. As Scherman et al. (*Op. cit.* 167) state, 'Offline and online actions are complementary forms of participation—not competitive ones'. The Speaker's Commission on Digital Democracy illustrates how politicians are keen to explore the possibilities for political engagement expedited by new technology. The Commission investigated the opportunities offered for political participation/parliamentary democracy by digital technology. It reported in January 2015. The views of young people appear particularly important to the Speaker's Commission on Digital Democracy, and specific events were held to elicit those views. For example, a round-table discussion was held at *Facebook* in London and focused upon the following questions, 'What comes to mind when you think of politics and politicians?, What could MPs do to involve young people in talking about politics and making decisions that affect you? What is the best way for you to access information about politics and government?'.[14] In addition, the Speaker's Commission on Digital Democracy held a national online student forum coordinated by Commissioner Cristina Leston-Bandeira, with student representatives from eight UK universities. Their remit was to discuss the challenges of digital democracy.[15] It is evident that students and young people *per se* were of central importance to the Speaker's Commission on Digital Democracy. The Commission's findings (published 26 January 2015) constitute an interesting read. As well as recommending online voting, the Report urges 'better' and 'more effective engagement' between the public and Parliament. The Report is explicit in stating, 'The House of Commons should take further steps to improve active involvement by young people' (2015: 10).

Young people (18–24-year-olds) constitute approximately 14 per cent of the UK electorate (Moira Swinbank, chief executive of vInspired, cited in Watts 2014). Given that 194 seats could change hands with just a 5 per cent swing, this potential power should not be underestimated (cf. Swinbank 2014). This is a sizeable proportion and could, in fact, illustrate that they potentially constitute an extremely powerful force in British politics. The youth volunteering charity, vInspired, launched the 'Swing the Vote' campaign to encourage young people to vote in 2015. As CEO Moira Swinbank states, vInspired is 'challenging politicians to recognise the power young people have to swing the election and to start communicating with them using the language and the mediums that young people use' (Swinbank 2014). She reveals that '69 per cent of young people claim a politician could actually win their vote if they were to embrace social media to communicate their principles and promises ... as a start, we have challenged all party leaders to present their top five policies affecting young people in five tweets' (Ibid.). This constitutes a direct challenge to politicians to connect with young people. The plea for the party leaders to use new technology and particular channels of communication with which young people are perhaps more familiar is an interesting dimension. As Loader et al. concur, 'Politicians wishing to connect with and build a constituency of young citizens ... need to understand contemporary youth culture and the central role social media plays within it' (2016: 404). Having said this, Nigel Jackson (2003) illuminated, more than a decade ago, how politicians could utilise new technology to get their message across and connect with the people so MPs have hardly rushed to embrace the full potential of Web-based technologies.

Conclusion

New technology might be the way for young people to mobilise and acti-vate that potential power and for them to utilise the strength afforded to them by their numbers. After explaining what is meant by new media, this chapter proceeded to analyse how it might be utilised to aid greater political participation. This was then assessed in relation, specifically, to young people and political participation. As Jonathan Birdwell, Charlie Cadywould and Louis Reynolds point out, 'Social media are a critical new space for political discourse and engagement, which political institu-tions cannot afford to neglect' (Birdwell et al. 2014: 61). The notion of an online community or e-democracy might be a factor that particularly appeals to young people. They may not necessarily vote in huge numbers, but digital democracy may have a particular appeal to the younger gen-erations. One possibility worthy of further exploration is former Labour Leader Ed Miliband's suggestion of a public question time, whereby members of the public interrogate the Prime Minister. If this does comes to fruition (new Labour leader, Jeremy Corbyn, asked Labour members to send him their questions for Prime Minister's Question Time), new technology may facilitate that process and young people might form a large proportion of the questioners. Technological advancement has the undoubted potential to revolutionise how politics takes place, and it is evident that this is happening already.

It is necessary, at this juncture, to examine another key aspect with respect to young people and political participation, namely, the vexed question of whether or not the voting age should be lowered to 16 years—which we discuss in Chap. 5.

Notes

1. http://www.guardian.co.uk/technology/2012/may/15/twitter-uk-users-10m accessed 16 November 2012.
2. http://mashable.com/2012/03/21/twitter-has-140-million-users/ accessed 16 November 2012.
3. Ibid.
4. http://www.guardian.co.uk/technology/2012/may/15/twitter-uk-users-10m accessed 16 November 2012.
5. http://www.salon.com/2012/11/15/in_uk_twitter_facebook_rants_land_some_in_jail/ accessed 16 November 2012.

6. See Ronson (2015) for the pros and cons of social media.
7. See http://www.statista.com/statistics/308746/snapchat-usage-among-social-media-users-by-age-uk/ accessed 9 May 2016.
8. See http://avocadosocial.com/1095-2/ accessed 9 May 2016.
9. See http://socialmedialondon.co.uk/facebook-instagram-usage-2015/ accessed 9 May 2016.
10. See Duggan, M. (2015). The demographics of social media users, 19 August. http://www.pewinternet.org/2015/08/19/the-demographics-of-social-media-users/ accessed 30 April 2016.
11. http://www.itpro.co.uk/624724/silver-surfers-dominate-uk-web-use accessed 18 November 2012.
12. http://www.telegraph.co.uk/technology/internet/7862234/Silver-surfers-increase-by-one-million-over-the-last-year.html published 30 June 2010, accessed 18 November 2012.
13. Ibid.
14. See: http://www.parliament.uk/business/commons/the-speaker/speakers-commission-on-digital-democracy/ddc-news/young-persons-roundtable-at-facebook/accessed 12 July 2014.
15. See summaries of the online student forum: http://www.parliament.uk/business/commons/the-speaker/speakers-commission-on-digital-democracy/publications/student-forum-summaries/ accessed 27 July 2014.

BIBLIOGRAPHY

Ali, R. (2014). In the real world. *RSA Journal,* Issue 1, 44–45.
Bakker, T. P., & de Vreese, C. H. (2011). Good news for the future? Young people, Internet use, and political participation. *Communication Research, 38*(4), 451–470.
Banaji, S., & Buckingham, D. (2012). Young people and online civic participation: Key finding from a pan-European research project. In P. Loncle, M. Cuconato, V. Muniglia, & A. Walther (Eds.), *Youth participation in Europe: Beyond discourses, practices and realities* (pp. 159–172). Bristol: The Policy Press.
Bell, E. (2013). Commentary: All the world's an outside broadcast. *The Guardian,* 24 May.
Birdwell, J., & Bani, M. (2014). *Introducing generation citizen.* London: Demos.
Birdwell, J., Cadywould, C., & Reynolds, L. (2014). *Tune in, turn out.* London: Demos. Retrieved September 18, 2015, from http://www.demos.co.uk/files/Tune_in_-_web.pdf?1419813387

Calenda, D., & Meijer, A. (2009). Young people, the internet and political participation. *Information, Communication and Society*, *12*(6), 879–898.

Cuconata, M., & Waechter, N. (2012). Interplay of youth culture, Web 2.0 and political participation in Europe: New reflections after the 'youth quake' in Northern Africa and the Middle East. In P. Loncle, M. Cuconato, V. Muniglia, & A. Walther (Eds.), *Youth participation in Europe: Beyond discourses, practices and realities* (pp. 143–158). Bristol: The Policy Press.

della Porta, D. (2013). *Can democracy be saved?* Cambridge: Polity Press.

Eliasoph, N. (2013). *The politics of volunteering*. Cambridge: Polity Press.

Furlong, A., & Cartmel, F. (2012). Social change and political engagement among young people: Generation and the 2009/2010 British Election Survey. *Parliamentary Affairs*, *65*, 13–28.

Gibson, R. K., & McAllister, I. (2015). Normalising or equalising party competitition? Assessing the impact of the web on election campaigning. *Political Studies*, *63*, 529–547.

Hansard Society. (2012). *What next for e-petitions?* London: Hansard Society.

Hestres, L. E. (2013). App neutrality: Apple's app store and freedom of expression online. *International Journal of Communication*, *7*, 1265–1280.

Jackson, N. (2003). MPs and Web technologies: An untapped opportunity? *Journal of Public Affairs*, *3*(2), 124–137.

Lee, H. (2015). *Go set a watchman*. London: Heinemann.

Lilleker, D., & Jackson, N. A. (2010). Towards a more participatory style of election campaigning: The impact of Web 2.0 on the UK 2010 general election. *Policy and Internet*, *2*(3), article 4, 69–98.

Loader, B. D., Vromen, A., & Xenos, M. A. (2016). Performing for the young networked citizen? Celebrity politics, social networking and the political engagement of young people. *Media, Culture and Society*, *38*(3), 400–419.

Moss, G., & Coleman, S. (2014). Deliberative manoeuvres in the digital darkness: E-democracy policy in the UK. *British Journal of Politics and International Relations*, *16*, 410–427.

O'Toole, T. (2014). Political engagement among ethnic minority young people. In A. Mycock & J. Tonge (Eds.), *Beyond the youth citizenship commission: Young people and politics* (pp. 28–31). London: Political Studies Association.

Raoof, J. K., Zaman, H. B., Ahmad, A., & Al-Qaraghuli, A. (2013). Using social network systems as a tool for political change. *International Journal of Physical Sciences*, *8*(21), 1143–1148.

Ronson, J. (2015). *So you've been publicly shamed*. London: Picador.

Savage, J. (2014). Time up for the teenager? *RSA Journal*, Issue 1, 16–19.

Scherman, A., Arriagada, A., & Valenzuela, S. (2015). Student and environmental protests in Chile: The role of social media. *Politics*, *35*(2), 151–171.

Shephard, M., Quinlan, S., Tagg, S., & Paterson, L. (2014). Engaging the brain as well as the heart: Political literacy and social media platforms. In A. Mycock

& J. Tonge (Eds.), *Beyond the youth citizenship commission: Young people and politics* (pp. 37–41). London: Political Studies Association.

Swinbank, M. (2014). What will get Britain's youth voting? *The Telegraph*, 5 June. Retrieved July 29, 2014, from http://www.telegraph.co.uk/education/educationopinion/10874359/What-will-get-Britains-youth-voting.html

Theocharis, Y. (2010). Young people, political participation and online postmaterialism in Greece. *New Media and Society, 13*, 203–223.

Theocharis, Y. (2012). Cuts, tweets, solidarity and mobilisation: How the Internet shaped the student occupations. *Parliamentary Affairs, 65*(1), 162–194.

Tormey, S. (2015). *The end of representative politics*. Cambridge: Polity Press.

Ward, J., & de Vreese, C. (2011). Political consumerism, young citizens and the Internet. *Media, Culture and Society, 33*(3), 399–413.

Watts, J. (2014). David Cameron's Cabinet reshuffle 'made young more likely to vote'—Poll suggests. *The London Evening Standard*, 28 July. Retrieved July 29, 2014, from http://www.standard.co.uk/news/london/david-camerons-cabinet-reshuffle-made-young-more-likely-to-vote-9632851.html

Webb, P. (2015). Construct interactive populist platforms. *Times Higher Education*, 7 May, p. 41.

White, S., & McAllister, I. (2014). Did Russia (nearly) have a Facebook revolution in 2011? Social media's challenge to authoritarianism. *Politics, 34*, 72–84.

World Bank Report. (2012, July 17). Mobile phone access reaches three-quarters of the planet's population. Retrieved May 1, 2013, from http://www.worldbank.org/en/news/press-release/2012/07/17/mobile-phone-access-reaches-three-quarters-planets-population

CHAPTER 5

Should 16- and 17-Year Olds Be Given the Right to Vote?

LOWERING THE VOTING AGE TO 16

This chapter involves a detailed analysis of the key arguments for and against lowering the voting age to 16. The focus is upon a case study of Austria where, in 2007, the voting age was lowered to 16 (the first country out of the then 27 members of the European Union to do so for national elections). In addition, detailed investigation is made of the situation closer to home in Jersey, Guernsey and the Isle of Man where the voting age has been lowered to 16 years too. There is a vocal campaign in the UK to lower the voting age to 16 (cf. the *Votes at 16* Coalition) but many oppose this and both sides of the discussion are subject to in-depth analysis in this chapter. Two more examples from mainland Europe are incorporated into the study. These are Germany and Bosnia. The reason why this chapter investigates these two countries is that, firstly, with respect to Germany, it constitutes an interesting case study because there 16-year-olds can vote in some municipal elections in some states. Bosnia is chosen as the second country, the reason being that, in Bosnia, 16-year-olds can vote if they are employed. Examination is made of the way in which various bodies support lowering the voting age to 16. Equal consideration is given to the arguments espoused by those opposed to the idea of lowering the voting age. Analysis is provided as to why the majority of young people have not expressed support for this idea. Opinion tends to be polarised on this topic and this is what makes it such an interesting issue and worthy of detailed examination. It is not intended that the book becomes a vehicle

© The Author(s) 2017
J. Briggs, *Young People and Political Participation*,
DOI 10.1057/978-1-137-31385-0_5

for arguing in favour of lowering the voting age but, rather, that it illuminates the key arguments across the debate.

This chapter discusses briefly the notion of the right to vote, the history of the franchise, who can and cannot vote, more recent debates about extending the franchise, such as whether or not voting should be compulsory and in relation to prisoners' rights, before moving to analyse the lowering of the voting age to 16.

THE RIGHT TO VOTE

In order to analyse the arguments for and against lowering the voting age to 16 (cf. for example, Berry and Kippin 2014), it is worthwhile, first of all, analysing who currently has the right to vote. Voting is regarded as a basic human right. The right to participate politically, at the most basic level, voting, is a key determinant of citizenship. Democratic governance is based on the power of the people; indeed, the word emanates from the Greek words for people and power, 'demos' and 'kratos', respectively, and a key factor in that power relates to the possession of the vote and the ability to exercise that right. In terms of voting, most democracies permit elections at national level at least once every four of five years. In the UK, there has to be a general election at least once every five years. The Fixed-term Parliaments Act 2011 stipulates that the gap between general elections is five years, held the first Thursday in May with the next one set to take place on Thursday, 7 May 2020. The two exceptions are as follows: if a motion of no confidence in the government is passed by a simple majority and after 14 days a confidence motion has not been passed in any new government or if a motion for a general election is agreed by two-thirds of MPs (434 out of 650). The history of the franchise points to a long and arduous struggle for those without the vote to eventually become in possession of that right. Disenfranchised groups have usually had to struggle to attain the franchise. Witness, for example, the lengthy struggle of working class men for the vote. This took place primarily via organisations such as the nineteenth-century Chartist Movement, and through the early years of the Labour Party. The struggle for women to attain the vote, likewise, is well documented with the bitter, and often violent, struggles at the turn of the last century. The Women's Social and Political Union and the Suffragette Movement were key facilitators behind the push for votes for women. It is argued that these cases illustrate that those without the vote have not suddenly been given/gifted the vote by those with the political power to be able to do so. Disenfranchised groups have had to struggle to attain that right. The majority of working class men gained the vote in the 1918 Representation of the People Act (it rectified the fact millions of soldiers returning home after the First World War were not eligible to vote). The Act abolished almost all property qualifications for men and gave women, who met minimum property qualifications, the right to vote at the age of 30. The electorate trebled from 7.7 million to 21.4 million and women made up 43 per cent of the electorate. The age requirement meant that women did not, overnight, become the majority of the electorate—as they would have done had they been granted the vote on the same terms as men, especially given the numbers of men lost during the First World War. The Act also brought in the annual electoral register and the system of general elections being held on one specific day (see Parliamentary Archives).[1] It was not until ten years later via the 1928 Representation of the People (Equal Franchise) Act[2] that women gained the right to vote at the age of 21, on the same terms as men. The 1929 General Election was the first one, therefore, where women and men were equally entitled to vote. This Act also erased the ten-year anomaly (from 1918 until 1928) where, in theory at least and it never actually happened in practice, a woman could have stood for Parliament at the age of 21 but would not have been able to vote for herself until the age of 30! The voting age was further reduced to the age of 18, for both sexes, in 1969 under the Representation of the People Act of that year; this was in response to the review of the age of majority undertaken by the Latey Commission whose Report was presented to Parliament in July 1967. Part of the rationale behind this reduction in the voting age was that there were some in the Labour Party who believed that younger voters would be more likely to vote for them as opposed to the opposition. In reality, this was not the case and, although not just due to younger voters, and contrary to most of the opinion polls, Harold Wilson's Labour Government lost the subsequent 1970 General Election.

In terms of who can and who cannot vote, currently most people over the age of 18 have the opportunity, should they so wish, to vote for the candidates/political parties of their choosing. According to the Electoral Commission, therefore, those who have the right to vote in the UK must be registered to vote and be over age of 18, resident in the UK, a British citizen, a qualifying Commonwealth citizen or a citizen of the Republic of Ireland, not subject to any legal incapacity to vote. Those who cannot vote include members of the Lords (although they can vote in local elections and in elections to the devolved assemblies and the European elections), anyone other than a British, Irish or qualifying Commonwealth citizen, convicted prisoners serving their sentence (although those on remand, if they register by making a declaration of local connection, unconvicted prisoners and those serving civil sentences can vote if they are on the electoral register), anyone found guilty within the previous five years of corrupt or illegal electoral practice.[3] Eligible British citizens living abroad were enfranchised by the Representation of the People Act 1985. This gave them the right to vote in UK Parliamentary and European elections for up to five years after they had left the UK. This qualifying period has since been extended to 15 years. Homeless people can register to vote by making a declaration of local connection to their local electoral registration office. Patients in psychiatric units can register to vote provided that they are not detained under specific sections of the 1983 Mental Health Act; or if they are convicted offenders. There is no literacy test or qualification required regarding eligibility to vote. If people are illiterate, they can ask the Presiding Officer at the polling station to mark their ballot paper on their behalf or else they can take a friend with them to the polling station to help them.[4]

COMPULSORY VOTING

In addition, it is correct to say 'should they so wish' because in the UK, the decision whether or not to vote is a personal one. Compulsory voting does not exist in this country even though there are a significant number of countries worldwide where citizens are compelled to vote. Belgium, for example, has had compulsory voting since 1893 and Australia has had it since 1924 (1915 in the state of Queensland). To be fair, compulsory voting is a misnomer because they do not compel people to 'vote' as such. In these countries, however, people are compelled to turn out to vote. A better descriptor, therefore, might be the label compulsory turnout. In states where voting is compulsory, it is actually attendance at the polling station that is compulsory and not the physical act of voting for one political party or another. Under a system of compulsion, there has to be the opportunity too for voters to place their cross in a box labelled 'None of the Above' (NOTA). This enables them to express their dissatisfaction with all of the candidates and political parties, should they so desire, and might, in fact, give a truer reflection of the wishes of the people. Voting is characterised by both positive and negative abstention. Negative abstention includes factors such as rains on polling day, something good on television (indeed,

'*Til Death Us Do Part* written by Johnny Speight and featuring the character Alf Garnett and an episode of *Eastenders* where a central character, Phil Mitchell, was shot are both said to have impacted the electoral turnout levels) or simply the 'can't be bothered' argument. Positive factors behind abstention relate to, for example, voters weighing up the merits and demerits of candidates and/or parties and making a definite decision whether or not to vote on the basis of factors such as specific personalities, policies and image.

Central debates surrounding compulsory voting relate to whether to be forced to vote constitutes an infringement of one's civil liberties, as some see it, arguing that the right not to vote is just as important as the right to vote (cf. Briggs and Celis 2010; Lever 2008). Others (cf. Watson and Tami 2000; Hill 2004) regard the exercise of one's vote as being more of a duty as opposed to a right and that people should be forced to fulfil their civic duty. They spotlight other areas in life where citizens are forced to fulfil their duties, such as, for example, sending one's children to school, paying taxes or serving on a jury. The state intervenes into our daily lives in a myriad of ways, they maintain, and compulsory voting is just an extension of that state coercion. There is an expanding literature on the topic of compulsory voting (cf. Electoral Commission 2006; White and Young 2007; Lacroix 2007; Lever 2008; Birch 2009; Briggs and Celis 2010); no doubt, politicians, policymakers and academics will continue to focus upon this debate, especially where turnout levels appear to have fallen dramatically.

General, local and European elections have all given cause for concern in terms of declining levels of turnout. Despite just under a 4 percentage point increase in 2010, only 65.1 per cent of those eligible to vote actually did so at the General Election, and 2015 was only marginally better at 66.1 per cent. Part of the issue too relates to differential turnout, with some sectors of society being more likely to vote than others. Women, traditionally, were one sector of the electorate least likely to vote. This 'gender gap' has now changed, in terms of political turnout. Given this potential power, it is worth noting that women in specific categories, such as young women, are traditionally less likely to vote. It is evident, therefore, that this potential power could be easily wiped out. At the 2001 General Election, for example, nearly two-thirds of 18–24-year-old women did not vote. At the 2005 General Election, for example, only 37 per cent of 18–24-year-olds turned out to vote, and this figure declines even further when young women are singled out. In 2010, 39 per cent of young women voted, and in 2015 a total of 44 per cent of young women voted (see Chap. 7). According to the Electoral Commission's survey on Gender and Political Participation,[5] women from ethnic minorities are also less likely to vote than men. What then is the answer? The Fawcett Society, for example, acknowledges that capturing the female vote is important for all parties. For some, the way forward lies in compulsory voting. Compulsion immediately alienates the mavericks and rebels amongst us. 'How dare the nanny state coerce us into the act of casting our vote?', we cry. A lifetime of fighting conformity is no easy task to ignore. Yet, let us not forget, as mentioned earlier, how we are compelled by the state in many other ways, from paying taxes through to serving on a jury or sending our children to school. Some critics simply see it as an infringement of our civil liberties, why should the state force us to participate or that apathetic and ill-informed voters hold too much sway (cf. White and Young 2007). To reiterate, it remains an important point that compulsory voting is somewhat of a misnomer, with some commentators (cf. Keaney and Rogers 2006) believing that it is better to refer to it as compulsory turnout, given that the voters are not compelled to actually vote but that they have to present themselves at the polling station. In addition, a box classified as 'None of the Above' would give a more accurate picture of the electorate's preferences rather than assuming that non-attendance at the polls signifies the 'politics of contentment' as Margaret Beckett stated when she referred to the phenomenon of Labour supporters not turning out to vote.

Supporters of compulsory voting believe, primarily, that electors should be forced to fulfil their civic duty. As Lord Kinnock, former leader of the Labour Party from 1983 until 1992, says, it is 'not only that people don't use their vote, they don't *think* about not using their vote'.[6] Compulsory voting would help to re-establish the voting norm. It would need, however, to be accompanied by an emphasis upon ensuring that the electoral register was as accurate as possible. The introduction of 'rolling registration', by the former Blair Government, has possibly helped. Advocates of compulsory voting also cite other arguments such as it being more democratic given that more people will be participating in the political process, decisions taken may have a greater degree of legitimacy, that it may have an educative effect if people are compelled to vote—encouraging people to take more of an interest in politics. There is also potentially a financial aspect in that parties do not need to spend money mobilising the voters (although they will need to try to tempt voters to vote for their party). The equality argument is also important in that all groups in society will participate—thus countering one of the pitfalls of voluntary voting whereby certain groups are more likely to vote than others (older people, for example), leading to differential turnout amongst certain sectors of society. Those of a countervailing viewpoint believe that compulsory voting is an infringement of one's civil liberties, that surely the freedom not to vote is just as important as the freedom to vote. They question whether an ill-informed and possibly poorly educated electorate is actually enhancing the democratic process, compulsion could be making apathetic and ill-informed voters structure political life. Far from educating people, compulsion may result in alienation and resentment, given that people are being forced to participate. There are also cost implications with a system of compulsory voting. Some seek to negate the equality argument in that even if certain groups are less likely to vote than others, they still remain potential voters and have the option of voting should they so desire. There are vocal supporters on either side of the debate; Peter Hain, Geoff Hoon (both former Labour cabinet ministers in the Blair and Brown governments) and, the aforementioned former Labour leader, Lord Kinnock have all been outspoken in their support of compulsory voting.

A further point to consider with compulsory voting is the question of what does the state do with non-voters. The notion of punishments or incentives is important here. Most states that operate a system of compulsory voting have in place a system of fines (Australia is an interesting case here, the fine is around AUD 20—about £9—but can be increased significantly if the non-voter goes to court). Other punishments include withdrawal of certain rights, for example, the right to a passport (as can happen in Brazil) and may even be as severe as imprisonment (rarely used but a sanction open to the authorities in Greece). In place of punishments (or the stick-approach), there is also the possibility of using an incentive ('carrot' approach) to encourage the electors to cast their vote.

In the USA, Jessica Alba, the actress and model, fronted a rather raunchy poster campaign to encourage young people to vote. Here, Hazel Blears (former Labour cabinet minister) outlined a lottery idea to get people vote at local level. This local lottery idea also found support amongst the independent Councillors Commission in the UK. There are echoes of California where, taking this notion of 'carrots' to the extreme, bribes have included free doughnuts, free chiropractor visits and even free chicken dinners! The use of incentives is not a new approach; indeed, Ancient Athens paid three 'obols' for each day of attendance at the Assembly. Incentive schemes could be the way forward or should we be advocating an approach that is tantamount to bribing electors to fulfil their democratic duty?

It remains the case, however, that certain people are more likely to vote than others; older people and those who have professional or non/manual occupations are more likely to vote. A Hansard Society poll in 2015 found that only 16 per cent of 18–24-year-olds were most likely to vote compared with 70 per cent of those aged more than 65 (Hansard Society 2015: 48). Women were very much the key to Labour winning the 2005 General Election; politicians ignore certain sectors, such as young voters and women at their peril. Females still only constitute 29.38 per cent of our MPs at Westminster and 31.5 per cent of our local councillors—hardly a resounding presence. Compulsory voting would encourage/coerce all groups to be counted but it would certainly mean more women would participate in the electoral process—particularly young women and women from the ethnic minorities; it may also mean that more women are (s)elected to political office. One result from the Electoral Commission's survey, *Gender and Political Participation*, is that where a constituency had a female MP, women were more likely to be politically active. More women as representatives could have a politically galvanising effect on women *per se*.

Martin Wattenberg believes that compulsory voting may be the key to increasing turnout amongst young people. He states, 'The best argument for the adoption of compulsory voting is simply that it works extremely well' (Wattenberg 2012: 197). He continues, 'Unlike many other democracies that are suffering from abysmally low youth turnout, these four countries [Australia, Belgium, Greece and Luxembourg] have recently experienced turnout rates ranging from 89 to 97 percent among citizens aged 18 to 29' (Wattenberg 2012: 197). Wattenberg joins other advocates of compulsory voting, such as Arend Lijphart,[7] in illuminating the reduction of differential turnout rates if voters are compelled to attend the polls.

As stated, older people are more likely to cast their vote. Anatole Kaletsky advises that we look to Hungary where the government proposed 'a truly significant reform. Hungarian mothers could be given extra votes on behalf of their children, to redress the imbalance in favour of older voters, which is increasing in all democracies with the ageing of the post-war baby-boom generation'. He argues that 'any system of genuine universal suffrage should recognise the interests of children who are too young to vote' and continues 'our present system fails to accord due weight to the interests of future generations and that bias against the young has recently become more extreme, threatening the future of democratic societies and economies'. Underlining how the baby boomers, born since 1946, are now retiring and benefitting from the austerity measures at the expense of other sectors of society, Kaletsky cites 'Free bus passes, television licences, winter fuel payments and age allowances have all been left untouched' (Kaletsky 2011: 23). He argues that the National Health Service has been protected in real terms and that the increase in public debt is in large measure due to increased spending on pensions, spending on health and care costs. The contention is that the fiscal crisis that would probably have come to the fore around 2020 has occurred earlier due to the recession/credit crunch.

Michael Sani, co-founder of the social enterprise *Bite the Ballot* (mentioned in Chap. 1), is in agreement with Kaletsky's observations. Sani observes that 'Ninety-six per cent of over 65s are registered to vote and there's an inherent link between voter registration and policies'. 'There's a reason the winter fuel allowance, free bus passes, free eye tests and free prescriptions aren't taken away—politicians fear being punished at the ballot box' (Sani cited in *Metro* 2014). Add in free TV licences for those aged more than 75 years too! Compare these high levels of older voter registration with younger registration and it is evident that a rational politician would focus upon the older voter if they were being purely instrumental. The drive to get young people to register to vote is even more important given the move from household registration to new voter registration self-regulation. The onus is on the individual to ensure that they are registered.

The Institute of Public Policy Research (IPPR) think tank has suggested compulsory voting for first timers (see Birch et al. 2013; Lawrence and Birch 2015). This is an interesting aspect to the compulsory voting debate—to introduce it solely for first-time voters. This might get them into the 'habit' of voting, to appreciate that voting is not so difficult and, possibly, to instil a sense of civic duty. Academic Mat Lawrence, research fellow for think-tank IPPR, believes first-time voters should be forced to vote, 'A distinctive non-voting population—generally younger and poorer—heightens political inequality by giving some groups far greater influence at the ballot box' (Lawrence, in *Yorkshire Post* 2015: 4). Compulsory voting was also the second most popular suggestion in the *Audit of Political Engagement 12* report, after online voting, as way of 'encouraging' electoral participation (Hansard Society 2015: 64). Matt Henn and Nick Foard have also examined this issue and point out that a problem with this approach is that 'it singles them out as "different" from the rest of the adult population, helping to reinforce the stereotype of this current youth generation as apathetic and politically irresponsible' (2014b: 19). The 'problem' is laid at the feet of the young people as opposed to with the political system. Perhaps this is a price worth contemplating if it enables young people to engage with politics. Interestingly, as an Intergenerational Foundation Report reveals, 'The only exception to the rule that young people are less likely to vote than the general population among the EU28 countries is Belgium, where younger people are slightly *more* likely to vote than the population average. Belgium is one of the few democracies which imposes compulsory voting on its citizens, where not voting carries fines of up to 50 Euros for a first offence and 125 Euros for a second one' (Leach et al. 2016: 27).

PRISONERS AND THE VOTE

A number of developments have resulted in increased momentum to the debate surrounding whether convicted prisoners should have the right to vote. Isobel White and Alexander Horne provide a succinct summary of those developments, cross-national comparisons and key arguments espoused by proponents and opponents (White and Horne 2014). A Parliamentary Joint Select Committee was set up to investigate votes for prisoners; it reported on 18 December 2013. The Committee requested, in essence, that the government should comply with the European Court of Human Right's judgement and enact legislation to give the right to vote to certain prisoners, those sentenced to 12 months or less. It also advocated that, six months before a scheduled release date, prisoners ought to be able to apply to register to vote. It recommended that a Bill be introduced in the 2014/2015 session of Parliament. The government did not, however, bring forward such a Bill in the 2014 Queen's Speech (see White and Horne 2014: 47–49). Furthermore, the UK Supreme Court rejected (July 2014) a bid by two convicted prisoners, Leslie Moohan and Andrew Gillon, to be able to vote in the independence referendum in Scotland in September 2014 (see Johnson 2014). As mentioned earlier, prisoners on remand can vote provided that they register by making a declaration of local connection. The European Court of Human Rights has ruled that it breaches the European Convention on Human Rights to prevent prisoners from being able to vote. In terms of whether or not prisoners should be allowed to vote, there are arguments in favour and against. These include the point that the punishment is the loss of liberty itself and to deprive prisoners of other rights is to go beyond punishing the crime. Those who oppose giving prisoners the right to vote believe that it is morally wrong that convicted criminals should be allowed to participate in the electoral process. Some proponents of votes for 16- and 17-year-olds argue that debate should centre on their concerns as opposed to focusing upon the needs/rights of prisoners. Others argue that both groups can argue their case from a rights-based perspective. Regardless, Prime Minister David Cameron was given a six-month ultimatum by the European Court of Human Rights, in April 2011, to legislate to end the ban on votes for convicted prisoners. Many Tory backbenchers were outraged by this ultimatum. The academic Susan Easton, however, believes that 'restoring the right to vote to convicted prisoners would be a positive step in affirming a commitment to fundamental rights' (Easton 2009: 224). She emphasises the social inclusion issue and how a denial of voting 'undermines civic respect and respect for the rule of law and thereby erodes the process of prisoner rehabilitation' (Easton 2009: 232). Easton also believes that 'The public's lack of sympathy may reflect their ignorance of the advantages of allowing enfranchisement, as well as their general punitiveness, so any changes would need to be carefully presented' (Easton 2009: 234). The government responded to the European Court ruling by announcing that prisoners serving less than four years would be eligible to vote but the former Minister for Political and Constitutional Reform Mark Harper said this was 'not a choice, it is a legal obligation' (Woodcock 2010). The European Court of Justice ruled, in October 2015, that sanctions must be proportionate, potentially paving the way for a legal challenge from prisoners convicted of lesser crimes. Sonja Grover reveals how 'the women's "suffrage" movement and the movement to gain the right to vote for felons (the latter still ongoing in some jurisdictions) both have relied on human rights rhetoric' (Grover 2010: 50). The human rights polemic furnishes a strong argument, but, clearly, opinion is polarised on the question of whether or not prisoners should be given the right to vote in elections. There are certainly parallels with the struggle for the vote for 16- and 17-year-olds.

YOUNG PEOPLE AND THE VOTE

A number of people and organisations have argued for the voting age to be lowered to 16. Amongst those who support lowering the voting age to 16 are politicians from all parties, the Welsh Assembly, the Scottish

Parliament, House of Lords and all the leading youth organisations. The Votes at 16 Campaign declares the fact that over 1.5 million 16- and 17-year-olds are currently denied the vote in the UK. The Votes at 16 Campaign reveals the various ways in which young people already participate politically and that, in their opinion, young people are far from apathetic. They state that '85 % of secondary schools have school councils, about 20,000 young people are active in local youth councils, often working in close collaboration with local councils and public services, there are 600 elected MYPs (Members of Youth Parliament) in the UK, each serving for 12 months and voted in by their peers. Established in 2000, the UK Youth Parliament has held debates in Parliament since 2008' (www. votesat16.org). The belief is that this indicates that young people have energy and passion, and that they deserve to be able to vote. As the former Shadow Minister for Justice Chris Bryant, MP, stated, we expect young people 'to take on significant levels of debt, and to consider doing so before they go to university, and I honestly believe that if they can make decisions about whether they can parent, about whether they have children, I think that they should also be able to decide who governs the country' (Bryant, House of Commons Debate 18 October 2010 cited in White 2011: 8). The struggle for the vote partly centres on the fact that, at the age of 16, people attain a number of other rights. Given that, at age 16, one can legally do many activities, such as, for example, leave school and enter work or training, they believe that a case can be made for acquiring the vote at 16. At age 16, a young person can leave school, give full consent to medical treatment, pay income tax and National Insurance, obtain tax credits and welfare benefits in their own right, consent to sexual relationships, get married or enter a civil partnership, join the armed forces, change the name by deed poll, become a director of a company, become a member of a trade union or a cooperative society, buy a lottery ticket (the youngest winner was a 16-year-old who won £2 million), pay adult fare on a bus. If that old adage 'No taxation without representation', coined by the Reverend Jonathan Mayhew in 1750 and prevalent during the American War of Independence 1775–1783, is to retain relevancy, then 16-year-olds paying taxes should be able to vote.[8] In terms of taxation, Reeves and Nadesan state that, 'Between November 2009 and January 2010, 380,000 16–17 year olds were in some sort of employment. The Department for Work and Pensions estimates that in the past decade the total tax liability for 16 and 17 year olds was over £550 million pounds (based on 563,000 16–17 year olds in some sort of work). During

2005–2006 alone this was approximately £47 million pounds' (Reeves and Nadesan 2010: 10). The figure of 380,000 equates to 25.3 per cent of those aged 16 and 17 years in the UK—estimated at around 1.5 million. Clearly, a significant amount of tax is being paid by 16- and 17-year-olds and which has a definite impact on the economy.

In terms of what one can and cannot do at various ages, there are a number of anomalies and oddities. At the age of 16, for example, one can buy liqueur chocolates, buy aerosol paint, buy a lottery ticket, participate in the Jeremy Kyle Show on television, join a trade union, drink wine or beer with a meal in a restaurant and drive a moped, amongst other things. At 17, a young person can take driving lessons. A person can own a pet from the age of 12, although some shops have a policy of not selling to those aged less than 16 years. At 13, a young person can legally work up to five hours on a Saturday or during the school holidays.[9] One issue to flag up is the lack of consistency between countries on these various ages of responsibility, for example, alcohol consumption. The comedian and writer Dawn French captures the feelings of many young people upon attaining these various milestones, in her novel *A Tiny Bit Marvellous*, when one character reels off a list of what she can now do at 18 including that she 'can vote, get married, join armed forces with parents' consent, buy cigarettes and alcohol, open a bank account without parents' signature, can change my name by deed poll, serve on a jury, buy a house, sue or be sued, make a will, place a bet, buy fireworks' (French 2011: 177–183). This character flags up the random quality of many of these 'rights' and it does make one question as to whether the state is correct to make her wait for some of these until she is 18 years, whereas some are attained at 16 years. Alex Folkes makes a fair point about the discrepancy of age limits when he says, 'Doesn't it send out the wrong message when in the eyes of the law voting requires more maturity than having a child and taking care of them for at least the next 16 years?' (2004: 53).

Amongst those who have expressed a desire to lower the voting age to 16, is the late Charles Kennedy, former leader of the Liberal Democratic Party. He is quoted as saying, 'When we call for votes at 16, we're drawing on a very fundamental Liberal Democrat belief'. He continues, 'We trust people to make decisions for themselves—the more responsibility you give them, the more responsible they will be' (BBC News 2002). Kennedy believed that lowering the voting age will make more people engage with politics and will make politicians take greater heed of the views of young people.

Arguments in Favour

In terms of key arguments in favour of lowering the voting age, these include the rights-based arguments. Simply put, to deny 16- and 17-year-olds the vote is to deny them their basic human rights. Lord Lucas, who introduced a Private Member's Bill on the topic in 2003, said the key reasons were for 'equity and justice' but also for the 'revival of active democratic politics' (cited in White 2011: 5). It is also, therefore, about democracy. Put simply, it is more democratic if more people are able to vote. It would mean that youth issues and the views of young people are included in politics and the policy-making agenda. It, therefore, expands democracy if this sector of society has the vote. Alex Folkes (2004:52) says it will 're-connect an entire generation of young people with our country's democratic structures'. Folkes describes research carried out by the Votes at 16 Campaign which has undertaken a number of focus group exercises with 11–24-year-olds and exposes how 'all but a tiny number claimed to have taken part in political acts such as going on marches, signing a petition or writing to an elected politician' (2004: 53). Clearly, many young people are already participating politically, is it right, therefore, to deny them the vote? Ben Kisby (2014a, b) believes, 'extending the franchise to this age group would create an excellent opportunity to increase youth interest and participation in mainstream and especially electoral politics', and that it would 'help re-focus citizenship education lessons that were introduced by Labour in 2002 and which, despite being revised and slimmed-down by the current Coalition Government, continue to contain an important political participative dimension'. Stephen Williams, the Liberal Democrat MP, who introduced a Private Member's Bill on this topic in November 2005, argued that it would foster young people's interest in politics, an interest that had ironically been fuelled by the Iraq war (White 2011: 6). It is claimed that lowering the voting age also increases the representativeness of those elected—if more people are able and have voted for them. It might encourage more participation in politics if young people feel they have some influence. Alex Folkes points out the way in which young people are sometimes manipulated, 'it is more common for young people to be used in photo opportunities than genuine consultation exercises' (2004: 55). As revealed by the Power Report, which recommended reducing both the voting and the candidacy age to 16,[10] lowering the voting age to 16 increases the 'likelihood of their taking an interest, and taking part, in political and democratic debate' (Power

Commission 2006: 199). Politicians might be encouraged, feel compelled to produce policies that address the concerns of young people and ensure that youth issues get on to the political agenda. Politicians are more likely to take note if they know they have the vote. As Kaletsky (2011: 23) states, 'The rapidly rising proportion of old voters, combined with their higher propensity to vote, virtually guarantees that public policies will increasingly be distorted against the interests of children, families and young workers'. Policies aimed at tackling rising living costs, helping young parents with childcare, measures to reduce youth unemployment or aid to get young people on to the housing ladder ought to attract the youth vote.[11] Hart and Atkins also divulge how demographic trends work against the interests of young people, 'The proportion of the American population composed of children has declined dramatically in the past 40 years, while the fraction of older voters, who are less inclined to support policies beneficial to the interests of children and youth, is increasing rapidly' (2011: 220). Martin Wattenberg depicts a nationwide survey of 18–24-year-old Americans whereby '74 percent agreed that "Voting is something older people do"' (Wattenberg 2012: 4). Clearly, this is a phenomenon that crosses national borders.

Stephen Williams, the MP for Bristol West, as mentioned above, is a long-time supporter of lowering the voting age. His key arguments include 'Equality of Expression. Not letting 16 and 17 year olds express their political views through the ballot box gives the impression ... that their views are not valid'; 'Consistency ... there is a great inconsistency about the age at which a person can vote (18), compared with the age at which young people are old enough to marry or enter a civil partnership, be able to leave school, have children, work full time, pay taxes, leave home, join the armed forces and receive social security benefits (all 16)'; 'Moral right. The arguments put forward for denying 16 and 17 year olds the vote are the same as those put forward previously denying women and children the right to vote ... those arguments are as wrong now as they were then'.[12] Clearly, Williams supports lowering the voting age based on a multiplicity of reasons.

There is an argument that if young people don't participate then they are unlikely to do so at a later stage—so apathy would travel through the generations. Giving 16- and 17-year-olds the right to vote might be a way to address this. According to the Electoral Reform Society,[13] giving them the right to vote might mean they are more likely to continue to vote as they get older too. Research looking at the consequences of lowering the voting age in three German Länder appears to support this idea, with the youngest voters having higher levels of turnout than slightly older cohorts.[14] Similarly, in Austria, researchers have found that in the 2008 General Election, turnout amongst 16- and 17-year-olds was about the same as the rest of the electorate, about 73 per cent.[15] According to Hart and Atkins, 'preliminary analyses of the consequences of this decision [to give the vote to 16-year-olds in Austria] are positive. Austrian researchers polled a representative sample of Austrian teenagers between the ages of 16 and 18, following the first national election for which 16- and 17-year-olds were eligible to vote, and found that the newly enfranchised voters reported voting at approximately the rate of the general population ... Moreover, the researchers found little evidence to indicate that 16- and 17-year-olds made voting decisions that reflected immaturity ... There are no reports, thus far, indicating that mistakes were made by awarding the vote to 16- and 17-year-olds in countries that have done so' (Hart and Atkins 2011: 218).

The Power Report also believes that young people are, in fact, mature enough to make decisions, attesting that the main objection to lowering the voting age rests on the belief that 16- and 17-year-olds are 'less able to take "mature" decisions about political issues than those aged over 18' (Power Report 2006: 2000). They state that they 'have seen no evidence to support this assertion and our own experience contradicts it' (Power Report 2006: 200). Hart and Atkins also refute claims that 16- and 17-year-olds are intellectually immature. They cite research from Steinberg et al. that little cognitive development occurs after the age of 16 and that 16- and 17-year-olds are just as cognitively sophisticated as others. They found an absence of age difference in cognitive capacity after the age of 16 and use this 'to argue for the propriety of 16-year-olds to make important health care decisions on their own' (Hart and Atkins 2011: 218). Perhaps a case can be made to expand upon this and say that 16- and 17-year-olds are competent enough to make judgements on a whole range of issues and not just in relation to health care matters.

Paul Thompson, writing in the Fabian Review (2002: 8), argued that we often seek the views of young people and yet we don't allow them to vote. As he says, the 'views and opinions of young people are much sought after in these days of consultation, deliberation and participation. In the areas of criminal justice, health, the arts, social exclusion and more, young people inform government with sensible and innovative ideas'. And yet even though we seek the views of young people, 'there is a certain illogicality in the fact that the views of young people are much sought after on the implications of public policy, their opinions matter in the formulation of government policy, but yet they cannot vote' (Ibid: 8). Thompson believes that lowering the voting age might get young people engaged in politics and it might also help to reinvigorate local democracy too.

Some say, why stop at 16, but others respond that 16 is the end of compulsory education in most states so there is a logical argument for the age being set at 16. There does have to be a cut-off point, and the central debate is over whether or not that cut-off point should be lowered to 16. Folkes says that young people are 'growing up faster than ever before and it is wrong to prevent them from airing views which are just as legitimate … as everyone else's' (2004: 55).

Lowering the voting age might help to redress the demographic trends. With more people living longer, there is an increasing sector of the population that is over the age of 65. Lowering the voting age might help to redress that imbalance somewhat. Young people constitute a smaller sector of society. By granting the vote to 16- and 17-year-olds, there will, potentially, be more young people able to vote for issues and concerns that affect them and their peers.

One argument might be to have different age thresholds for different elections. Say, vote at 16 in local elections but at 18 in national elections, as happens in Germany and Switzerland, or to link it to other aspects such as employment or marital status, as already happens in Slovenia and Hungary. These differentials might be unconstitutional in some states.

Alongside arguing for the right to vote at 16, many commentators stress the need for young people to receive a political education. The aim was that this would occur through the teaching of citizenship in schools, introduced in secondary schools in England in September 2002. The reality has been somewhat different in that the type of citizenship that has taken place has differed from that envisaged by its original advocate, the late Professor Bernard Crick. The idea was that citizenship would teach the basics of politics, how the legislative process operates, how elections operate and so forth. The reality is that many citizenship classes focus upon teaching topics such as drugs awareness, anti-bullying strategies and handling personal relationships—all laudable aims and of value to young people but not what was originally envisaged when citizenship teaching was first proposed. In addition, many citizenship classes are not taught by subject specialists or are fitted in to the personal tutorial system or in Personal, Social, Health Education (PSHE) classes, almost as an afterthought or on an *ad hoc* basis. The Speaker's Conference (on Parliamentary Representation) Final Report extrapolates this problem, 'The Association of Citizenship teachers told us, however, that there was also an urgent need for school heads to take citizenship more seriously, and for more specialist citizenship teachers to be trained. A recent study had found that more than half of citizenship teachers (55 %) had received no formal training in the subject' (2010: 25). Alex Folkes (2004: 53) believes that it's a Catch-22 situation in that 'Many educators would argue that citizenship education lessons will only reach their full potential when the "prize" of a vote exists at the end of the process'. A review of citizenship education, however, reveals it is not an entirely negative picture. Indeed, research by Tonge et al. (2012: 599) claims that 'citizenship education *has* made a significant impact upon political understanding and engagement'. Their study 'demonstrates that young people who have received Citizenship classes are more likely to engage in civic activism, contributing to a healthier polity' (Ibid.). There are, therefore, positives associated with citizenship education. The citizenship curriculum was revised and slimmed down by the Coalition Government in 2013 (and has been taught since September 2014). It was criticised by various people (cf. Kisby 2014b) for promoting a rather individualised, consumerist agenda, for example, including a new focus on teaching about personal finance and financial services and products.[16] Although citizenship was retained as a national curriculum subject, citizenship education campaigners are worried about the quality and extent of citizenship teaching going forward, since academies do not have to follow the national curriculum. All schools, after the government's change of mind in May 2016, are not now compelled to become academies but will still be strongly encouraged to do so.

Linking in with citizenship education, the Labour Party pledged to introduce a new so-called democracy portal if they were elected to power in 2015. In a speech to the Electoral Reform Society, Angela Eagle, MP, outlined her focus upon understanding apathy via her 'People's Politics Inquiry'. One outcome of this Inquiry is the suggestion of a comprehensive democracy portal that would provide information about elections and political parties and help people as they decide how to vote. Eagle refers to her perception that the 'intervention of culturally significant people like Russell Brand[17] urging young people not to vote has set the alarm bells ringing' (Eagle 2014: http://press.labour.org.uk/post/89069034189/angela-eagle-speech-to-electoral-reform-society). The portal would provide an accessible site of basic information about the political system and the voting process. For Eagle, this may encourage more people to participate in politics. As she states, 'all the evidence from the Inquiry tells me that citizenship education in schools is often just not up to scratch. Too often it is dry and unexciting. If it takes place at all it focuses on the mechanics of voting, but not on the value or the nature of the choices on offer. Too many young people are leaving school none the wiser about how our democracy works, how important it is or how they could get involved if they wished to' (Ibid.). The democracy portal would be part of a new approach to political education and might lead to online voting. As Eagle asserts, 'Person after person I met during the Inquiry just couldn't understand why when they can shop online, bank online, meet their partner online—they can't vote online' (Ibid.). There are potential problems associated with online voting, including the possibility of fraud or the greater propensity towards patriarchal/familial voting. The democracy portal is, however, another attempt to encourage more people, particularly young people, to participate in mainstream politics. Having said this, some young people believe that citizenship teaching is not the issue. Joel Pearce, aged 17 (cited in Harris 2013: 12), is of the opinion that 'People are aware of the issues; people are aware of politics. But they make an active choice, that there's nobody on the ballot paper who represents them'. Likewise, Harris affirms that 'plenty of under-25s are eminently politically aware, but increasingly fail to see the point of either the rituals of Westminster, or elections' (Ibid.). The democracy portal may, therefore, provide more information, but it remains to be seen whether it will re-engage people with politics.

Some commentators (cf. Cowley and Denver 2004; Mycock and Tonge 2014) illuminate the argument that young people themselves don't actually want the vote at 16 but, according to research undertaken by MORI for Nestlé UK in 2003, most young people do want the vote to be lowered; three out of five think it should be lowered, with 53 per cent wanting it at 16 or below (Nestlé UK 2003). In addition, the Electoral Reform Society makes the point that 'No other age group or other demographic (e.g. gender, ethnicity, class) is required to demonstrate majority support among their peers in order to have the right to vote. The case for lowering the voting age is made on the basis that 16 and 17 year olds are capable of voting, and it is on this basis that change should be made' (Electoral Reform Society 2009: 4).

ARGUMENTS AGAINST

Arguments against lowering the voting age to 16 include the following. Some say (cf. Cowley and Denver 2004), if 16-year-olds are given the right to vote, where does one draw the line?' The clichéd line 'thin end of the wedge' comes into play here. In this sense, the argument rests on the notion that an age limit has to be chosen and therefore an arbitrary age has to be picked and there would be debate whatever age was chosen—if it goes down to 16, will the next debate centre upon the disenfranchisement of 15- or even 14-year-olds? A counterargument is that the age simply stops at 16 as this is no more or less arbitrary than 18. Some say, it will increase low turnout as this sector of society is the group least likely to vote. David Denver makes this point, arguing that 'It would lower the turn-out because the lowest age group always has the lowest turn-out'.[18] This argument was rejected by the Power Report which stated, this 'suggests that a significant reform should be rejected on the grounds that its results may embarrass politicians and reinforce the widespread view that the party and electoral system are disliked. This cannot be accepted by the Commission as an adequate reason to reject reform' (Power Report 2006: 201). Membership of political parties by young people is falling too. Emily Rainsford argues for young people to have greater power with regards to decision-making within political parties (Rainsford 2014: 50). 'Political parties have not been the preferred way for young people to engage in politics over the past couple of years. It is hard to find exact reliable figures of membership levels, but opinion polls suggest that young people do not trust political parties and politicians. Recently some young people seem to have been enthused somewhat by Jeremy Corbyn, where reports suggest that his mandate came mostly from new young members joining the party to vote for him as labour leader. Not only is the irony of an old white haired man getting the youth vote a surprise to most youth scholars, but the question is also whether it will last'.[19] Rainsford continues, 'Political engagement is not only a matter of the demand from citizens to engage politically, but also what kind of opportunities the political system supplies to citizens. Many are concerned with the electability of Corbyn, but there is also a tension in what happens to the new members. These enthusiastic, energetic young people who want to do things will join an organisation that offer them opportunities to do the electoral legwork for the party in forms of leafleting, door knocking and phone banks. There is thus a mismatch between what the citizens demand (to do things that matter in the world) and the opportunities that are on offer by the political parties (activities that will get the party elected). Further to this, the opportunities young people have to get involved in political parties is limited by the fact that they automatically become members of the youth faction that is at the margins of the political party, where only Liberal Youth has a constitutional right to exist. Young people have shown that with the right (?) leader and message they will engage in political parties, the challenge is now on the political parties to offer young people real opportunities to engage politically'.[20] James Sloam quantifies, 'less than 2 % of 18–24 year olds are members of political parties' (Sloam 2015). Those opposed to lowering the voting age argue that giving 16- and 17-year-olds the right to vote is not addressing the real problem of young people feeling disengaged from mainstream politics and politicians.

Voter turnout is often contingent upon whether someone started voting first time round (it becomes a pattern). If youth are mobile, possibly not registered, and do not vote, then the chances are voter turnout will continue to drop due to a contagion of behaviour from the outset. This is a key argument espoused by the 'no' side of the debate. Others (cf. White 2008, 2013) argue that 16-year-olds are not mature enough to cast their vote, that they do not have enough experience of politics and of 'life' in general, most still live at home and go to school, they need parental permission to marry and leave home, they also need parental consent to join the armed forces and do not go on the frontline if they are in the armed forces. With regards to marriage, Andrew Russell enlightens that 'in 2009 there were just 18 men and 88 women getting married at age 16' (Russell 2014). The numbers are, therefore, statistically insignificant. Russell also exposes as 'bizarre' the argument 'that rights requiring "parental permission" justify further rights' (Ibid.). As Cowley and Denver (2004: 60) state, 'The great bulk of 16 and 17-year olds, therefore, are financially dependent upon their parents and guardians'. Rights at various ages change, for example, witness the campaigns to raise the age for buying cigarettes and fireworks (16-year-olds can buy category one fireworks such as party poppers, 18-year-olds can buy category two fireworks such as garden and display fireworks). Andrew Russell reveals that 'the UK has legislated so that the age at which one can legally buy tobacco, fireworks, have a tattoo, or visit a tanning booth has been raised to 18' (Russell 2014). The Citizenship Foundation has opposed lowering the voting age on these maturity grounds. Chan and Clayton (2006: 555) oppose lowering the voting age as they believe that 'there is an age gradient with respect to political maturity ... we claim there is a *prima facie* case against lowering the voting age'. They do, however, admit the need for more normative and empirical research to demonstrate their argument conclusively.

Alex Hardy, in *The Times*, cites a BBC programme headed up by the former *Eastenders* actress, Melissa Suffield, entitled '16: Too Young to Vote?'. Hardy states 'When a neuroscientist later suggested that voting powers should perhaps be delayed until 21, when our neural networks become fully formed, I almost shouted: take the prize, Melissa! Be 16! Run away from responsibility!' (Hardy 2009: 13). Suffield, who used to play Lucy Beale, tried to organise a flash mob of supporters in Trafalgar Square but efforts were thwarted both by the street cleaners who wipe away the X on the floor and by the fact that relatively few supporters of lowering the voting age turn up.

Ellie Levenson, former Editor of *Fabian Review*, also focused upon the maturity issue in a letter to the *Guardian*, 'At 16 and 17, teenagers should be able to try out new ideas and start to think politically without having to take responsibility for their actions by voting on their beliefs. The maturity levels of 16-year-olds vary immensely—as the law is arbitrary, we must choose the highest common denominator. Eighteen is a better line than 16' (The *Guardian* 2003). The issue of whether most 16- and 17-year-olds are mature enough to cast their vote is a key argument of those opposed to lowering the voting age. Levenson had also used this argument in the *Fabian Review* (2002: 9), and she states that young people need to 'accept that there is a level of maturity and understanding needed to vote'. She proclaims differing rates of maturity amongst teenagers, amongst males and females, but believes that, by 18, there is 'more of a chance that most voters will have reached at least a minimum level of maturity' (Ibid: 9). She also counters the arguments about young people being able to get married and join the armed forces at 16 by saying that this is only with parental consent and that if there is an issue with differing ages where one is allowed to do certain things then why not raise the ages? As she specifies, 'How many of us really think a sixteen year old is capable of making a life changing and legally binding decision such as marriage? Financial institutions certainly do not think so. You must be eighteen to sign binding contracts ... or to own land in your own name'. Levenson concludes by saying that 16-year-olds 'do not have enough experience of life. They should use this time to consider their views without the responsibility of voting' (Levenson 2002: 9). Cowley and Denver do not see anything intrinsically wrong with having differing age limits, 'Determining a cut-off age for anything is an arbitrary decision rather than a moral question. How, for example, could there be a moral case for votes at 16 but not at 15 or 14?' (2004: 61). Opinion is clearly divided on levels of maturity of 16- and 17-year-olds. If it is claimed they are not responsible, surely this assertion can be made in relation to any age group?

The 16- and 17-year-olds pay taxes argument is often taken to its logical conclusion by those who say even very young children pay taxes on pocket-money purchases such as VAT on toys and sweets. Does this mean that we should enfranchise four-year-olds? Cowley and Denver claim that the taxation arguments collapse 'both because of the high percentage of children who already pay VAT (are those who spend their pocket money on sweets or CDs to be granted the vote because they are taxed?) and because of the low percentage of 16 year-olds who pay income tax. Just 5 % of 16-year olds and 17 % of 17-year olds are full-time employees, according to the 2001 census' (2004: 59). What Cowley and Denver are saying, in essence, is that the 'great bulk of 16 and 17-year olds, therefore, are financially dependent upon their parents and guardians' (2004: 60). Likewise, Andrew Russell points out the key arguments against lowering the voting age and affirms that, according to his previous research, 'relatively high tax thresholds and poor youth wages meant that only around 9 % of 16–17 year olds actually earned enough to qualify to pay income tax' (Russell 2014). Counter-critics say that, in respect to the taxation argument, the level of taxation that some 16- and 17-year-olds pay cannot simply be compared with the occasional small purchase that incurs VAT.

The Electoral Commission's 2004 Report, *Age of Electoral Majority*, does not believe that there is sufficient evidence to warrant a lowering of the voting age to 16, concluding 'the Commission has looked for clear evidence on which to base any change in the current voting age, and to date has found insufficient justification for such change' (2004a: 61). Michael White, writing in the *Guardian*, asks, 'what evidence is there that most normal 16-year-olds want to vote, let alone that they are old enough or experienced enough to do so—or that grown-ups should let them, any more than we would let them backpack around Europe with their best friend until they are a little older' (White 2008). Cowley and Denver describe the arguments of the Votes at 16 Campaign as 'muddled and incoherent' (2004: 61) but they do commend them for having mobilised a lot of supporters behind their cause.

In reporting the key arguments against lowering the voting age, the Youth Citizenship Commission states that one of the arguments against change is that the current age limit of 18 does not breach human rights law. They also claim that only a small majority of 16–18-year-olds actually want change, and they also say that it is still early days in terms of analysing the impact of lowering the voting age elsewhere (Youth Citizenship Commission 2009: 15). Grover's work analyses whether the denial of the youth vote undermines the human rights of young people. She relates it to participation and the ability to affect policy and law. She focuses upon international perspectives in relation to the voting age.

A survey by the Children's Society, prior to the General Election in 2010, found that Stephen Fry was their most popular choice for Prime Minister. It also discovered that fewer than one in ten young people think that politicians can be trusted. They polled more than 1000 people aged 11–25 years and found that 30 per cent believed Stephen Fry would be the best Prime Minister—compared with 21 per cent who chose one of the three current party leaders. Only 9 per cent felt that politicians could be trusted and only 8 per cent felt that politicians cared about the views of young people.[21]

Table 5.1 provides a summary of the key arguments in favour of and opposed to lowering the voting age to 16 years.

CONSIDERATION OF WHETHER IT SHOULD BE LOWERED

The issue of whether or not to lower the voting age to 16 has been considered on numerous occasions. For example, the Howarth Working Party on Electoral Procedures in 1999 (see White 2011: 3), an amendment, was added during the Committee Stage of the Representation of the People Bill in 1999 but it was defeated; the Conservative Peer, Lord Lucas, introduced a Private Member's Bill, and it had its Second Reading on 9 January 2003; the Welsh Affairs Select Committee recommended lowering the voting age in its 2003–2004 Report; an Early Day Motion (19 October 2005) tried to get an amendment passed to the Electoral Administration Bill lowering the voting age but it was unsuccessful; on 29 November 2005, the Liberal Democratic MP for Bristol West, Stephen Williams, introduced a Private Member's Bill to try to lower the vote, but it did not gain a Second Reading; in June 2007, the Liberal Democrats published a list of 20 proposals to reinvigorate British democracy, entitled *Real Democracy for Britain*, one of these was to lower the vote to 16; another Private Member's Bill on the topic was introduced on 5 December 2007, this time by the Labour MP for Cardiff North, Julie Morgan, who had also

Table 5.1 Summary of key arguments for and against lowering the voting age to 16

Arguments *For*

1. Rights-based arguments (i.e. it is their 'right' to be able to do so)
2. Out of sync with 'other' rights one has at 16 (e.g. can marry with the consent of one of your parents, can serve in the armed forces, pay taxes)
3. Part of a momentum—other countries and principalities have lowered the voting age to 16 (e.g. Austria, Isle of Man, Jersey, Guernsey, recent Scottish referendum on Independence). It is only a matter of time. Inevitable now
4. Having the vote might lead to more interest in politics and greater levels of political engagement
5. Specifically, it might lead to more young women becoming active/interested in politics as they have been the group least likely to vote

Arguments *Against*

1. Goes against recent trends, for example, tanning parlours up to 18, stay on at school until 18, purchasing cigarettes
2. It would not necessarily increase turnout, given low levels of political engagement amongst young people
3. Young people are not arguing for this in significant numbers
4. Young people are not sufficiently mature at 16
5. Where do you draw the line? Thin end of the wedge argument? Next, arguing for 14-year-olds, 12-year-olds?
6. Young people already pay taxes on pocket-money purchases

tabled an Early Day Motion (which received 111 signatures) on the same day. Morgan's Bill had its Second Reading on 6 June 2008 but did not progress beyond there. Another Early Day Motion was tabled by Stephen Williams in October 2008, recording the fact that Jersey had lowered the vote and arguing for it in UK elections. More recently, the Parliamentary Voting System and Constituencies Bill 2010–2011 had an amendment proposed by the Labour MP for North East Derbyshire, Natascha Engel, so that those aged 16 on the day of the referendum (5 May 2011) about Alternative Vote (AV) would have been able to vote, it was not successful but the case was aired again and received support from Chris Bryant, the former Shadow Minister for Justice. MPs debated Engel's proposal on 18 October 2010, defeated by 346 to 196 votes, it was widely regarded as a positive debate. Two further amendments to try to get the vote for 16- and 17-year-olds in the AV referendum were attempted in the Lords, by Baroness Hayter of Kentish Town, in December 2010, and by Lord Howarth of Newport, in February 2011, but both were withdrawn. In Scotland, the voting age was lowered to 16 for the referendum on independence, held on 18 September 2014, and, subsequently, lowered for the Scottish Parliamentary elections 2016 and Scottish local elections from 2017. Relating to the UK as a whole, the issue was debated on 18 June 2015 (see Hansard Debates) as an amendment to the EU referendum but the vote was 265 in favour, 310 against. After much debate, 16- and 17-year-olds did not vote in the referendum on continued membership of the European Union held on 23 June 2016. The issue has clearly been raised on numerous occasions and, no doubt, will be raised again.

Discussion of the issue with Andy Thornton,[22] Chief Executive Officer of the Citizenship Foundation, revealed some interesting points. Thornton raises four key points in relation to the debate and which he believes ought to be factored into the equation: Firstly, he states that 'the raising of the compulsory education and training age to 18 means that it is a good time for students to vote at 16 because they will be in a supported context where the political option can be discussed with adults who would guide young people to comprehend the system and encourage them to adopt this use of political rights'. Secondly, he makes the point that 'In a school setting this can be amplified to the whole of the school in that the opportunity to vote for 16 years + will give the school good reason to discuss the election and political options in more detail—even running an equivalent of a mock-election across the school in order to generate debate'. The third argument espoused by Thornton is that the 'inclusion of citizenship as a national curriculum subject should enable young people to make more informed choices earlier in their lives and to logically harmonise these with other rights that are available at 16'. Finally, he states, 'When this was last discussed by the previous Labour administration it was supported by a youth citizenship commission which focused primarily upon this issue. To our dismay, that commission saw this as an issue for 16–18 year olds to decide. This was not a good democratic framework to my mind—it should be a decision for the whole electorate aged 18 to 100 whether or not we want to extend this entitlement down to 16 year olds. As it happened, 16–18 year olds believed that they "weren't ready" to vote. Older people may have concluded differently'. Whilst the Citizenship Foundation *per se* has not historically taken a policy view of the topic, its CEO, Thornton, does raise a number of interesting and thought-provoking arguments.

Democratic Audit's Stewart Wilks-Heeg states that he is 'deeply ambivalent' about lowering the voting age. He examines the situation with regards to the Scottish independence referendum and cites research which points out that 'of the 229 countries and dependent territories for which information is available, 202 (88 %) have a minimum voting age of 18. Only 11 states (5 %) worldwide have votes at 16 or 17 (intriguingly, these 11 include Jersey, Guernsey and the Isle of Man, all of which lowered the voting age to 16 during the 2000s). Of the 27 members of the EU and the 34 members of the OECD, only Austria has a voting age under 18. There are 16 cases (7 %) where the voting age is between 19 and 21, with these overwhelmingly being found in Asia and Africa'. In statistical terms, therefore, states which do permit votes at 16 are in a minority. Having said this, Sonja Grover reveals that, as well as 'the Isle of Man in July 2006; Jersey in July, 2007 and Guernsey in December 2007 ... Bosnia, Serbia and Montenegro permit voting at 16 years if the voter is employed and there is voting at 16 in select German states' (Grover 2010: 76). This is an interesting angle on lowering the voting age to 16 debate, giving the right to vote to those 16- and 17-year-olds who are in employment. This raises the issue of what happens to those who are actively seeking work. Presumably, this could result in the double whammy in that a 16-year-old could find themselves both unemployed and disenfranchised.

UK

Lowering the voting age to 16 and 17, in the UK, would boost the electorate by about 1.5 million and might possibly engage young people in politics. The issue was debated in December 1999. In committee, the Commons considered an amendment to the Representation of the People Bill. It was the first time a vote on lowering the voting age to below 18 had ever been put to the Commons. The government opposed it and it was defeated by 434 votes to 36.

On 19 April 2004, the Electoral Commission published a report on voting and candidacy ages, which recommended that the voting age stay at 18. The Commission carried out its consultations over the summer of 2003, divulging in a press release how fewer than four out of ten young voters had voted in the 2001 General Election and how this had dropped to just 11 per cent in the 2002 local elections.[23] In November 2005, the Commons voted by 136 to 128 (on a free vote) against Stephen Williams' Private Member's Bill that wanted the voting age to lower to 16. The Electoral Administration Act was passed in July 2006, which lowered the age of candidacy from 21 to 18 but did not have a provision to lower the voting age to 16.

The Power Inquiry, in February 2006, called, in Recommendation 16, for the voting age to be reduced to 16 and also the candidacy age for the House of Commons to be reduced to 16. Gordon Brown, then Chancellor of the Exchequer, in a *Guardian* article on the same day said he favoured a reduction, provided that it was accompanied by citizenship education.

In June 2007, a Green Paper entitled *The Governance of Britain* was published by the Ministry of Justice. It proposed the setting up of the Youth Citizenship Commission which, amongst other issues, would examine 'whether reducing the voting age would increase participation in the political process'.[24] The Youth Citizenship Commission was set up in July 2007. Part of its remit was to investigate lowering the voting age to 16. In October 2008, a consultation paper was published. Responses were requested by January 2009. In April 2009, the Youth Citizenship Commission published its recommendations; it did not recommend lowering the voting age to 16, citing an 'evidence gap' and preferring to leave the matter to politicians.

In their 2010 manifesto, the UK Labour Party promised a free vote in parliament on lowering the voting age to 16 and also promised to improve citizenship education. The Liberal Democrats promised to do the same and, as a party, have supported lowering the voting age. In Scotland, the Scottish National Party, at their conference in October 2007, voted unanimously to lower the voting age to 16. The Welsh Assembly debated lowering the voting age in February 2008, and there was significant support for the idea. Westminster MPs, however, did not seek to lower the voting age for the referendum, held in May 2011, on whether the AV electoral system should be brought in for Westminster elections. The Conservative Government have also said that 16- and 17-year-olds will not be able to vote in the referendum on continued UK membership of the European Union. Labour Party Leader, Ed Miliband, expressed support, at the 2013 Labour Party Conference, for lowering the voting age to 16 and 17 years and it was a manifesto pledge in 2015.

DEBATE AT EUROPEAN LEVEL

A 2011 report by the Parliamentary Assembly of Europe entitled 'Expansion of democracy by lowering the voting age to 16'[25] found that the young people should be encouraged to participate in democratic life. In particular, 16- and 17-year-olds who already have responsibilities within society but who do not have the right to vote should be encouraged to participate. The report encourages member states of the European Union to consider lowering the voting age to 16. Education and community involvement are regarded as key ways in which young people should be encouraged to participate. The Parliamentary Assembly has discussed this issue on numerous occasions, for example, in 2008 (Resolution 1630) relating to the youth agenda of the Council of Europe. The Report also proclaims the fear that young people's issues and concerns are likely to be overtaken by issues of concern to older people. This aspect was mentioned in May 2009, in a motion for a resolution on lowering the voting age presented to the Parliamentary Assembly. This stated, 'According to EUROSTAT statistics we will for instance see a 44.5 percentage increase in the 65–79 year olds and a 24.3 percent decline in the 15–24 year olds by year 2050. There is a real risk that young people will be marginalised in the political process, both on specific level as they will be numerically outnumbered, but also because the political agenda risks becoming dominated by issues that are primarily interesting for older people' (Parliamentary Assembly 2009). This development might impact social cohesion and stability if young people feel that their rights and concerns are being neglected. Again, the low turnouts amongst 18–24-year-olds in European elections can be regarded a concern for the future of democracy.

The Parliamentary Assembly asserts the fact that Recommendation 1019 (1985) seeks to encourage political participation by young people. It points out that greater involvement by young people means elections are more representative; 16- and 17-year-olds often have responsibilities but cannot vote; more participation will make young people more aware; education systems must provide better citizenship education; schools could provide a model for political participation by facilitating the greater involvement of young people and that lowering the voting age to 16 would lead to a higher turnout amongst first-time voters and, therefore, a higher turnout overall. In Recommendation 1019 (1985), about the participation of young people in political and institutional life, the Assembly stated that 'if democracy is to survive and develop', it should consider ' the importance of the active and effective awareness, understanding, participation and commitment of young people in political and institutional life at local, national and European levels'. In Recommendation 1286 (1996), about a European strategy for children, the Assembly stated that 'to enable the views of children to be heard in all decision-making which affects them' and also it urged re-consideration of 'the age at which young people can vote'. The Assembly adopted order number 523, in June 1996, and noted key areas for discussion at national level included whether or how to 'lower the minimum age for voting'. In 1997, Recommendation 1315 on the minimum age for voting, the Assembly did not recommend lowering the voting age to 16 but did recommend that members all set the voting age and age at which one can stand for election at 18 for all elections and also to encourage youth participation via the education system and through community involvement. A further example of where the European Union has looked at this issue was in 2008, in Resolution 1630, which looked at the youth agenda of the Council of Europe. This emphasised the encouragement of the active participation of young people in political institutional life as being a central part of the Council of Europe's youth policy.

Essentially, therefore, the Parliamentary Assembly called upon member states to 'investigate the possibility of lowering the voting age to 16 years in all countries and for all kinds of elections' and to 'examine the possibility of lowering the minimum ages to stand for different kinds of elections (local and regional bodies, parliament, senate, presidency) whenever advisable' (Parliamentary Assembly 2011: 2).

A motion entitled 'Expansion of democracy by lowering the voting age to 16' was tabled with the Parliamentary Assembly in May 2009. It was then referred to the Political Affairs Committee. It was debated in September 2010 in Belgrade and in Paris in December 2010, where a representative of the European Youth Forum was present.

EUROPE

Currently, most European countries have settled upon 18 as the age at which young people are eligible to vote. This mainly took place in the 1970s when many countries lowered their voting ages from 21 to 18. The debate nowadays is as to whether or not this should be further reduced to 16. Only Italy has a higher voting age, where young people have to be 25 to vote in elections to the Senate. They can, however, vote for the Italian lower house (the *Camera deideputati*) at the age of 18.

THE CASE OF AUSTRIA

Austria became the first country in the European Union to allow 16- and 17-year-olds to vote in 2007. This change was supported by four of the five parties in the Austrian parliament; it was opposed by the right-wing

Freedom Party. This was for all municipal, state and national elections. By 2003, three Federal states, Burgenland, Carinthia and Styria, had lowered the vote. In May 2003, Vienna became the fourth Federal state to do so, next it was Salzburg. Five states out of the total of nine had lowered the voting age to 16 by 2005. In Burgenland, Salzburg and Vienna, the lowering of the voting age to 16 in municipal elections led to the lowering of the voting age in state elections too. After the 2006 legislative elections, the winning coalition, SPÖ-ÖVP, said that it would reduce the voting age for all elections to 16 in all Austrian states. A bill was presented to the legislature in May 2007. The Constitution Committee recommended approval to its National Council, and the National Council duly approved the proposal in June 2007. There was very little opposition; four out of the five parties actively supported it, indeed disputing who had first proposed it. At the same time, the candidacy age was also reduced from 19 to 18. The Bill was approved on 21 June 2007. No party voted against it. Marcus Wagner and Eva Zeglovits (2014: 19–20) provide an interesting analysis of the Austrian experience believing it to be generally positive. They found, for example, that 'political interest among young people aged 16 and 17 increased after they were granted the right to vote' (Ibid: 19).

According to Sarah Birch, when the voting age was reduced to 16 in Austria, 'turnout rates were found to be comparable to those of the electorate at large' and 'turnout was found to *decrease* with age from 16 to 20, with older teenagers exhibiting less civic appetite than their juniors' (Birch 2013). Eva Zeglovits supports this analysis, 'Results from Austria show, that turnout of 16 and 17 year olds is in fact higher than turnout of older first time voters, and it is nearly as high as overall turnout' (Zeglovits 2013). In part, as Birch posits, this could be because more 16- and 17-year-olds live with their parents and attend school. Birch also states that if people vote in the first election for which they are eligible, they are more likely to continue to vote.

Germany lowered the voting age in some Länder. Lower Saxony lowered the voting age for some municipal elections in 1995. Since then, the following Länder, Mecklenburg-Western Pomerania, North Rhine-Westphalia, Saxony and Schleswig-Holstein, have all followed. Aarts and van Hees (2003) testify that 'In Germany, 6 of the 16 states have, in the past seven years, actually lowered the active voting age for local elections to 16 ... All six German states ... were governed at the time of the change by coalitions of Social Democrats (Sozialdemokratische Partei Deutschland) and Greens (Die Grünen)'. Aarts and van Hees refute the argument, espoused by some opponents of lowering the voting age, that young voters tend to be more extremist in their voting patterns. They state that research into voting patterns in these German states, shows that 'these new voters do vote in different patterns than older voters; however a uniform trend is absent'. They continue, 'Electoral statistics from the 1999 local elections in North Rhine-Westphalia show that the Greens and the liberal FDP (Freiedemokratische Partei) are more popular among young people, at the expense of the SPD and CDU (Christlichdemokratische Union Deutschlands). But in the 1996 Lower Saxony local elections, surveys in the cities of Hannover and Braunschweig show that the CDU and Greens received more votes among the young. Finally, in the 1999 Saxony-Anhalt local elections, the differences in party preferences were hardly noticeable. It is important to note that in none of these states is there a strong tendency among the young to vote for parties of the extreme left or right'. Evidence from Germany should, therefore, dispel fears that young voters would behave radically in their voting choices. In terms of turnout too, Aarts and van Hees' evidence from Germany informs how the youngest voters had slightly higher levels of turnout than the next age categorisation. In Lower Saxony, for example, their voting levels were on a par with the 35–45-year-old age group. In relation to Germany lowering the voting age in local elections and Austria lowering it for all elections, the UK Youth Citizenship Commission, however, believes that it is 'still too early to say what the effect of this has been so it's hard to know what it would be like to do this in the UK' (Youth Citizenship Commission 2009: 15). As already stated in Chap. 3, Martina Gille,[26] a German academic who has written about young people, states that 'in Germany, national voting is only allowed for persons who are 18 years old or older. Voting for people up to [from] 16 years is only allowed for some local elections (community level). And only in one "Länd"—Bremen—voting on Länder level is allowed for young people up to [from] 16 years. Beyond that, national and Länder elections are only allowed for persons with German nationality'.

In Switzerland, the Canton of Glarus lowered the voting age to 16 for local and regional elections in 2007. Several other member states have also debated the issue. In Slovenia, 16-year-olds can vote if they are employed. In Norway, 16-year-olds can vote in 20 municipalities in the 2011 local elections as part of a drive to make young people more interested in politics. In Hungary, 16-year-olds can vote under certain circumstances, for example, if they are married. They are deemed to have attained full adult legal rights and can, therefore, vote.

The three British Crown dependences, Isle of Man, Jersey and Guernsey, all allow 16-year-olds to vote. In July 2006, the Isle of Man lowered the age to 16 in its general elections. As White elucidates, however, 'with a month to go before the general election held on the 23 November 2006, less than half of those aged between 16 and 18 who were able to register to vote, (698 out of a possible 1800), had actually registered to vote' (White 2011: 9). At the Election, only around one in four young people voted. As the Youth Citizenship Commission states, this is 'quite a low number' (Youth Citizenship Commission 2009: 15). Those who did vote, however, became the first European Union citizens to vote at the age of 16 or 17 in a general election. In July 2007, Jersey followed when it approved a reduction in principle. The law changed in Jersey in April 2008 prior to the general election being held later that year. According to White, it added 'around 2000 names to the electoral roll [for the election] of senators and deputies in October and November 2008 respectively' (White 2011: 10). Guernsey had a proposal for a lowering of age in October 2007, put forward by the House Committee of the States of Guernsey. It was approved by the States' Policy Committee and adopted by the States of Deliberation. The law was sanctioned in December 2007, in time for the 2008 Guernsey general election.[27] Former Chief Minister of Guernsey, Lyndon Trott, who held the position from 2008 until 2012, reveals, 'I am a strong supporter of the extension of the franchise to those aged 16 and above. In Guernsey, this has provided a valuable opportunity to engage the younger generation in government and political matters'.[28] He continues, 'I recently attended a session in the island's schools where a number of interesting, current and valid issues were raised to which I was asked to respond, this has reinforced my view that the extension of the franchise is having a positive effect on further strengthening confidence in Guernsey's democratic government'.[29] Trott states that '2008 was the first election with this voting age and this April's general election, in 2008, it made some 1800 individuals eligible to vote'.[30] For Trott, the lowering of the vote in Guernsey has had an educative effect through engaging young people in the political process.[31]

OTHER COUNTRIES CONSIDER CHANGE

The Irish Parliament's joint committee on the constitution, in July 2010, recommended that 17-year-olds should be able to vote in the lower house, the Dail Eireann. In Finland, their government has been investigating lowering the voting age to 16. In Denmark, the Folketing (Danish Parliament) has received motions for a suffrage commission to be set up to investigate, amongst others aspects, lowering the voting age to 16. This was set up and is made up of representatives from political parties, trade unions, think tanks, youth organisations and the media, amongst others. It was due to report in late 2011. In Finland in the local election in 2009, a total of 31 areas organised shadow elections for 16- and 17-year-olds. The Czech Republic had, in September 2008, a motion by their Minister for Human Rights and Ethnic Minorities, to lower the vote to 16 in local elections. Malta has discussed lowering the voting age.

Scotland's Referendum: 18 September 2014

It was decided that 16- and 17-year-olds were able to vote in Scotland's referendum in the autumn of 2014. This was included in the legislation emanating from the Scottish Parliament paving the way for the referendum. The so-called Edinburgh Agreement setting out this legislation was signed by Alex Salmond, then First Minister of Scotland and David Cameron Prime Minister, on 15 October 2012 (it was also signed by Michael Moore MP, Secretary of State for Scotland, and Nicola Sturgeon MSP, Deputy First Minister of Scotland). This move enfranchised 8.2 per cent of the UK's 16- and 17-year-olds. There are over 1,530,000 youth aged 16 and 17 in the UK as a whole and Scotland has 123,000 youth aged 16 and 17—yet, according to the *Guardian*, only around 44,000 of these are 'attainers' (teenagers eligible to register in advance) already on the electoral roll. Some feel that this question of registration will be an issue in terms of 16- and 17-year-olds. As Carrell states in the *Guardian*, 'Constitutional experts and lawyers have warned, however, there are still significant issues on extending the franchise, including the lack of an electoral register, which are far from solved' (2012: 5). Illuminating the fact that Scotland has allowed some under 18 to vote in health board and crofting elections, Carrell says it 'will also have to pay for a big registration drive to encourage children now 14 and 15 to register for a vote in 2014' (Ibid.). In addition to 16- and 17-year-olds having the right to vote, mechanisms need to be in place to ensure that this functions effectively in reality.

The i-newspaper (15 October 2012: 12) cites Janet Street-Porter as saying, 'By 16, young people are fully engaged with issues ... That they find mainstream politics a turn-off is the fault of our colourless three main parties and not the young'. Catherine Bennett in the *Observer* as saying 'We would compromise: make it 17. So that teenagers only had a year to wait, after they had already married, donated an organ, bought fireworks, left home and signed up to fight for their country, before they were allowed to choose, alone in an exposed voting booth, between one nation and aspiration nation. To judge by the resistance, you'd think we were doing them a great big favour' (14 October 2012).

This move, to lower the vote in Scotland, is said to have infuriated many Tory MPs in particular. Opinion varies as to whether this will pave the way for a lowering of the vote in the rest of the UK; the former Tory Scottish Secretary, Lord Forsyth, claimed it would have 'huge implications' for the rest of the UK.[32] The Liberal Democratic peer, Lord Wallace, has said there is 'nothing inevitable',[33] and others agree that it is not setting a precedent as it just refers to the specific vote on independence. Willie Sullivan, the Scottish director of the Electoral Reform Society, is quoted as saying 'If 16-year-olds are to be granted a vote on the future of the Union, it would be ridiculous not to give them a say on the trifling matter of their next local MP'.[34] Michael Moore, Secretary of State for Scotland, refutes this claim and says that there is no consensus for this in Westminster. It is debatable as to whether or not it will lead to it being rolled out to the rest of the UK. According to Graham Jones, the Labour MP for Haslingden and Hyndburn, who is supportive of lowering the voting age, this move is a continuation of other measures. As he states, over 590,000 young people voted in youth elections in 2011/2012, and 85 per cent of young people go to schools where they have a school council so they (potentially) have a voice. Jones believes that many young people are 'knowledgeable and passionate about the world in which they live'. For Jones, participation in free elections is a 'fundamental human right'.

In the amusingly entitled article, 'Alex Salmond's Bannock Bairns', Andrew Mycock and Jon Tonge (2012b), extrapolate that the Scottish National Party (SNP) has supported this issue for a long time but that it is a 'calculated' decision that it is now on the political agenda. Proceeding to spotlight two clear advantages for the SNP, firstly, that this flags up Scotland's 'difference from England', thus showcasing Scotland as a modern democracy in comparison with the UK Parliament as 'archaic', and secondly, they report how in opinion polls support for independence has been highest amongst the youngest voters, so perhaps 16- and 17-year-olds might be in favour too. According to Peter Kellner, president of the polling company YouGov, evidence suggests that giving the vote to 16-

and 17-year-olds will only increase the Yes vote by about 0.2 per cent. The Youth Citizenship Commission (Chaired by Tonge and including Mycock) recommended that the UK government considered devolving responsibility for voting age to the devolved legislatures for sub-state and local elections. Yet, SNP-led Scottish government did not adopt their recommendation in neither its 2010 General Election manifesto nor for the 2011 local elections. This further fuels the argument of those who believe that the SNP's move is inspired by purely political motives rather than a real desire to enfranchise 16- and 17-year-olds. Mycock and Tonge (2012b) state that the SNP has not tried to equalise ages of responsibility to rationalise citizenship rights. They underline the 'general *upward* trajectory' of many other age limits and verbalise the irony of a 'two-tier citizenship' where 16- and 17-year-olds will be able to vote but, if independence is secured, they could not buy fireworks, alcohol or a cigar to celebrate!

As with the rest of the UK, debate about lowering the voting age also includes discussion of political education. In Scotland, citizenship classes are not a statutory element of the curriculum, unlike in England. According to Mycock and Tonge (2012b), there is a wide variation in terms of quality and quantity. Modern Studies does provide some political education but only about one-third of pupils opt to take this subject. There is an ongoing debate in relation to Scottish Studies being a compulsory subject, but this is more about history and culture as opposed to providing a political education. There will be a need to re-visit the amount and type of political education that young people in Scotland receive given their enfranchisement.

In terms of the UK as a whole, a number of initiatives have spotlighted young people and political participation. For example, a Coalition Government document, entitled *Positive for Youth*, was published in April 2012. As Mycock and Tonge (2012b) point out, it encouraged youth representation frameworks across the UK, such as the UK Youth Parliament, so-called youth-proofing of government policies at national and local levels, and facilitating young people to scrutinise local youth service provision. It did not, however, mention the right to vote at age 16. As Mycock and Tonge (Ibid.) assert, politicians need to address the 'peripheral status of youth within our democracy'.

In terms of what has happened regarding 16- and 17-year-olds since the Scottish independence referendum, the Scottish Parliament in Holyrood voted (18 June 2015) to allow 16- and 17-year-olds to vote in Scottish

Parliamentary and local elections. Ironically, on the same day, 16- and 17-year-olds across the UK were refused the vote in the EU referendum. An amendment to give youth aged 16 and 17 the right to vote in the EU Referendum was rejected by Members of the House of Commons, by 310 against to 265 in favour. Meanwhile, Members of the Scottish Parliament passed the Scottish Elections (Reduction of Voting Age) Act granting 16- and 17-year-olds the vote to elect the 129 members of the Scottish Parliament (the next one being on Thursday, 5 May 2016) and local elections. Lowering the voting age in Scotland was also supported by the Smith Commission on further devolution for Scotland. The Commission, headed by Lord Smith of Kelvin, reported on 27 November 2014, and one of its recommendations was that the Scottish Parliament should be able to give those aged 16 and 17 the right to vote if it wished to do so. Therefore, young people in Scotland cannot vote in a UK general election, nor in the EU Referendum, but can vote in Scottish elections. Part of the drive behind moves to lower the voting age in Scotland is the fact that in the Scottish independence referendum, held on 18 September 2014, there was an 84.6 per cent turnout; 109,553 youth aged 16 and 17 put themselves on the electoral register for the referendum (about 2.5 per cent of the electorate). According to the Electoral Commission, more 16- and 17-year-olds voted than those aged 18–24 years, estimated at 75 per cent compared with 54 per cent. This may be due to the '"novelty value" and publicity given to 16–17s being allowed to vote for the first time' (Electoral Commission 2014: 11) and also to the work undertaken in schools regarding registration. The Scottish referendum was widely considered a success in engaging young people in politics (see Eichhorn and Mycock 2015). According to Jan Eichhorn from Edinburgh University, 16- and 17-year-olds were as equally influenced by the economy as older voters. Eichhorn's work also shows that classroom discussion is good for engaging young people politically (Kemp 2015: 35). Eichhorn claims that many worries are unfounded according to their research on under-18s and the Scottish independence referendum, '16–17 year olds showed similar interests to adults, used a great variety of information sources (not, as often wrongly asserted, only social media) and engaged in extensive discussions with family and friends. Over 40 per cent held a different view to a parent and we actually found indications that young people influenced their parents as well' (Eichhorn and Mycock 2015: 22). On the contrary, Philip Cowley believes the Scottish referendum is hard to draw lessons from as it was 'very high-octane … an existential system where the stakes were incredibly high on both sides' (Barford 2014), therefore not the same as a general election. Likewise, Andrew Mycock is equally sceptical, believing the Edinburgh study does not provide enough longitudinal data, contending that the 'often febrile and divisive nature of the debate may have actually schooled younger citizens in a form of binary politics that is deeply adversarial and reductive' (Eichhorn and Mycock, *Op. Cit.* 23). Mycock believes that there is a need 'to consider the question of voting age within a broader debate about the age-related rights and responsibilities of citizenship' (Ibid.). Opinion is divided, therefore, regarding lessons to be learnt from the Scottish independence referendum.

The decision has already been taken in relation to *not* lowering the voting age to 16 in the 2016 UK referendum on continued membership of the European Union (due 23 June). It had been anticipated that the House of Lords would vote to enfranchise 16- and 17-year-olds in this referendum. The Electoral Commission said that enfranchising 16- and 17-year-olds might delay the referendum by up to a year—requiring six months to get ready after the EU Referendum Bill gets Royal Assent and another six months for a registration push to take place (see Stratton and Clayton 2015). The £9 million it cost to send a leaflet to every household promoting EU membership is deemed, by the government, to be a price worth paying. In a crude synergy, this figure is 50 per cent more expensive than the £6 million that the government claimed it would cost to allow 16- and 17-year-olds the opportunity to vote in the referendum—and used, in part, as an argument against doing so. On 18 November 2015, members of the House of Lords had the opportunity to rectify this omission when the European Union 2015–2016 Referendum Bill reached its Report Stage in the Lords. Indeed, they voted by 293 votes to 211 to allow this to happen. In early December, however, the Commons by 303 to 253 votes (a majority of 50) chose to block the Lords' proposals—one of the arguments expounded was that the cost of registering 16- and 17-year-olds would amount to, as the government noted, 'in excess of £6m of additional public expenditure' (see www.bbc.co.uk, 7 December 2015). On 14 December 2015, the Lords voted, by 263 votes to 246, to reject an amendment that challenged government figures on the cost of registering 16- and 17-year-olds, thereby curtailing the debate. The £9 million found in the coffers to send the leaflet may illustrate that this debate was never really about money.

Given that David Cameron referred to the referendum, as 'perhaps the biggest decision we will make in our lifetimes', it could be argued that it is only right that 16- and 17-year-olds should play their part in that decision-making process. In addition, polls indicate that younger voters are more likely to vote to remain in the European Union—a fact that ought to have appealed to Cameron. Younger voters have known nothing other than being inside the EU, and it is, possibly, hardly surprising that they would vote for maintenance of the *status quo*.[35] In Scotland, 16- and 17-year-olds will, again, be able to vote—this time in the Scottish Parliamentary elections in 2016 and in local elections from 2017—but not in UK-wide votes. This could be regarded as a two-tier system of citizenship in the UK. Enfranchising 16- and 17-year-olds would mean that they too, in Cameron's words, 'hold this country's destiny in [their] hands'. In all likelihood, the outcome of this plebiscite will impact young people and their futures for a far longer period than it will those old enough to remember the last time the UK voted on continued membership of Europe.

VOTES AT 16 COALITION

Launched on 29 January 2003, and made up of over 70 leading youth and democracy organisations, the Votes at 16 coalition includes UK youth organisations, parties and others. Amongst others, it includes Barnardo's, the Children's Society, YMCA, National Youth Agency, National Children's Bureau, Scottish National Party, Plaid Cymru, Funky Dragon (Wales), Liberal Democrats Youth and Students, the British Youth Council, the Children's Rights Alliance for England, UNITE, the Scottish Youth Parliament, the UK Youth Parliament and the National Union of Students. The NUS has been campaigning for a lowering of the voting age for a number of years. UNISON has also supported Votes at 16. Clearly, there is a wide and disparate variety of groups in favour of lowering the voting age to 16.

The Liberal Democrats had a commitment to lowering the voting age to 16 in their 2001, 2005 and 2010 manifestoes, but it was omitted from the Coalition Agreement published after the 2010 General Election.

BEYOND EUROPE

If we look beyond the European Union boundaries, we can see that a number of countries have already enfranchised 16- and 17-year-olds. These include Iran—they lowered it to 15 but put it back up to 18 in January 2007. In Venezuela—they tried to lower the vote in 2007, but it was lost in a referendum. In Canberra in Australia—a motion was tabled to lower the vote to 16 in September 2007, in the territorial legislature, but it was defeated. In Australia—in 2009, they published a Green Paper on electoral reform launched including possibility of lowering voting age to 16. In Brazil, Cuba, Ecuador, Nicaragua—one can vote at 16. In East Timor, Sudan, Seychelles, North Korea and Indonesia—one can vote at 17. Israel—one can vote at 17 in local elections. In the Philippines—16-year-olds can vote in all elections, if they are married.[36] In Slovenia, they can vote if they are employed. Argentina passed a bill, on 1 November 2012, to lower the voting age. An interview with a Brazilian academic, M.B., who teaches law, reveals that 16-year-olds have the vote in Brazil but they are not compelled to vote unlike those aged 18 and over and below 70.[37] Those aged 16 and 17 may register and may actually vote but they are not compelled to do so. According to M.B., one of the reasons they have many 16- and 17-year-olds registered to vote is that this then enables them to exercise their democratic and personal rights. Speaking about her own experiences, she provides this example, 'The University I have studied at was a Federal one. It means that all my studies were sponsored by the taxpayers. To be able to exercise my right, I have to be updated in my obligations as a citizen. I remember that when I was doing my exams for university, I realised that I would reach 18 in the meantime. Due to this, I did my enlistment [register to vote] before reaching 18. Most of my friends did the same. Therefore, the main motivation to do my enlistment before I was compelled to, was the fact that I wanted to avoid problems rather than political motivation'. M.B. continues that with regards to young people and politics in Brazil, 'because of the size of Brazil, we do not have any accurate data of how young people vote. The matter regarding elections in Brazil is much more related to economical status than age, and that is where the available research tends to focus. However, authors support the idea that young people tend to support "modern" candidates, but they fail to actually vote'. She also says that even though voting is compulsory in Brazil, the fine is small. She forgot that she had not voted in 2008 until she was reminded of this fact when she went to renew her passport and encountered questions. She continues, 'I can say that every single person that I know failed to attend in at least one election'. Her comments on young people and politics in Brazil continue thus, 'Regarding young people again, in this particular election that I failed to attend, one of the candidates was a very modern guy, of the Green Party, very "legalize" and the polls were saying that he would succeed easily. Actually, he did not. Many articles blamed this for the lack of attendance on the elections by the young people that were his main supporters. I remember reading an article where the writer said that the same people that supported this candidate, Gabeira, were the ones that could not be bothered to leave the beach earlier, where they were smoking weed, to attend the elections. The fact that the elections are always on the first Sunday of October, where it is always sunny and hot, does not help!' So, although 16-year-olds can vote in Brazil, M.B.'s testimony is not a resounding nod in the direction of youth political engagement.

Granted not to 16 but in a downward trajectory, Japan lowered the voting age from 20 to 18 years in June 2015. This added 2.4 million potential voters to the 104 million electorate in time for the 2016 election to the upper house. The last time Japan changed the voting age was in 1945 when they lowered it from 25 to 20.

In the USA, 17-year-olds can vote in some primaries and caucuses in a large number of states, including Alaska, Delaware, Iowa, Nevada and North Carolina. Bernie Sanders, Vermont Senator and a Democratic candidate for President in 2016 praised a ruling that allowed 17-year-olds to vote in Ohio.[38]

POLITICAL CANDIDACY

In addition to lowering the voting age, debate has also centred on the age of candidacy. Generally, it is 18 years (as it is in Denmark, Finland, Germany, the Netherlands, Portugal, Spain and Sweden, Australia, Canada). It is 19 in Austria and 21 years in Belgium. In France, it's 18 in the local elections but 23 for the national legislature and 23 to run for president. In Italy, a person has to be 50 to run for President, 40 to be a senator, 25 a deputy, 18 years for the regions.[39] In the UK, the candidacy age was lowered to 18 from 21 years under the Electoral Administration Act 2006, and one of the first people to benefit from this change in the law was Emily Benn, the granddaughter of the late Labour politician, Tony Benn. She was selected, in September 2007, three weeks before her 18th birthday, to stand in the 2010 General Election in the constituency of Worthing East and Shoreham. She did not win the election but had paved the way for younger candidates. At the 2015 UK General Election, 20-year-old Mhairi Black, a political science student at the University of Glasgow, was elected to serve Paisley and Renfrewshire South for the Scottish National Party. It had been claimed that she is the youngest MP elected since 1667.

This is refuted by Lord Philip Norton of Louth. He revealed on his blog *The Norton View* that there were many previous young parliamentarians including, for example, 'Viscount Jocelyn, returned in 1806 as the MP for county Louth, "was barely 18 years old"' (*The Times Higher Education*, 21 May 2015: 25). Mhairi Black did not want to dwell on her age but did concede 'Maybe it [her age] captures the way there is a new, youthful engagement in politics in this country, and the way Scotland is changing politically' (McIntosh and Macdonnell 2015: 13).

CONCLUSION

This chapter assesses the debate surrounding whether or not the voting age should be lowered to 16 years. Following on from a discussion of related key issues regarding the franchise, such as whether voting should be compulsory and whether or not prisoners should have the right to vote, the key arguments for and against lowering the voting age to 16 are outlined in detail. There are arguments in favour of and against lowering the voting age and vocal advocates on both sides of the debate. In relation to the UK, the Youth Citizenship Commission, in its final Report found 'not enough evidence to recommend lowering the voting age to 16', they advocated leaving it as an issue for 'political parties to decide for themselves' and also cited a lack of evidence that 'just by lowering the voting age to 16, young people would be really encouraged to become interested and involved in politics' (Youth Citizenship Commission 2009: 15). Others, such as the *Votes at 16 Campaign*, refute this and argue vociferously for the voting age to be lowered for 16- and 17-year-olds. Clearly, this debate has gathered momentum due, in part, to the Scottish independence referendum, the fact that 16- and 17-year-olds will be able to vote in forthcoming Scottish elections and due to debate surrounding the referendum on continued UK membership of the European Union. It will be fascinating to see what happens in the near future.

NOTES

1. http://www.parliament.uk/about/living-heritage/transforming-society/electionsvoting/womenvote/parliamentary-collections/representation-of-the-people-act-1918/ accessed 21 October 2015.

2. http://www.parliament.uk/about/living-heritage/transforming-society/electionsvoting/womenvote/parliamentary-collections/equal-franchise-act-1928/ accessed 21 October 2015.

3. http://www.electoralcommission.org.uk/faq/voting-and-registration/who-is-eligible-to-vote-at-a-general-election accessed 21 October 2015.

4. For further details regarding the eligibility to vote, see http://www.electoralcommission.org.uk/__data/assets/electoral_commission_pdf_file/0017/13274/0906whocanvote_23253-6144__E__N__S__W__pdf

5. Electoral Commission. (2004). *Gender and Political Participation*. London: Electoral Commission.

6. Interview with author, 10 October 2006.

7. See Lijphart (1997).

8. See Votes at 16 (2008) *16 for 16: 16 reasons for votes at 16*, London, Votes at 16 Coalition, reason 6.

9. For further details see Childline at http://www.childline.org.uk/explore/crimelaw/pages/rights.aspx or http://www.bbc.co.uk/radio1/advice/factfile_az/law_overview both accessed 21 October 2015.

10. Recommendation number 16. See White (2006: 6).

11. See Birdwell et al. (2014: 53) for information about issues of concern to young people.

12. Email correspondence with Stephen Williams' Parliamentary Assistant, 16 October 2013. See also, http://stephenwilliams.org.uk/en/page/campaigns-votes-at-16

13. http://www.electoral-reform.org.uk/votesat16/

14. Parliamentary Assembly report 'Expansion of democracy by lowering the voting age to 16', document number 12546, 22 March 2011: 6.

15. Ibid: 7.

16. See: https://www.gov.uk/government/publications/national-curriculum-in-england-citizenship-programmes-of-study

17. Interestingly, former Labour Leader, Ed Miliband, met up with Russell Brand during the 2015 General Election campaign.

18. Cited in Burrell (1997) Teenagers too naïve, say critics, the *Independent*, 31 January.

19. Email correspondence, 9 November 2015, with Emily Rainsford, Research Associate, University of Newcastle.

20. Ibid.
21. Cited in *The Times*, 1 March 2010.
22. Email interview with Andy Thornton, Chief Executive Officer, Citizenship Foundation, 30 October 2012.
23. http://www.electoralcommission.org.uk/news-and-media/news-releases/electoral-commission-media-centre/news-releases-reviews-and-research/electoral-commission-to-review-minimum-voting-age
24. *The Governance of Britain*, CM 7170, July 2007.
25. Parliamentary Assembly report 'Expansion of democracy by lowering the voting age to 16', document number 12546, 22 March 2011.
26. Email interview with Martina Gille, Zentrum für Dauerbeobachtung und Methoden Deutsches Jugendinstitut (Research Associate in the German Youth Institute's Social Monitoring and Methodology Department), e. V., 3 September 2012.
27. See Parliamentary Assembly of Europe.(2011).*Expansion of democracy by lowering the voting age to 16*.document number 12546, 22 March, p.4 for further details.
28. Email correspondence with author, 17 February 2012.
29. Ibid.
30. Ibid.
31. Seehttp://www.guernseylegalresources.gg/article/96983/Reform-Guernsey-Amendment-Law-2007 for the relevant legislation, accessed 18 February 2012.
32. 'Votes for 16-year-olds 'not inevitable', *BBC News Scotland*, 10 October 2012.
33. Ibid.
34. Willie Sullivan cited in, Morris, N. (2012). Give 16-year-olds the right to vote, government told, *i-newspaper*, Thursday, 11 October 2012: 5.
35. In a poll, 53 per cent of 18–34-year-olds would vote to stay in the EU, compared with 54 per cent of the over 55s who would vote to leave. Apathy appears to be an issue, however, in that only 52 per cent of the 18–34-year-olds are certain to vote, compared with 81 per cent of the over 55s (see Opinium/Observer Poll http://www.theguardian.com/politics/2016/apr/02/eu-referendum-young-voters-brexit-leave, 2 April 2016).

36. See Parliamentary Assembly of Europe.(2011).*Expansion of democracy by lowering the voting age to 16*.Document number 12546, 22 March (pp. 4–6) for further details and cross-national comparisons.
37. M.B., Interview with Author, March 2010.
38. See tweet by #NYT Politics (*New York Times* political team), 12 March 2016.
39. See Ibid: 8 for further details.

BIBLIOGRAPHY

Aarts, K., & van Hees, C. (2003). Lowering the voting age: European debates and experiences. *Electoral Insight*, July. Retrieved from http://www.elections.ca/res/eim/article_search/article.asp?id=54&lang=e&frmPageSize

Barford, V. (2014). Should 16-year-olds get the vote following referendum? *BBC News*, 23 September. Retrieved from http://www.bbc.co.uk/news/uk-29327912

BBC News. (2002). Allow voting at 16—Kennedy. Retrieved from http://news.bbc.co.uk/hi/english/uk_politics/newsid_1800100/1801693.stm

Berry, R., & Kippin, S. (Eds.) (2014). *Should the UK lower the voting age to 16?* London: Democratic Audit Retrieved from http://eprints.lse.ac.uk/59110/1/__lse.ac.uk_storage_LIBRARY_Secondary_libfile_shared_repository_Content_Democratic%20Audit%20blog_2014_July%202014_Votes-at-16.pdf.

Birch, S. (2009). *Full participation: A comparative study of compulsory voting.* Manchester: Manchester University Press.

Birch, S. (2013). Votes at 16: What the UK can learn from Austria, Norway and the Crown Dependencies. *Democratic Audit* Blog, 28 September. Retrieved April 21, 2016, from http://www.democraticaudit.com/?p=1536

Birch, S., Gottfried, G., & Lodge, G. (2013). *Divided democracy: Political inequality in the UK and why it matters.* London: Institute of Public Policy Research.

Birdwell, J., Cadywould, C., & Reynolds, L. (2014). *Tune in, turn out.* London: Demos. Retrieved September 18, 2015, from http://www.demos.co.uk/files/Tune_in_-_web.pdf?1419813387

Briggs, J. E., & Celis, K. (2010). For or against: Compulsory voting in Britain and Belgium. *Social and Public Policy Review, 4*(1), 1–33.

Burrell, I. (1997). Teenagers too naïve, say critics. *The Independent*, 31 January.

Carrell, S. (2012). Holyrood faces snags over teen voters in poll. *The Guardian*, 12 October, p. 5.

Chan, T. W., & Clayton, M. (2006). Should the voting age be lowered to sixteen? Normative and empirical considerations. *Political Studies, 54*, 533–558.

Cowley, P., & Denver, D. (2004). Votes at 16? The case against. *Representation*, *41*, 57–62.

Eagle, A. (2014). Speech to electoral reform society. Retrieved June 18, 2014, from http://press.labour.org.uk/post/89069034189/angela-eagle-speech-to-electoral-reform-society

Easton, S. (2009). The prisoner's right to vote and civic responsibility: Reaffirming the social contract? *Probation Journal*, *56*(3), 224–237.

Eichhorn, J., & Mycock, A. (2015, September). Debate: Should the voting age be lowered to 16 for UK elections? *Political Insight*, *6*(2), 22–23.

Electoral Commission. (2004a). *Age of electoral majority: Report and recommendations*. London: Electoral Commission.

Electoral Commission. (2006). *Compulsory voting around the world*. London: The Electoral Commission.

Electoral Commission. (2014, November). *Scottish independence referendum research* (pp. 1–72). Edinburgh: Electoral Commission. Retrieved May 6, 2016, from http://www.electoralcommission.org.uk/__data/assets/pdf_file/0005/179807/Scottish-referendum-Public-Opinion-survey-ICM-Report-WEBSITE.pdf

Electoral Reform Society. (2009). *Response to the youth citizenship commission's consultation on the voting age: "Old enough to make a mark?"*. London: Electoral Reform Society.

Folkes, A. (2004). The case for votes at 16. *Representation*, *41*(1), 52–56.

French, D. (2011). *A tiny bit marvellous*. London: Penguin.

Grover, S. C. (2010). *Young people's human rights and the politics of the voting age: Comparative perspectives on law and justice*. Dordrecht, Netherlands: Springer Verlag.

Hansard Society. (2015). *Audit of political engagement 12*. London: Hansard Society.

Hardy, A. (2009). Generation no X. *The Times*, 5 August: *Times2*, p. 13.

Harris, J. (2013). 'Stop being old men!' Yawning generation gap alienates young. *The Guardian*, 27 December, p. 12.

Hart, D., & Atkins, R. (2011, January). American sixteen- and seventeen-year-olds are ready to vote. *The ANNALS of the American Academy of Political and Social Science*, *633*, 201–222.

Henn, M., & Foard, N. (2014b). Will compulsory voting fix the disconnect between young people and the political process? In A. Mycock & J. Tonge (Eds.), *Beyond the youth citizenship commission: Young people and politics* (pp. 18–22). London: Political Studies Association.

Hill, L. (2004). Compulsory voting in Australia: A basis for a "best practice" regime. *Federal Law Review*, *32*, 479–497.

Johnson, S. (2014). Killers lose bid to vote in Scottish independence referendum. *The Telegraph*, 24 July. Retrieved July 27, 2014, from http://www.telegraph.

co.uk/news/uknews/10989412/Killers-lose-bid-to-vote-in-Scottish-independence-referendum.html

Joyce, P. (2002). *The politics of protest: Extra-parliamentary politics in Britain since 1970*. Basingstoke: Palgrave.

Kaletsky, A. (2011). Pensioners' votes should be given to children. *The Times*, 27 April, p. 23.

Keaney, E., & Rogers, B. (2006). *A citizen's duty: Voter inequality and the case for compulsory turnout*. London: Institute for Public Policy Research.

Kemp, J. (2015). Yes or no to openly discussing politics in class? *The Guardian*, 9 September, p. 35.

Kisby, B. (2014a). Why 16 year olds should get the vote. *New Statesman*, 22 August. Retrieved September 3, 2014, from http://www.newstatesman.com/politics/2014/08/why-16-year-olds-should-get-vote

Kisby, B. (2014b). Citizenship education in England in an era of perceived globalisation: Recent developments and future prospects. In J. Petrovic & A. Kuntz (Eds.), *Citizenship education around the world: Local contexts and global possibilities* (pp. 1–21). New York: Routledge.

Lacroix, J. (2007). A liberal defence of compulsory voting. *Politics, 27*(3), 190–195.

Lawrence, M., & Birch, S. (2015, August). *The democracy commission: Reforming democracy to combat political inequality*. London: Institute for Public Policy Research.

Leach, J., Broeks, M., Østensvik, K., & Kingman, D. (2016). *European intergenerational fairness index: A crisis for the young*. London: The Intergenerational Foundation Retrieved from www.if.org.uk.

Levenson, E. (2002). Vote early, vote often? *Fabian Review*, Winter, p. 9.

Lever, A. (2008). A liberal defence of compulsory voting: Some reasons for scepticism. *Politics, 28*(1), 61–64.

Lijphart, A. (1997). Unequal participation: Democracy's unresolved dilemma. *American Political Science Review, 19*(1), 1–14.

McIntosh, L., & Macdonell, H. (2015). Let's stay together, Cameron tells SNP. *The Times*, 9 May, p. 13.

Metro. (2014). Time to bite the ballot: Young people wanted for National Voter registration day, 21 January. Retrieved February 21, 2014, from http://metro.co.uk/2014/01/21/time-to-bite-the-ballot-young-people-wanted-for-national-voter-registration-day-4267238/

Mycock, A., & Tonge, J. (2012b). Alex Salmond's Bannock's bairns. *Open Democracy*, 20 February. Retrieved November 20, 2012, from http://opendemocracy.net

Mycock, A., & Tonge, J. (Eds.) (2014). *Beyond the youth citizenship commission: Young people and politics*. London: Political Studies Association.

Nestlé Family Monitor. (2003). *Young people's attitudes to politics*. Croydon: Nestlé UK.

Parliamentary Assembly of Europe. (2009). *Expansion of democracy by lowering the voting age to 16: Motion for a resolution*. Document number 11895, 4 May.

Parliamentary Assembly of Europe. (2011). *Expansion of democracy by lowering the voting age to 16*. Document number 12546, 22 March.

The Power Commission. (2006, February). *Power to the people*. York: Joseph Rowntree Reform Trust.

Power Inquiry. (2006). *Executive summary and recommendations of the report of power: An independent inquiry into Britain's democracy*. York: Joseph Rowntree Trust.

Rainsford, E. (2014). Young people and political parties. In A. Mycock & J. Tonge (Eds.), *Beyond the youth citizenship commission: Young people and politics* (pp. 48–51). London: Political Studies Association.

Reeves, R., & Nadesan, T. (2010). *The new frontier: Votes at 16*. London: Demos Retrieved from http://www.demos.co.uk/files/The_New_Frontier_EMARGOED.pdf?1270385835.

Russell, A. (2014). The time has come—But not for votes at 16. *Manchester Policy Blogs: Westminster Watch*. Retrieved April 21, 2014, from http://blog.policy.manchester.ac.uk/featured/2014/04/the-time-has-come-but-not-for-votes-at-16/

Sloam, J. (2015). Political parties are neglecting young people—It's time for unis to step in. *The Guardian*, 25 February. Retrieved September 27, 2015, from http://www.theguardian.com/higher-education-network/2015/feb/25/political-parties-are-neglecting-young-people-its-time-for-unis-to-step-in

Speaker's Conference on Parliamentary Representation. (2010). *Speaker's conference on parliamentary representation: Final report, HC 239-1*. London: House of Commons.

Stratton, A., & Clayton, J. (2015). EU poll 'may be pushed back' if 16 and 17-year olds get vote. *BBC News*, 3 November. Retrieved November 8, 2015, from http://www.bbc.co.uk/news/uk-politics-34708742

The Governance of Britain. (2007). House of Commons Library Research Paper, Cm 7170, 3 July. London: The Stationery Office. ISBN 9780101717021.

The Times Higher Education. (2015). *The Times Higher Education*, 21 May, p. 25.

Thompson, P. (2002). Vote early, vote often? *Fabian Review*, Winter, p. 8.

Tonge, J., Mycock, A., & Jeffery, B. (2012). Does citizenship education make young people better-engaged citizens? *Political Studies*, 60(3), 578–602. Retrieved from http://onlinelibrary.wiley.com/doi/10.1111/j.1467-9248.2011.00931.x/pdf

Votes at 16. (2008). *16 for 16: 16 reasons for votes at 16*. London: Votes at 16 Coalition.

Votes cast for teenagers. (2003). *The Guardian*, 15 October. Retrieved from http://www.guardian.co.uk/politics/2003/oct/15/voterapathy.uk/print

Wagner, M., & Zeglovits, E. (2014). The Austrian experience shows that there is little risk and much to gain from giving 16-year-olds the vote. In R. Berry & S. Kippin (Eds.), *Should the UK lower the voting age to 16?* (pp. 19–20). London: Democratic Audit Retrieved from http://eprints.lse.ac.uk/59110/1/__lse. ac.uk_storage_LIBRARY_Secondary_libfile_shared_repository_Content_ Democratic%20Audit%20blog_2014_July%202014_Votes-at-16.pdf.

Watson, T., & Tami, M. (2000). *Votes for all*. London: The Fabian Society.

Wattenberg, M. P. (2012). *Is voting for young people?* (3rd ed.). New York: Longman Pearson.

White, I. (2006). *Power to the people: The report of power, an independent inquiry into Britain's democracy*. London: Parliament and Constitution Centre. SN/ PC/3948.

White, I. (2011). *Voting age*. London: House of Commons Library. Standard Note: SN/PC/1747.

White, I., & Horne, A. (2014). *Prisoners' voting rights—In brief*. London: Commons Library Standard Note. SN/PC/01764, 8 July. Retrieved July 11, 2014, from http://www.parliament.uk/business/publications/research/ briefing-papers/SN01764/prisoners-voting-rights

White, M. (2008). Allowing 16-year-olds to vote is neither wise nor sensible. *The Guardian*, 29 July. Retrieved from http://www.guardian.co.uk/politics/ blog/2008/jul/29/michaelwhitespoliticalblog211

White, M. (2013). Political anger and apathy a reflection of voter "kidiocy". *The Guardian*, 27 December. Retrieved January 14, 2014, from http://www.the-guardian.com/politics/2013/dec/27/political-anger-apathy-voter-kidiocy

Woodcock, A. (2010). Prisoners serving less than four years to get vote. *The Independent*, 17 December. Retrieved from http://www.independent.co.uk/ news/uk/crime/prisoners-serving-less-than-four-years-to-get-vote-2163224. html#

Yorkshire Post. (2015). Democracy threatened by voting gap says think-tank. *Yorkshire Post*, 6 April, p. 4.

Youth Citizenship Commission. (2009). *Making the connection: Building youth citizenship in the UK*. Final report. London: Youth Citizenship Commission.

Zeglovits, E. (2013). Votes at 16: What the UK can learn from Austria, Norway and the crown dependencies. *Democratic Audit* Blog, 28 September. Retrieved April 21, 2016, from http://www.democraticaudit.com/?p=1536

CHAPTER 6

Youth Political Participation at Local Level

Youth political participation, at the local level, is the subject of Chap. 6. Comparative data will be used here, but the central focus is upon Lincolnshire Youth Cabinet. This provides a detailed case study of youth political participation at the local level. Based upon qualitative methodology, namely, in-depth interviews, the latter part of this chapter utilises a study of the members of Lincolnshire Youth Cabinet. In particular, examination is made of why these young people participate in politics to a much greater extent than their peers. The chapter assesses the types of policy areas upon which young politicos prefer to focus. The young people's motivations, alongside whether the reality meets their original expectations, are investigated. In addition, the career pathways that these young people hope to pursue in the future and the extent to which 'politics' features in their future career plans, are recorded.

This chapter examines young people's experiences of political participation via a focus upon their motivations, expectations and experiences of involvement in a youth cabinet, specifically, a case study of Lincolnshire's Youth Cabinet. The case study approach is used as, whilst recognising that it does not claim to represent every youth body, it furnishes a useful insight into some of the key issues impacting young people and politics and illuminates some of their key concerns that do have a wider applicability. There is a wealth of research methodology literature that examines case studies (cf. Gomm et al. 2000; Gomm 2009; Hamel 1993; Hammersley 2008; Thomas 2009a, b; Travers 2001; Yin 2009, by way of example). As Yin states, the

© The Author(s) 2017
J. Briggs, *Young People and Political Participation*,
DOI 10.1057/978-1-137-31385-0_6

case study 'is preferred in examining contemporary events, but when the relevant behaviours cannot be manipulated' (2009: 11). Thomas points out the potential pitfalls, however, by stating that 'generalisation is not possible; detail and contextual understanding are essential. It is the rich picture with "thick description" ... that we need' (2009a, b: 116). Using the case study of Lincolnshire Youth Cabinet, therefore, young people and their political participation are explored. As stated in earlier chapters, youth political participation is a topical issue in the twenty-first century. Not only are politicians and political scientists alike interested in whether younger voters will turn out to vote (in elections at all levels of governance) but there is an ongoing debate as to whether the voting age should be lowered to 16 years—which, as stated in Chap. 5, happened in the referendum over Scottish independence, held in the autumn of 2014, and in the 2016 Scottish Parliamentary elections. In part, this drive, in some quarters, to lower the voting age is driven by a desire to re-engage young people with the political process.

Young people have expressed the view that they would be more likely to make use of Internet voting. One suggestion, examined in Chap. 4, is that greater usage of new technology (such as voting via the Internet or SMS text messaging) may encourage young people to participate in politics. In any case, the issue is often about facilitating the physical act of casting one's vote and does not relate to encouraging the youth vote to re-engage with politics. Young people need to believe that politics is relevant to their lives (White et al. 2000: 45). This is a challenge for politicians and educators alike. The debate about whether newer methods of voting would encourage greater levels of political participation is an interesting one (Gibson et al. 2005: 565). In essence, however, the contemporary debate in much of the political science literature centres around whether and how we can facilitate the physical act of casting one's vote. This fails to tackle the crux of the issue, however, which relates to how do we, as a nation, try to re-engage a politically disengaged and apathetic electorate (as illustrated by electoral participation)? Possibly one way to re-engage young people is to encourage their participation at local level.

GENERATION I[POD]: POLITICAL PARTICIPATION AMONGST YOUNG PEOPLE

Debate often centres on the extent to which young people are interested in politics. Research conducted by political scientists (cf. Henn et al. 2005; Marsh et al. 2007; Sloam 2015) has discovered that young people are not necessarily apathetic but that they are uninterested and disillusioned with mainstream politics. As Alex Delaney, the 25-year-old former Chair of the British Youth Council, stated, 'Young people are not apathetic about politics but perhaps they are about politicians' (Watson 2010: 13). Young people are often, for example, concerned about issues like animal rights and environmentalism and will tend to focus upon single-issue campaigns. They are often active in informal politics and participate in boycotts, protests and campaigns. It cannot be argued, therefore, that young people dislike political issues and political debate but more that they are far from enamoured by the major political parties. Aside from the Parliamentary expenses scandal (that came to light in 2009) given that the average age of an MP elected in 2015, across all the political parties, is 51 years (up from 50 in 2010), it is no wonder perhaps that young people do not feel a great connection. Labour MPs are on average (at 53) 3 years old than Conservative MPs (50) and 1 year older than Liberal Democratic MPs (at 52), and the SNP average age is 46 (Hawkins et al. 2015: 62). Indeed, according to the Smith Institute, 20 per cent of MPs elected in 2010 were aged less than 40, with 61 per cent aged 40–59 and 19 per cent aged 60 and more (Hackett and Hunter 2010: 4). As Martin Wattenberg articulates, in relation to the States but applicable in the UK too, 'older people are running the government while [the younger] generation is ignored due to its low turnout rate' (2012: 204). Perhaps the election of more, younger MPs, such as the election of the youngest MP elected in 2010, 25-year-old Pamela Nash for Airdrie and Shotts in 2010 (Cracknell et al. 2011: 43–44), or the election of 20-year-old Mhairi Black in 2015, the youngest MP since the candidacy age was reduced from 21 to 18 under the 2006 Electoral Administration Act (see p. 143), may go some way towards redressing the balance but there is still a long way to go before the green benches have a youthful look to them. No wonder perhaps that many young people feel that politics is not for them and that politicians do not represent them. Can a 51 year old claim (or 84, as in the case of the oldest MP elected in 2015, Gerald Kaufman) to fully understand the experiences of a twenty-first-century teenager or a person in his or her 20s? Clearly, the concept of representation is important here (cf. Pitkin). With a focus upon descriptive representation 'what seems important is less what the legislature does than how it is composed' (Pitkin 1967: 61). Parliamentary and other representative institutions do not need to be an exact microcosm of society at large but, surely, questions need to be asked about the extent of the imbalance.

METHODOLOGY

The primary research, in Chap. 6, is based upon in-depth interviews with a number of politically active, young people. Each interview lasted, on average, 30 minutes and was recorded using a digital audio recorder. The recordings were solely for the benefit of the researcher, who was able to actively listen to the responses, as opposed to attempting to take detailed notes. If any interviewee objected to being recorded, then the digital voice recorder would not have been used. In terms of confidentiality, the names of all the young people in this study were changed to ensure anonymity. It is worth stating, however, that many of them did not wish to remain anonymous. The key ethical issue here is based upon the fact that the majority of the interviewees were younger than 18 years of age. They were given clear information as to the purpose of the study and were able to withdraw from the study at any time. No inducements were offered to people to participate. The researcher had a significant amount of experience (of both ordinary and élite interviews) upon which to base and approach these interviews. In terms of location, the interviews took place in the Youth Cabinet venue or at the interviewee's school.

LINCOLNSHIRE YOUTH CABINET

In Lincolnshire, in 2015, there were 167,652 youth aged 11–18 years, according to the *Make Your Mark 2015 Results Report* by the British Youth Council. In the fourth set of elections, held in 2008, a total of 7500 young people voted for the youth cabinet. The fifth set of elections, held in 2010, resulted in a significant increase in turnout, with 15,334 votes being cast. There were 47 candidates in 2010 (two withdrew). In 2010, there were 16 members of Lincolnshire's Youth Cabinet, their age ranging from 12 to 19 years. The elections held in 2012 had up to four people being elected from each of the seven districts in Lincolnshire, and some vacancies still existed.[1] Usually, there are a minimum of fourteen members of the Youth Cabinet (at least two from each of the seven districts within Lincolnshire County Council). There can be up to a maximum of 28 members (some of these are ring-fenced for special interests, such as, young carers). Lincolnshire has four seats on the UK Youth Parliament, as Andrew Garbutt, County Participation Lead Officer, states 'the three area winners and a fourth nominated and voted for from a number of priority groups'[2]; they meet regionally in the East Midlands. Elections to

Lincolnshire Youth Cabinet were held in 2009, 2010, 2012 and 2013. There were no elections in 2014 or 2015 and there has, according to Andrew Garbutt,[3] been a move to an 'open-door' policy. Anyone who is interested in becoming a member of the Youth Cabinet is able to do so. They still have elections to the UK Youth Parliament (UKYP) and currently have three members of the UKYP who will be attending the Commons debate on 13 November 2015. The expectation is that these young people will contribute and represent the views of their Lincolnshire peers as well as of themselves. All the young people receive an induction pack that helps with planning and organising; training, such as for public speaking, is on the agenda. Membership of the Youth Parliament is no longer organised through schools but through youth groups, such as young carers, young farmers, scout groups and district youth councils. According to Garbutt, members of the Youth Cabinet wanted stronger links with decision makers. To this end, two local councillors attended a recent meeting, and the young people were able to provide feedback as key stakeholders. Lincolnshire Youth Cabinet has eleven regular attendees and two or three others who attend on a sporadic basis. According to the Youth Cabinet's Constitution, it aims to give young people a 'voice which will be listened to and acted upon by local government, service providers and agencies ... in accordance with the United Nations Convention on the Rights of the Child (particularly Articles 3, 12 and 13)'.[4] In terms of the number of schools covered by Lincolnshire Youth Cabinet, there are '21 special schools, 58 secondary schools but there are 60 secondary sites. St George's Academy are in Ruskington and Sleaford and the Priory Ruskin is also over two sites too in Grantham'.[5] As Andrew Garbutt, explains, 'The work of representing young people in their area will begin ... It is an opportunity for pupil voice and school councils in their area to link in with them and will provide evidence for schools thinking about the School Council Awards through Healthy Schools enhancements among other things'.[6] Garbutt's role involves overseeing the activities of the Youth Cabinet. He deals with formal governance, supports the Youth Cabinet and deals with the developmental programme. It seems that young people are becoming increasingly aware and understanding of what the youth cabinet entails. The quality of personal manifestos have improved and more young people are now putting themselves forward, according to Colin Hopkirk, former Principal Participation Officer, Participation and Inclusion Team, Lincolnshire County Council Children's Services, now Programme Officer for Community Engagement. In addition, almost every school now has a school council. There are approximately 400 school councils, each having ten pupil representatives (it is worth noting that the Parliamentary Education Service runs an annual Speaker's School Council Awards for innovative projects).[7] There are also Youth Councils in each of the seven districts; the local district councils support these. Other bodies and organisations which also contribute to youth political participation in Lincolnshire include Speaking Up, Rural Youth, the Children in Care Council, Action for Young Carers, Pupil Voice in Lincolnshire and Tell Us. Lincolnshire County Council also offers training for the young representatives. A four-day programme is offered, but this can be condensed to suit the young people's needs and availability.

Colin Hopkirk is emphatic about the need for children and young people's participation. As he states, 'The participation of children and young people is not just ethically or morally "sound". Through genuine engagement, recognising and valuing children and young people as "citizens now, not citizens in waiting", we can make better decisions about the services we provide and the people we employ'.[8] He continues, 'The organisational benefits are clear. Of equal importance is the public recognition and experience of children and young people as positive citizens "taking part", making this visible and helping modify public perceptions and challenge stereotypes'. This is clearly an important aspect as far as Hopkirk is concerned. Other benefits outlined by him are the fact that it can also 'help strengthen communities. At an individual level, children and young people who are taken seriously and whose experience is that their views and ideas are made real, are more likely to contribute further, become future voters, develop new skills, have faith in adults and the "adult world" and grow personally in their sense of worth and confidence'. Hopkirk does concede, however, that 'None of this is straightforward. It requires committed and skilled individuals at professional, community and political levels to be this inclusive, react and respond openly and genuinely to children and young people's "straight talking" about issues and concerns, and to be real about sharing power and control over resources and budgets'.[9] Likewise, Andrew Garbutt[10] states, 'We have a duty to listen to children and young people about matters that affect them, particularly when it is about services designed to meet their needs'. He continues, 'Lincolnshire Youth Cabinet have an important role to play in bringing young people's voices to top decision makers. They must ensure that their peers' opinions are expressed, not just their own, by entering into dialogue with other young people's groups and individuals from their areas'. Garbutt recognises that, 'There is a balance to strike between consultation by officers and elected members and young people driving forward their own priorities and campaigns. When young people's priorities are recognised, joint working and an emphasis to include them in both central plans and targets increases the likelihood of their impact and success'. As was demonstrated with the analysis of the theoretical underpinnings of political participation in Chap. 2, both Hopkirk and Garbutt's comments clearly 'fit' with notions of what constitutes real, genuine and meaningful participation.

A case study of Lincolnshire Youth Cabinet reveals these young politicos to be erudite, vibrant and full of ideas. One of these young politicos stated that for her the key issue is transport. Her priority is 'getting better transport and better travel prices for young people in Lincolnshire'. This issue is all the more important given the rural nature of Lincolnshire and the fact that young people, in particular, need access to reliable, affordable transport. Another interviewee expressed an interest in the 'media image of young people' and in 'trying to change the way the media portray us'.[11] Young people participating politically may constitute a minority, but clearly these young people display a keen awareness of issues that affect themselves and their peers.

Lincolnshire Youth Cabinet furnishes an interesting case study. Chosen, initially, because of locality and accessibility, it provides a valuable insight into youth political participation. The county faces similar issues as those faced at national level, for example, youth unemployment in Lincolnshire where there is a slightly 'higher than average proportion of 16–24 year olds among Lincolnshire's unemployed' (Dunn and Roach 2013: 1). In addition, 'there has been little or no decrease in the numbers of young unemployed in the Lincoln City area for six years' (Ibid.). This is an issue that Lincoln City Council is keen to rectify and measures are in place to focus specially upon the question of youth unemployment—not least of which is an impressive in-depth survey, based on qualitative and quantitative research methodologies, carried out by Dunn and Roach. There is a recognition that a multi-agency approach is key to tackling this issue. In 2014, there was reason for optimism, a '4 per cent decrease from July to August in youth claimant numbers in Lincolnshire was broadly in line with the decrease nationally. However, in Lincolnshire the 16–24 age group presently form 29 per cent of all claimants, compared to 24 per cent nationally' (Lincolnshire Research Observatory 2014: 2). As mentioned in Chap. 1, youth unemployment is of key concern to policymakers and politicians across the spectrum and is an issue not just at the local level but also at the national and international levels in these times of global economic uncertainty. As Mark Shephard and Stratos Patrikios point out in their comparative study of EU youth parliaments, youth parliaments provide a mechanism for 'locating youth at the heart of political decision making' (2012: 1), acknowledging this is especially important 'given the acute levels of youth unemployment following the global financial crisis' (Ibid.).

In-depth interviews with young people who participate politically at the local level reveal a number of interesting phenomena. One young man, Julian H,[12] stated:

> Basically, I was elected to the Lincolnshire Youth Cabinet … I am a serving member of the UK Youth Parliament so I also work on the national agenda as well.

In terms of his own personal history of political involvement, Julian stated that he had served for a couple of years on the Lincolnshire Youth Cabinet and that he:

> was on the School Council before that but I wasn't an elected member and I didn't really think much to it if I am honest as well. I have got a negative perspective on [youth councils] to be honest. I feel that they are, there's two elements to it, they can either be very proactive, very empowering or they can be a tick box for a school … I think it's very easy for head teachers to show off to Ofsted, to the inspectors but what do they actually achieve? And the worst thing is, we are not feeding into our local youth councils, the youth cabinets and the UK Youth Parliament.

It is noteworthy, therefore, that whilst Julian is an active participant at local level and has a history of involvement at the school council level, he remains rather cynical in terms of the power possessed by such councils and by their potential to achieve their goals. In terms of what made him want to get involved in politics, Julian stated:

> I was fed up with complaining about the circumstances I found myself in and the circumstances of those around me. You know, a very negative society, lack of aspiration and hope and a real, the impression was you can't do anything about the world around you … I wanted to make a difference.

It is evident that Julian's experiences in the Youth Parliament have meant that he has had to re-assess his previously held opinions in terms of what he is able to achieve. When asked to clarify whether he was disappointed with his experiences on the school council but impressed with the youth parliament, he had this to say:

> Yes, I thought, well, I was when I got into it. That's been an interesting journey in itself ... I think there is a clear line between the Youth Cabinet and the Youth Parliament.

In terms of what made him interested in politics, the response was as follows:

> I think I have always been interested in the news and I do feel that certainly the lead up to the last general election, whilst there were a lot of false promises, it was an interesting time. For a second, it did feel or certainly I did feel that young people were engaged in politics. I remember being in the Common Room and people were talking about the Election and I really did believe that we were going to see a change, a change in terms of young people's views would be considered and accounted for, I think also I am very much a believer you can always do better and to know that politics gives you that potential ... it inspired me and interested me to make a difference.

This theme of wanting to 'make a difference' is apparent in many of the interviews.

When asked to rank his level of interest on a continuum, a scale of one to ten, with one being relatively little interest in politics and ten being the maximum interest, Julian responded by saying:

> I'd say eight and a half [on a scale]. I am an optimist but there is always that side to you that makes you believe that it is for the élite few and can you actually make a difference.

In terms of specific areas of interest, he cites the following:

> Yes, I have run three campaigns. One is surrounding rural transport, the transport infrastructure in Lincolnshire. The second was about, not so especially Lincolnshire, but it was about sex and relationship education tying into child exploitation. And the third campaign I ran was about enterprise pro-

motion and aspiration-building in terms of looking at self-employment as an option for NEETS [those Not in Education, Employment or Training].

Clearly, this young man is very interested and aware of specific areas of concern and specific policy areas. He continues in terms of one area that really engages him:

Yes, I certainly think youth unemployment and what I believe to be a niche there, enterprise amongst young people is something that, well, it's what I do now.

When asked about whether the voting age should be lowered to 16, Julian was very supportive but felt that it needs to be accompanied by political education. He answered:

I am for it, on the basis that political education is reformed in this country [but] I do feel that we would see a lot of young people voting for a party that they may not necessarily fully appreciate or understand what the ethos truly is.

In his eloquent response, Julian clearly supports the lowering of the voting age to 16 years but, in line with many other political commentators (see Chap. 5), acknowledges that it needs to be accompanied by a programme of political education so that young people are at least aware of the key issues and what each of the major political parties represent. He recognises that it is not appropriate to simply lower the voting age without ensuring that young people have at least a basic understanding of politics and the political system. Aligned to this is the issue of citizenship teaching as a way of ensuring that young people possess an awareness of key events, issues and processes with regards to the political system. In relation to the teaching of citizenship in secondary school, Julian's response was, to say the least, a little dismissive:

Citizenship [laughs] Absolute shambles. Absolute shambles. [Own experience?] Yes, I think that if we go down the SRE [sex and relationship education] route, for example, that I campaigned on, we know that peer-to-peer SRE education is absolutely essential and I think that the same thing applies in any areas of citizenship. How can you teach young people, you know, the value of politics, the value of budgeting, the value of social responsibility, if we haven't got realistic role models or peers that we can admire.

Julian believes that the way forward is to ensure that mechanisms are in place so that young people feel that their views are being taken seriously and that it's not just that lip-service is being paid to their views and opinions but that their views really count. This ties with theoretical analyses of political participation (see Chap. 2 whereby different aspects of political participation are examined in detail). Sherry Arnstein's 'Ladder of Participation' (1969) is important at this juncture. This is to say that there are degrees of participation and that some participation may just be manipulation or therapy and not actually proper participation.

In terms of whether his friends are interested in politics, his response was:

> I associate with like-minded people so I'd say yes but when I was in sixth-form, were people interested in mainstream politics? No … they realised the impact and the empowerment that young people can have, if they don't shut up and if they don't take no for an answer. Yes, I think they were [interested in political issues].

He proceeds to state that, 'At the end of the day, jobs, university applications, everything that was important to them, is a political decision that was in their hands. You know, we were seeing the transition of EMA and, you know, Uni fees and whether you agree with it or not, it affects young people so yes, they were interested in current affairs'. It is worth bearing in mind that young people may be interested in politics but they have other, possibly more pressing issues that impact their lives. They are starting out on their career trajectory and have to focus on issues like examinations, university applications and securing employment, not to mention this is also a time in their lives when making new friends and entering into relationships come to the forefront.

Julian's final overall comments relate to the future and how he hopes his personal experiences of youth political participation will serve him well. 'I am trying to get as much experience as possible and then work'. Clearly, this young man has been able to put his experiences in youth politics to good usage. An articulate and intelligent young man, he had certainly given and gained a great deal from his political involvement to date and had clearly defined ambitions for future involvement. This is not to claim that he is representative of all young people, or even all young people in Lincolnshire, but he does provide us with an interesting case study.

Another case study involving an interview with another member of the Youth Cabinet, 19-year-old university student, James,[13] reveals some interesting insights into youth political involvement. When asked whether he had been on the school council, he answered:

> Not school councils but when I came to University that's when I started to get involved in politics and stuff. Well, I got involved in Socialist Students at the start of this academic year. I certainly slotted into it. I had always been quite moderate and I'd grown up in a Conservative household and a Conservative stronghold. I just all of a sudden realised that I didn't agree with it anymore. Starting to talk to a certain friend and he showed me socialism and what it meant and I started to realise that I was a socialist. They [parents] find it quite funny. They think it's something I will grow out of.

It is surprising perhaps that, for James, university coincided with a complete *volte-face* in terms of his political opinions, thoughts and beliefs. In terms of whether this was just a manifestation of his need to rebel, James answered:

> No, I just decided to go my own way and see what was out there politically. I didn't agree with the mainstream politics so I wanted to look at what else there was and socialism came up and I agreed with a lot of it ... I am really active in the Socialist Students Lincoln. I was nominated for Campaigns Officer in January so it's just kind of in the last year it's spiralled ... we went to the November set of student marches in London. That was interesting, very interesting.

This was to be James' first involvement in politics, so it seems to have almost just happened. As James articulates this phenomenon:

> I think everyone is interested in politics at some point but I don't think there's any point where someone suddenly decides they are interested in politics ... But as I grew up I realised that the more I knew, the more I had to get involved.

For him, it was a dawning realisation. There was no one single 'Eureka' moment—it was more of an incremental, 'drip', 'drip' effect. As he states this was how it was:

'I have been interested for more than two or three years. Five or longer, something like that'.

Again in response to the question of where he would place himself on that continuum of political interest, James stated:

> Probably about nine or ten on a scale of one to ten. Politics is now a big part of my life.

Asked whether he is interested in specific policy areas or issues, James states:

> I won't say specific ones [policies] but I just have an understanding of most. Certain ones, I have more of an idea upon. Military policy is something that I am very interested in … I suppose I am not the average socialist who is very anti-war and everything like that. I am more a strong believer in that you need a defence force and that to protect your nation. There are divisions within any political group.

This notion that political groupings and parties contain a variety of differing thoughts and beliefs is interesting. James recognises that parties and groupings constitute an amalgamation of opinion and that, presumably, they actually *need* to have within their ranks such a broad church of opinion, especially if they seek electoral success. They need to attract supporters from as wide a range as possible. In terms of studying politics, James had not chosen politics specifically but recognised that there will elements of this in the course that he had chosen:

> I did consider studying it [politics] but learning what Criminology entails, I did decide it covers politics as well, you know … I'd like to work for an international organisation such as the UN or the EU. Using my Criminology degree, I could go into things like the United Nations Drugs and Organised Crime or Interpol or something like that.

In terms of the contentious issue of whether or not the voting age should be lowered to 16 years, James responded thus:

> I think that there are many people who are very passionate about politics who are 16/17. I think the fact that we have places in the UK that allow voting at 16, such as Jersey, Guernsey and the Isle of Man, I think why don't we implement that on the rest of the country.

Once again, the teaching of citizenship was met with a less than enamoured response:

I always found that it [citizenship] was lacking a lot. It tended to be a bit of a doss. One hour a week and it was anybody really who taught it ... It tended to be a bit of a joke really, I think. There's a movement to install a politics class, an hour of politics a week, which I strongly agree with because I think the apathy of a lot of the youth today is because they don't understand politics ... they are disillusioned with politics as it is. Surely, they should realise that it is their democratic right to vote.

This ties in with scholarly analyses of citizenship teaching that has been undertaken over the past few years (cf. Kisby; Kisby and Sloam; Tonge and Mycock; Tonge, Mycock and Jeffery; Whiteley 2014). Whilst it is true that there have been plenty of criticisms of citizenship classes along these lines, evidence suggests that it has had some success in terms of increasing levels of civic engagement among young people (cf. Tonge et al., Ibid; Whiteley, Ibid).

In terms of his views in relation to the low turnout at the 2010 General Election James stated: 'Yes, it's terrible. It should be more than 60/70 per cent'.

In terms of whether he deliberately chooses friends due their similar politics, his response was negative:

No. I have friends from all over. They have all manner of different political persuasions, like Conservatives. I have never been like that [shunning people who support other parties] just not talking to someone because of their political beliefs. I think that's a very good thing, to have passionate debates ... I wouldn't discriminate and judge them just because of their political beliefs.

When asked about the disillusionment amongst young people and politics, James responded by saying:

I think that the youth is disillusioned with politics because they were so lied to by the Liberal Democrats that they didn't realise that politicians could lie like that and I think they became mistrusting of their mainstream politics. I think there needs to be a differing voting system for our country and the three mainstream parties don't really seem to be up to scratch because they have sold out their founding values ... So, there is plenty of other political parties that people could vote for but they just have to sift through to find which one they agree with. And the only way it is going to happen is if there is political education and this apathy is stopped.

He had not studied politics at school: 'No, I didn't do politics at A level at school. I did humanities subjects and that was it. We got some debates through that'. Again, this opinionated and articulate young man was able to provide reasoned arguments behind the lack of youth political participation and engagement in politics.

Another young interviewee, John,[14] was active in youth politics and when asked what position he currently held, he responded,

Within the Lib Dems, I am a youth officer but I basically just got given it because there weren't many other people doing it … I have been in the Lib Dems about a year and a half.

This is revealed as a relatively interesting phenomenon because the Liberal Democrats received a lot of criticism after the 2010 election, and yet this interviewee is still supporting them and is young and active. He replied,

Yes. I am 21. Well, I'd say the main reason I've joined them [i.e. the Liberal Democrats] is due to friends really … I know people have tried to recruit me to both Labour and Conservatives and they are all very keen just to give you cards.

When asked whether he was or had been a member of any other political bodies, he said,

I wasn't really active during school years because, to be honest, I didn't really know anything about politics, mainly because I wasn't really educated in it. I got educated in politics on a whim at college because it was just a course that I could take and then it came from that. I got to know more about it and it got me really interested. I am currently the Politics President here at University.

It appears to be the case that, with respect to this young person, studying politics had whetted his appetite and had made him interested and eager to get involved in politics. He claimed to have been interested in politics for about four years, 'Roughly four years, I have been interested'. On the scale of one to ten, he said, 'I'd say 7 or 8. I am interested in it but

I don't try to get to know the nitty gritty details of everything but I try to follow it when and where I can really'. Asked whether he was interested in specific policy areas, he said

> I am quite keen on the NHS. I am not for it being privatised and I am quite keen to possibly lobby against that. Tuition fees aren't really an issue ... the decision has already been made so it is quite difficult for it to be changed although people still seem to think that they have a chance'. With regards to specific policy areas in the locality, he said, 'I'd say, although it sounds boring, transport in Lincolnshire is a key one. Just because it is a local issue and it is never really brought up ... It affects us [young people] more because we have to use the transport.

He had chosen to study politics at university, by deciding to study a joint degree in History and Politics,

> Yes, I am studying History and Politics. I would love to be an MP. Well, recently running in the election for president here. It does get quite difficult, especially speaking in public and having to talk to potentially hundreds of people. I have done canvassing before and it does get a bit awkward when I'd say about three out of ten people don't even really want to talk to you ... I ran last year to try to be a local councillor. I lost atrociously.

In response to the question of whether or not he wishes to pursue a career in politics, he responded, 'Politically, it gets difficult because it comes in sort of like cycles. So, currently my career aspirations are trying to get a normal job and then doing a political job on the side ... there's a TV series called *In the Loop* whereas if you are out of the loop, it doesn't really matter, you've got to wait four years'.

Possibly surprisingly, in response to the question of whether or not the voting age should be lowered to 16 years, he replied, 'Personally, I am against it. Purely because you don't get educated in it unless you choose to. So, the longer you get a chance to learn about actual politics rather than just voting on a whim or on who looks good, the better it is politically. I think keep it 18, I just think people need educating ... I think it's better to wait'.

Allied to this, in relation to citizenship education, he stated, 'I think it [citizenship] is alright but I think that it needs to have political education in there as well. Because currently you get educated about religion and yet although politics isn't in the same sphere it's sort of on the same part and yet it's not really mentioned. And even if you ask teachers about it, they are trying to remain unbiased, especially in secondary schools. So, they don't really go into that much detail. The main focus of citizenship was about religion, just all the different religions out there. It could have been more interesting to learn more about all the different political parties or at least the main three and a little bit about the others'. So, the citizenship education that this young man had received in school very much centred upon religious education as opposed to focusing upon the political system and the policy-making process. Asked whether more could be done to engage young people with politics and ensure they had more of an understanding of what politics entails, he said, 'Yes, there could be a hell of a lot more done. As I said, education is a key issue but, as I said, they could organise parties coming in and talking about their political party and having some possible sign-up sheets for the youth there. To just discuss it. I know the Politics Society [at his university] is trying to organise something along those lines so that we get more young people involved in politics'. Asked about his University Politics Society and whether it was all-party, he responded, 'Yes, that's all the parties ... So, I get a lot of opinions from all the parties'.

In response to the question of whether he deliberately chooses his friends because they are interested in politics, he said,

> I'd say those on the same course as me are very interested in politics and the friends that I have from there are very interested in politics. Those outside that group don't really want to discuss it. They will talk about big news issues but when it comes down to like nitty gritty stuff they are like 'I don't know what you are talking about', 'I don't really want to talk about this'.

When asked whether he had other thoughts on young people and political participation, he stated that

> There are a couple of things that I wanted to sort of mention. I think, I have got this from a few youth reps now ... just given the job because they are young and they are like 'Oh, OK'. It can be quite patronising. I think it depends on the person and how they take it ... I think the worst thing we find is when they see a young person they think 'Oh, we've got a leaflet-ter (*sic*) here, let's use them to leaflet'. So, we are like going around knocking on doors and I just wanted to get interested and involved and you do feel a bit sort of used sometimes just to sort of leaflet. Sometimes it does feel like you are a sort of token. It's like I am interested in politics just like anybody

else because there is an age gap, especially in the Lib Dems of like twenty years between most of the members.

The issue of tokenism is an important issue. It could be that young people do find themselves drafted in to fulfil a quota. Parties need young people from the point of view of succession-planning and forming the next generation of politicians and party apparatchiks but it is thought-provoking when the young people themselves are saying that they feel that they are almost there as a tick-box exercise. As Bruter and Harrison acknowledge, political parties need young people to inject new life into their organisations, 'Young people are the future of old-style politics, and without their participation, some fear that our current model of governance might reach a point of no return' (2009: 2). As they say, 'Parties welcome this new blood with great enthusiasm and hope that it will restore their fragile legitimacy' (Ibid.).

Finally, when asked why he gets involved in politics, John stated 'I get involved and, because I am a youth member, I am on the Lib Dem cabinet. So, I get a vote in decisions ... you talk about local issues so basically you are trying to organise it and it does get quite interesting'. This young man may be unrepresentative of young people *per se* given the level of his involvement with one political party, in this instance, the Liberal Democrats. He does, however, clearly express his opinions in terms of what made him interested in politics and what policy issues he regards as being of importance.

Another interviewee, Beth,[15] a member of Lincolnshire Youth Cabinet, when asked when she was elected and how long she had served said, said, 'Since 2007. At the time, I was co-opted on because I came in the middle of the year. And I met Sophie who, at the time, was the lead worker and I said there should be a UK Youth parliament and she said "Well, there is". So she introduced me to the Lincolnshire Youth Cabinet and then co-opted me on. And then it was probably about six months later that they elected me as a Deputy Member of the UK Youth Parliament. Yes, because Wales, Scotland and Northern Ireland they have all got their own individual youth parliaments but England has only got the UK one'. When asked whether she had served on other political bodies stated, 'I was on the School Council probably about three years before I joined the Cabinet because I was sent by the School Council to a thing called *Heirs to the Future* which they don't have at the moment but they brought together people from all over Lincolnshire to talk about what young people want to see in the next year'. In terms of what made her interested in politics, she responded, 'Being on the cabinet and meeting people from the county council ... I went on the Annual Sitting and, by the time I came back, I had decided I wanted to do politics and I needed to change my A levels choices ... The Annual Sitting was in Exeter that year'. In terms of how long she had been interested in politics, she said, 'Probably about three years now'. In terms of the scale from one to ten, with ten being maximum interest, she said 'Probably about eight or nine', and in relation to being interested in specific policy areas on Lincolnshire Youth Cabinet, she said, 'Well, we have three main priorities that we work on every year and I've been the lead for the transport campaign which is aimed at you know getting better transport and better travel prices for young people in Lincoln'. Transport is clearly a key issue that affects young people in large rural area like Lincolnshire. The ability to be able to move around and meet up with friends, whilst being mitigated somewhat with the possibilities offered by the Internet and social networking sites (see Chap. 4), remains of key concern to many young people in Lincolnshire and similar rural communities. In terms of being interested in some areas more than others, Beth responded, 'I am more passionate about transport but our other issues were "media image of young people" which I do feel very strongly about as well. Trying to change the way the media portray us which is, especially after the House of Lords event, there was virtually no press coverage. Which, by the time it came to the debate in the House of Commons, we'd managed to fix because there was a lot more coverage ... The third area was youth talent, we were trying to showcase youth talent. Which I think kind of feeds into the *Brilliant Lincolnshire* scheme that the County Council does'. So, transport, the media portrayal of young people and nurturing the talents of young people remain, for Beth, the key issues that interest her and where she would like to see change and improvement. She is studying politics at university and claimed that she would like to pursue a career in politics. In terms of specific career aspirations, she said, 'It's vague but I am thinking probably working in local government, local council. I am not as ambitious as some who are thinking "Oh yes, I want to be Prime Minister" because I think being Prime Minister is one thing but I think it's doing all those little small things that is where things really get done ... because you see loads of people from the UK Youth parliament saying "Oh yes, I want to be Prime Minister" but that's all very well but are you actually going to get a huge amount done if you are prime minister? Because if everybody who said they wanted to be prime minister ended up prime minister, we'd have about 14,000 prime ministers!'.

More specifically, on the topical question of whether or not the voting age should be lowered to 16 years, Beth stated that she was

> 'For it. The thing is there is obviously a lot of legislation about not dis-criminating against people on age and sex and against votes at 16, you are discriminating on age. I don't think there should be a voting age at all but if we are going to have one, 16 is a good place because these young people some of them are paying taxes, if they have left full-time education, they are paying taxes, you know they can be training for the armed forces, they can get married, they can do all these things and they're not allowed to vote on the way that the country is run, especially like those who plan on going on to higher education, they want to be able to vote ... Well all these people who are 16 at the moment, they are going to go to university in a few years, universities have tuition fees, tuition fees are about to be raised. So they want to have a say on the party who'll be raising these tuition fees'.

> Allied to this the question of the teaching of citizenship in schools elicited this response from Beth, 'At the moment citizenship, when I left school it wasn't being taught. It was supposed to be done in tutor groups actually which were only about half an hour long in the first place. The teachers didn't want to teach it and nobody listened anyway. I think if it was a proper lesson in a proper place and not just shoved in as part of your tutor group activities. Like General Studies is compulsory for sixth form students so maybe if it was an actual lesson ... The teachers didn't care. It was half an hour, they didn't really care what people were doing'.

These comments from Beth accord with many of the comments in relation to citizenship from the other interviewees. Citizenship lessons simply do not appear to be doing or even attempting to do what was envisaged by Bernard Crick when he was instrumental in bringing about their introduction.

In relation to this, when asked what she thought could be done to make young people more aware of politics and political issues, Beth replied, 'Yes. I think they could be, well, like votes at 16, involving them more. If you're allowed to vote at 16, you're gonna think "Oh well I'd better, you know, find out what's going on", that kind of thing. I mean you get a lot of people they just hear one thing. A couple of people, I've talked to about the UK Youth Parliament, they've suddenly gone "Oh what's that?" and become really interested and wanting to know exactly what it is. I think if more people knew that there was a parliament for young people they would probably be more interested in real politics because they'd think, "Well, we've got our Parliament", especially when they can see some of the changes that have actually been made. Like the changes to Sex and Relationships Education, lowering the age of teaching it and the way it's taught. Well, the fact that it is now Sex and Relationships Education and not just Sex Education'.

In terms of her friends being interested in politics, Beth said,

> Some of them. It really does vary. I mean when we came to do the last lot of elections, it was local councils and it was the European elections, and I had one person who came up to me and asked why the local MP wasn't on the ballot because she wasn't sure what she was voting for, she still voted … she thought she was voting in a general election and somebody else said that she voted based on the prettiest advert that she could see on TV, so it does vary. It's the same though if you look at the cabinet members, you've got some cabinet members [i.e. Lincolnshire Youth cabinet] who are really, really interested in politics, who can sit and talk about it for hours and you have got others who are sort of indifferent.

She raises an interesting point here. The level of commitment required from young people who participate in youth politics is important. Travel to meetings, using up evenings and weekends all require a time commitment that many young people, no matter how interested they are in politics, may find too much of a sacrifice. It seems to be the case that it is only the really dedicated young people who get involved in the first place, never mind stay the course.

A further interview with an elected member of Lincolnshire Youth Cabinet, a young man called Louis,[16] produced the following responses. He was asked about members on the Youth Cabinet when he was first elected to Lincolnshire Youth Cabinet,

> I am not exactly sure of the numbers but I think there are around 14 [on Lincolnshire Youth Cabinet]. I am elected as a member of the UK Youth Parliament. Whilst I am not a member of the Youth Cabinet because I wasn't elected as a member of the Youth Cabinet, I am integrated into it and I can attend meetings and things like that. [ex-officio member]. The age range this year is 12 to 18. So, there is a broad range. I am 14. We are not allowed to show bias on the Youth Parliament but I support the Labour Party. In Lincolnshire, we are split into four different sections, there's the City of

Lincoln, South Lincolnshire, West Lincolnshire and East Lincolnshire and from them four areas, there's a member of the Youth Parliament and a Deputy. Two from each of the four areas that fill up the places of member and deputy. There are four members of the Youth Parliament and four deputies ... In Cabinet, we try to meet once a month but, for example, in exam terms and things like that we try to steer away from them and hold more meetings at other places and regional meetings with the regional parliament and the regional reps, they take place every, once every six weeks, or we try to... In my manifesto, my main aim was transport but also new parks and new areas for children to meet at and have something to do instead of being out on the streets, things like that and also to have Helplines, more Helplines to help children that are in need. I actually live in North Hykeham so I bike to school but at the weekends when I want to go into town, I use the bus and sometimes, I am charged as an adult, and other times I am charged as a kid and I know that this is a problem with a lot of people. Because I end up paying £1.50 sometimes to ride as an adult when I should only be classed as a child. It's just based on the bus driver and if I say, "Oh, I am only a child" they will say wait for the next bus or something like that and I just thought that. I think that in different counties, you know Beth [also a member of the Youth Cabinet] don't you? She did a campaign of the transport. She set out some aims along with someone else and they found out that in Derbyshire, they have a system that cost 1.2 million pounds a year which entitles all children to half price transport and fares and more people use the transport so the bus companies are earning more even though it was half price. And I just thought 'Well, why can't we do that here in Lincoln?'.

Clearly, similar issues are of concern to different members of the youth cabinet, and transport kept recurring as a central policy area.

In terms of serving on other bodies, Louis stated, 'Yes, I serve on the UK Youth Parliament, UK Youth Parliament rep for the City of Lincoln. I attend Youth Cabinet meetings and I am a member of the School Council as well. I have been a member of the School Council since Year Seven, three years now and I was also at my primary School I was involved in the School Council there, since Year two, since I was about seven. So I have been involved in school councils for about eight years. I think it was in Year One that I started my ambition that I wanted to be the Prime Minister'. Louis was one of the youngest interviewees and probably one of the most passionate in terms of his interest in politics.

With regards to what made him interested in politics, his response was as follows, 'I am not really sure because I remember my Granddad was a politician and he was Leader of the County Council and Mayor so I knew that he had been involved in politics. I remember speaking to him about things and that got me interested but I think really it was just the fact that I thought that things need to be changed for the good of everyone ... And I thought that people who are like me and just normal don't get enough. I mean their views are appreciated but nothing is actually passed in legislation ... There will be something that I just think "Wow, I don't think that's right". If I became a Member of Parliament, I will be able to change that'. In response to a question about family politics, Louis stated, 'Yes, my Granddad was Labour. My other Granddad on the other side of the family is Conservative and my Dad, he only votes sometimes in elections because he feels that, well like with the expenses scandal, he feels that, I always say to him that "You've got to vote, it's a waste of your vote". I try to convince him and he just thinks, "It's pointless me voting and all this" but my mum is, they are both interested in politics but not as much as I or my Granddad was but it's as if it's skipped a generation. My Mum's Dad was the County Councillor and my dad's Dad is a Conservative'. What is interesting here is that it is almost a role reversal with the young man trying to encourage his parent to cast his vote and participate!

In relation to how long he had been interested in politics, Louis responded, 'I started getting involved with politics about seven years ago as I said and I have been active in politics for about four years and I guess I started getting interested in it when I started in the School Council, just that small area and then it has grown since then'. In terms of the scale or continuum of interest, Louis said, 'I'd say nine or ten' and in terms of specific policy areas, he is interested in, 'Transport and ... well, at the moment on the Cabinet, there are three priorities transport, talent and media. Media is all about giving children and teenagers a better media outlook so instead of it being bad reports all the time about kids, it's to show that most of them are just, the majority of teenagers aren't like that. It's just a small minority. So, I am quite interested in that because I know when I bike to school sometimes and pass older people they seem scared. I just feel that they shouldn't have to feel like that ... Talent is good because it is recognising Lincolnshire talent and transport is my main priority'. For Louis, transport is the key policy area above all others.

As regards a career, Louis said, 'Yes, I would like to do something else before, like a Lawyer. I mean when I was younger, I thought I would like to go straight into it but as I have grown up, I have realised, along with the fact that I would like to experience other things before I do that, there is also, like if I was to go into an election as a 22 year old or something, people might think "Oh, he has never done anything before so how is he going to …". It will give me life experience as well as the fact that I will get to do something else that I like as well as doing that later on'. This is a very astute analysis from, as stated, a 14 year old. In terms of career aspirations, he said he'd 'like to go to University and study Law and Politics … I am not sure whether I would like to be a barrister or solicitor yet but I would like to go into the Law career maybe and then into Politics later on'.

With regards to lowering the voting age to 16 years, Louis stated, 'I am friends with another Member of the Youth Parliament, Craig [name changed], who represents, I think it's, Lincolnshire West and we were going to, I think it's Channel Four *Campaign Blast* or something—where you sign up, and if you get picked, you get to campaign for six months for something. And we were thinking about doing a campaign for lowering the voting age to 16. Now before I joined the Youth Parliament, I was against it because I just thought, "Oh, 18, it's when you become an adult" and that should be right. But then as you look more into it, when you are 16 you can legally join the army, so you can serve and die for your country, you can pay tax and raise a family, if you are in a family unit but you can't vote for your country. So, I just think well, if you can do all that, you can die for your country, you can pay for your country but you can't vote, then I think that it should be changed'. He continued, 'I think it's the Channel Four *Campaign Blast* [NB: it's called Battlefront] or something like that. You put your name down, forward your details and your idea to these people and they check through which ones they think are best and then they select. I think it's any young person'.

With regard to the teaching of citizenship in schools, Louis stated, 'I think the citizenship, we only get about forty minutes a week and it's not an actual lesson like, say, maths that we'd have for a solid hour. It's like a tutor group. And I think that whilst I'd love politics to be a lesson now, if the voting age was lowered to 16 then I guess that would be quite beneficial for everyone but I think that in citizenship, we do government and politics in one of our citizenships but we only have it for about four weeks … we do government and politics and then we've moved on to like finance. This is the first year we've done government and politics. We've never studied it before'. As to what could be done to make more young people aware of and possibly interested in politics, Louis said, 'Whilst I think more could be done, I also believe that it's up to the person them-selves to research it … I also think that the education people, the boards and things like that could do more to teach politics at school because for the people that think "Oh politics, that sounds quite interesting", like I have a lot of friends who are like, "Oh, I don't understand it". Some friends are like me, they like politics, others want to be, they want to know more but they can't because they are not taught it so I think that more can be done, yes'. It is striking the way he places the onus, at least in part, upon the young person themselves. He pursued his own interest in politics but recognises that schools ought to do more to cultivate that interest in young people.

In terms of where Louis receives his political education, he divulged how he is 'always watching the news on the Internet. I always have the news channel on. I watch Sky News on the Internet but I normally watch BBC news on the TV—6 and 10 o'clock but I don't really read newspapers, I do read newspapers when I get them but I just think newspapers are a bit, I mean the political influence on the newspapers kind of steers me away … at least when you are watching it or reading it on the website, there is no like massive bias … I am not really too fussed on which newspaper I read. I mean I read the *Lincolnshire Echo* sometimes but I mainly read *The Times* quite a lot. *The Times* if it is ever there—especially at my Conservative Granddad's house. He will buy *The Times*. My Labour Granddad buys, is it the *Mail*?' Louis does, therefore, recognise newspaper bias even if his analysis is perhaps a little naïve.

With regards to whether his friends are interested in politics, Louis states, 'Some are interested in politics. I mean in my class there are not as many who are as interested as I am but there are some that know a bit about politics … but I think that a lot of them *want* to know about politics'.

Finally, Louis added that he thinks that the

> … main thing that is interesting for me is this run-up to the Election with the fact that it is quite close now and I mean if there is something on the news about politics, I like rush through to my mum and say, 'Oh, have you heard about this?' and she will talk for about ten minutes about it but yes, I think it's the fact that when something big is happening in politics, my friends, even the ones who don't know much about politics, will say to me, 'Oh, have you seen this?' especially one of my friends, he had no interest in politics but now he's getting interested in it. He's always on about the news now and he's saying 'Oh, Louis, did you see this? It was on the news' … They want to know about it and then they'll come and speak to me and then that involves like debate and things in politics. Politics seems to link

everything together, even if you are opposing each other, like a different political party.

It is significant that media coverage does potentially make young people more interested in politics. The extent of that coverage does, as is illustrated in Louis' case, provide fertile topics for discussion and potentially spark an interest in politics.

A further interviewee, Eric,[17] when asked how long he had served on Lincolnshire Youth Cabinet said 'I was elected around the end of February. I have served about a month. So I am fairly new. I am twelve'. In terms of serving on other bodies, he came up through the school council route, 'I was on my primary school School Council for two years, year four and year five and then I was on North Kesteven Youth Council as well'. In terms of what sparked his interest, he said, 'It will probably be the election, the George the second election [George W. Bush]. I was in America at that time and I just bought every book to do with it'. In terms of how long he has been interested in politics, he responded, 'Probably as long as I can remember. Yes, there are people on the youth cabinet who are 16, 17. I am still ... I think I am the youngest by about eight days. There is another one, from South Holland, who is twelve. Everybody else is about 16. 14, 15, 16 is about the average age'. With regards to the continuum or scale of interest, Eric said, 'Probably 9, point 9 because I can get away from politics but I am still heavily into it'. In terms of policy areas, transport was, once again, mentioned, 'Well, there is transport but the priorities depend upon what the young people prefer and what they think is a problem so it's not usually up to us but transport. Because 16 year olds on the trains have to pay adult rates. So that needs to be changed that's what transport does'. In terms of specific areas of interest that interest him more than others, he replied, 'Probably improving, just tweaking it a little bit the youth facilities, making it a little bit better. It's ok but the thing is you walk into a youth centre and you've got chavs. If you know what I mean. Do you know what a chav is? And people don't want to walk in they think, people my age don't want to walk in because there are people a lot older. You don't want to make it intimidating; you want more of a homely environment'. As to whether he would like a career in politics, he replied unequivocally, 'Yes. Definitely' and that he would like to be a 'Barrister. This is probably going to sound a bit childish. Number ten-ish. Probably leader of the Conservative Party'. Given that this interviewee is only 12 year old, perhaps this is why he was so refreshingly outspoken about his career ambitions.

With regards to lowering the voting age to 16, Eric said, 'I think it should be lowered if there is political education, brought in. Because that is one of the priorities for the UK Youth Parliament and if political education is brought in then yes, 16 would be probably about the right age. Because the government thinks "They don't know anything about it". They'd probably find it boring but they'd learn something. Probably, a bit more political because at [name of school]'s we do PSHE which is politics for about two weeks and then we do citizenship and all these other things but now we do SEAL which is actually nothing to do with it. To find out what the role of the cabinet is, what the cabinet is and what government politics is involved in. I would love it but noone else in my class would. They would hate it, they would be like [pulls a face]. I just have to ignore people who think I am a bit of a boff for liking politics'. In terms of citizenship in schools, he said quite succinctly, 'It's alright but it's not politics'.

With regard to whether more could be done to make young people aware of politics and political issues, Eric said, 'Yes because at this school nothing is portrayed of politics. You would probably see it once in a million years in this school because it is so we'll do everything else except politics … at this school noone knows who Nick Clegg is, noone knows who David Cameron is. Some of them will but no one knows who's in power. Someone came up to me and they were arguing about and they brought me to one side and said who's in power and I was like "Oh, Ok". Not every day, I read the sports page of *The Sunday Times* and *The Times* on a Saturday. Or I watch BBC Parliament. Sometimes in science lessons or ICT I type in BBC Politics and look at that'. Clearly, Eric sees schools as having a key part to play in the political education of young people.

In terms of whether his friends are interested in politics, Eric said, 'No. [Friend's name] is. The people on the Youth Cabinet are really, really interested. You've got 16 people who like politics on the Youth Cabinet so it's really, really interesting … whereas in some things if you said "Oh, I like politics", they'd go "Ugh", whereas everyone likes politics. [Friend's name] and I are really good friends and we were talking on *Facebook* yesterday and even though we don't really like the same politics, he's a socialist, I'm a Conservative, we're still friends'. So, he has one or two close friends who are really interested in politics but the majority are not. He did appear, however, to like the educative role he was able to play in teaching his friends about politics. This interesting, articulate young man was only 12 years of age and was passionate about politics—possibly a key example for those who would like to see the voting age lowered to 16 years.

A further interviewee, Piers,[18] provided more thought-provoking insights into youth political participation. He said the 'first time I got involved in the youth cabinet, I was co-opted on to it … and I re-stood in the elections in February [2010] and I regained my place on the youth cabinet'. As for school councils, he was quite outspoken in saying, 'I tend to avoid school council mainly because people get voted on because they're popular, because they're cool, whatever. And you just get these boring, mundane, turgid debates about "Oh, we should have the school toilets a bit better" or "We should have the PE bags in a different site". I went to one and I was like, "Oh my God, this is just, this is what you do when you are five!". I'm not interested in school council because if they are not going to make it interesting for me why should I go if I find it to be mundane?' In terms of how long he had been interested in politics, he said, 'I have probably always seem to have been interested in politics but I think when I first started to take a little bit more of an interest was the 2005 General Election. So I would have been just about to finish Year Six by then'. In terms of his own political views he said, 'when I was younger, I was a very staunch Labour supporter … I have lost faith in my own party … I personally don't think Gordon Brown was the right man to put in as the leader. OK, he's got the brains, he's got the intelligence and every-thing but the fact is that he doesn't have the connections, doesn't have the people skills and also I think that, at times, especially with this whole bullying façade, I think that in politics if you're going to be successful, you have to detach yourself emotionally and obviously Gordon Brown is quite an emotional man so I think that doesn't play well in his favour either'. What is fascinating here is the perceptive analysis that Piers prof-fers in relation to politics. He is 16 years of age and provides an analysis that many, much older political commentators would envy. In terms of the continuum of political interest, he said, 'My life is not dictated by politics because I would be a hideous, boring person to be around. I would say around the eight and a half/nine mark, so quite a strong interest but it doesn't control my life'. He did concede, however, that 'it used to when I was about 12 or 13, I used to be able to reel off virtually every person's majority in the House of Commons, in their constituencies, but I am not that obsessed by it anymore because I've grown older'. In terms of poli-cies that he would like to pursue on the Lincolnshire youth cabinet, he said, 'I just want to open the minds of people in Lincolnshire ... we live in quite a closed-minded country anyway and Lincolnshire is the most closed-minded of the counties so that is going to be a very taxing thing to try to do but that is what I would like to do, ideally'. Part of trying to open up minds was to be involved in organising a Youth Cabinet Question Time, to enable young people to let their peers on the youth cabinet know what issues are important to them. He is also interested in international matters, stating 'I am quite passionate about how states are striving for independence, in Chechnya, Kosovo, even Scotland if you can call that an international matter, and Burma, the whole thing there is quite intriguing. And I've got quite strong opinions on Afghanistan'.

With regards to lowering the voting age to 16, Piers said, 'Personally, I am for it because I think that 16 year olds, there are some out there that have a fantastic understanding of politics and a lot of adults' views are based on the media, basically what the *Sun* puts into their head ... there's a lot of like younger people, 16, 17, that have got very open minds and would vote on their own merit'. He did concede, however, that 'equally, I can see the argument against because there would also be a lot of 16, 17 year olds, actually as we saw in the youth elections, a lot of them were voting for people with stupid names, who looked the best in their photo and you'd also get the factor that they would vote for who their parents would tell them to vote for. So, you would get like whole families voting Tory or something'. In relation to citizenship classes, Piers said, 'after Year Nine, you don't get it. I don't know if it's a legal requirement? In Year Ten, we got like a day on study skills and everything and they said that was citizenship. In Year Seven, you get PSHE. You obviously know what that is! I can't remember all of it but the vast majority is like puberty, yuck, and all that lovely biological stuff'. In terms of making people more aware of politics and political issues, he felt that more could be done but he wasn't sure what exactly. He said, 'we're always going to see politics as the Eton-educated, pipe-smoking, tweed hats, like really posh, really snooty and a lot of people are going to think they are out of touch'. As to whether his friends were interested in politics, he differentiated between friends and acquaintances, saying, 'Some of my acquaintances, like [name], are interested in politics. [Name], who is one of my friends, used to have quite a strong interest in politics when he was about 11 or 12, saying that we should change to the Euro and radical things like that and now that's kind of dwindled with him and there's another one, [name], who goes, "Oh, I'm just Tory because my parents are Tory", so I've got a right range of views of politics and everything'. He reiterated his point about opening minds saying, 'there's quite a lot of racism, of homophobia, and all that kind of prejudice and it's not very good … I think the opening of the mind is a very hard thing to do'. He felt that being in an all-male school did not help in terms of opening minds, and said, 'I don't think the fact that we're in an all-male environment helps because you get men, men … women have like different ways of working, … the psychological thing'. As with all the others, Piers was a fascinating interviewee and provided a unique insight into youth political participation.

Another Lincolnshire Youth Cabinet interviewee, Eva,[19] said she was 'first elected about last April [2009] so I have been on there just over a year now'. In terms of serving on other bodies, she said she had 'done in the past but I don't anymore because it all got, with all school and everything, I had to stop because with school and everything it all got too much. I used to be on the Boston Youth Council and from primary School, I was always like Head of the School Council there. I was about Year Five when I first started on the School Council'. She said she would have been about 9 years old. In terms of what made her interested in politics, she said, 'Well, my brother's disabled so I have always been like a naturally protective person. He is two years older. He's got Downs' Syndrome so I've always been like naturally protective over him. Like people look and laugh at him in the street and from the age I can remember, I've always turned round and stuck up for him. Like when I was four, I remember walking down the street and having a go at boys who were 16. So, it's just, I was always naturally defensive and so I thought I may as well use the defensiveness and try and make something good out of it'. It is possibly of relevance that Eva later became a young carer. In terms of an interest in politics, she said, 'I mean I wasn't never directly interested in politics, I'd say that was quite a recent thing. As I've got older and understood it. But I've always been interested in standing up for people's rights, for as long as I can really remember'. In terms of the continuum of political interest, Eva placed herself at 'about eight'. In terms of policy areas that interested her, she sated, 'Well because I'm representing all young carers in Lincolnshire, I've obviously got the whole County to think of and because there are only two of us, whereas everyone else represents a specific area within Lincolnshire and because I am doing the whole of Lincolnshire, I am trying to get involved in all areas so that I can achieve all young carer's aims and everything. On the system, we've got about 800 [young carers] in Lincolnshire. So, that's how many people I am representing at the minute'. With regards to specific policy areas, she reiterated,

> Obviously young carers but I think the transport in this area is absolutely shocking, in Lincolnshire. I go to London to visit my friend who I met on holiday a few years ago and they can use buses for free all round London. I just think it's absolutely ridiculous. For me to come home from work is three pounds, a single journey. Just from Boston to my local village and I have spoken to the Stagecoach Director about it and I said to him, 'Why are we charged so much?' I mean we're not adults at 15 and I went 'So, why are we being charged it?' and he said 'You take up an adult seat'. And I said like 'Oh, so does a child only sit on half a seat then?' And he looked at me and he went 'Well, no' and I was like 'So what's your point?' and he just didn't answer. It really kind of bugs me so I'd like to get that sorted. And to change, I met the Children's Commissioner of England, I met her at a Conference a couple of months ago and one of my quotes got put on the front of her monthly newsletter. And we were talking about how young people are represented and how we wanted it to be changed. And I made the point that just because I am walking down the street wearing a hoodie, just because I'm with my friends, it doesn't make me a thug, I am actually a caring person. I actually care for my brother at home, I am on the Lincolnshire Youth Cabinet and every Wednesday night I do volunteering at a disability youth centre. So I just made the point that you can't judge people by what they look like kind of thing. So I'd like to change that.

Eva was very adept at articulating her concerns in relation to specific policy areas. She continued in relation to transport, 'In terms of the transport, I think the frequency of the buses is good but there isn't, they don't go to enough places. I live in [Name's Lincolnshire village] and they don't go through surrounding villages. So when I want to go and see my friends, I've only got a bus from Wrangle and it goes straight through to Boston. Well, there's loads of surrounding villages where my friends live, where I can't get to on a bus. So, I think if they could introduce something for there, people would use it quite a lot'.

In relation to whether she would like to study politics at university, Eva replied, 'Well, I am in my Year twelve now so I am starting to apply to Uni and I want to do Speech and Language Therapy but I was thinking that as a back-up option, what did I want to do and I am looking into Politics at the minute, like doing History and Politics, I think, or English and Politics'. Her chosen career path is rather specific, speech therapy, and, as she explains is based upon altruism as a result of her own familial experiences, 'I've always wanted just to make, well my brother has like had to have it [speech therapy] so I have seen how it benefits people. I like the fact that it doesn't just benefit that one person when that person can communicate efficiently with someone, it affects like the parents, the family. If that person is in pain and they could tell you. I mean like as a family not knowing whether you son is in pain must be heart-breaking. So, I would like to improve that for people because I know how much of a difference it can make to our lives. So just to be able to give it back to other people really'.

With regards to a career in politics, Eva said,

> I am not sure ... I think it can be quite risky because you can say one thing and it can be completely twisted and your career can be over within a second .... So I think although it is good for the right reasons, I think it is quite risky. It's nearly 20 grand to go to uni and to have it wasted so I thought with Speech and Language Therapy, once you're out of uni, about 90 per cent come out with a job in the first couple of months. I'm looking at the employability as well.

Eva does seem to be very astute in relation to careers and employability.

In terms of the specific question regarding lowering the voting age to 16 years, Eva was in favour, 'I am definitely for it. Well, I say I am for it but then a lot of, I think it's because I've matured quite early, having to look after my brother, I have always naturally been a few years older to cover it. So I think, in a sense, I would be happy for me but I know there are so many people out there who would just vote willy-nilly, not even taking into consideration who they voted for and I mean I know it's only a few votes but them few votes can make a big difference. So if you've got a lot of people who don't actually know what they're voting for then it could possibly change how the country is run'. With regards to the related question of citizenship teaching, Eva was straight to the point, 'I don't like citizenship lessons. We call them life skills or PSHE, it's all the same. They just attach a fancy name to it basically. But, I mean some of it can be useful. But when teachers teach us it, I think they kind of think like we don't know. I mean when they teach us about bullying. They're like "Yeh, we know it happens" and I don't know. I think, I just think it's a waste of time. Like one time we had to do this like coffee shop thing and run a virtual coffee shop. I mean that has given me no skills whatsoever. I should do it for about six weeks. But the thing is it was the biggest waste of six hours, I could have been doing something a lot more valuable. But when it comes to like work experience and then the life skills lessons were really useful. And now we're like applying to uni and doing UCAS applications and we've been going through unis in that time, so in that sense it's been useful'.

In terms of measures to make young people more aware of politics, Eva said,

> Yes, I really do because at the end of the day everyone has got to learn about them sometime because if you're going to be one of these people who say 'Oh, well, I'm not voting' then you have no right whatsoever to moan about how the country is run. So I think everyone should definitely be taught it. … I wouldn't have listened in year 8 if someone said 'Oh, shall I teach you about politics?' I would be like, 'Why? I don't want to know I am in Year 8' but if they approached it in a different manner. Not even, say if they like had a lesson, don't tell you what the lesson is going to be about but make it like a fun debating lesson and at the end go 'That was all politics' and you've really enjoyed it. I think if you're told at the end of having enjoyed something that that was actually politics, it might make people think, 'Oh, if they'd have told me that at the beginning, I would have hated it'. I would immediately have been negative but because we weren't told until the end then had a really good lesson then like, sneaky!

Eva spotlights an interesting way of teaching political education. With regards to whether her friends are interested in politics, she said,

> I was interested in politics a lot, like making a change. I have always been you know the one who was seen as gobby. Like a teacher was calling me, personally, I saw it as politics at a lower level. We were in life-skills, a citizen assembly thing and she said 'You all need to stop being selfish and stop thinking about your own selfish little lives and think about other people for a change. Leave your hair straighteners alone' and all this. She was being really quite rude. And I just thought, she's associating 200 people in this room as being exactly the same. Stereotyping 200 people she knows nothing about. I mean I was personally quite offended by it. And everyone else was but they never said anything. And I just went up to her and I said, 'I was like who are you to talk to me like that' and she looked at me and I went 'How dare you call me selfish'. I went, 'I have raised thousands of pounds for disabled people and young carers' and I was like 'I am volunteering every Wednesday night for two hours just like helping disabled people'.

This confrontation with a tutor had clearly had an impact upon Eva, and upon her tutor too.

In terms of being elected on to Lincolnshire Youth Cabinet, Eva said,

> I was elected [on to the Lincolnshire Youth Cabinet]. We have a day called MAD Day. It's 'Make a Difference Day' and it's the day when we learn skills like how to cook healthy meals because a lot of people who care for their mum and dad have to do all the cleaning and cooking and that for their mum and dad and like wash their parents ... we do some aerobics to keep us fit and we will have like first aid sessions in case anything is to go wrong. We will do cooking to like give us ideas for what we can cook when we are at home.

In terms of final comments, Eva added, 'I am 17. I don't particularly support a political party at the moment. I am kind of keeping my options open seeing how they all do'.

Eva expressed a keen interest in politics and testified how her involvement with the youth cabinet had been sparked by her role as a young carer, an issue about which she feels passionately.

A further interview with a young man named Theo,[20] elicited the following responses, 'I am on two groups. One of them is a local youth parliament thing just run by the village members and the council members in the village. But the other one, a lady who works for the Lincolnshire County Council, she's got an elected body which is called the Lincolnshire Rural Youth Forum which is a collection of children from rural areas around Lincolnshire who have all come together to sort of make a point of going to meetings and things and just saying what, at the moment what's wrong with the rural areas and what we would like to improve. That's the Wellingore Kid's Council and that was just started up when a member of the village, he's called [name], I think it is, he was in the village and he saw a group of kids playing outside and he went out and said, "Do you enjoy being out here?" and we were sort of saying, "Well, there's not a lot to do", so that's how it all started really. It's just sort of us giving our ideas of what would improve the village really so we helped make a play park for the younger members of the village who done, meals for people, and it's not just the young people, it's like the elderly and the, we did a meal for them and things like that really just to sort of improve the area in which we live. I have been doing this for two years'. In terms of whether he had served on other bodies, Theo said, 'Yes, I am very interested in that [UK Youth Parliament], my older sister who is also a member of both the things that I am on, she is also the head of Wellingore Kid's Council. She has been involved with lots of meetings and things to do with the UK Youth Parliament and getting on that. I haven't been on School Council but one of my close friends has'. In relation to what made him interested in politics, Theo said, 'Well, I really like the idea, the fact that it gives people a voice who may not have one in other areas such as children who may not be asked a lot of things about what they would like to improve'. He became interested in politics 'when the group started and came together and I thought well, this is a really good idea and I would like to continue with this so when the idea for the Wellingore Kid's Council started that's when it sort of started'. In terms of the continuum of political interest, Theo said, 'I would say around an eight because I am very interested in the ideas of politics but a lot of other things that I am interested in … like I have got a big interest in things like Psychology and stuff like that but I do take a big interest in politics'. The policy areas that interest Theo are, 'The Lincolnshire Rural Youth Forum has three main areas that's better transport for areas—I am quite interested in that—and also better house pricing and higher employment in rural areas'. So, Theo's key contribution had been to help set up 'Wellingore Kids' Kouncil' (*sic*), contributing to getting a new set of play park equipment, but he has also helped to make a meal for the elderly people of the village and taken part in a rural youth exchange programme to Lithuania. He was also involved in organising an event called the Linx Summer Festival, held at the Lincolnshire Showground and aimed at young people.

Asked whether he would like to study politics at university, Theo was unsure. Likewise, in terms of a career in politics, Theo replied 'Yes, I would but … I would like to go a bit further into it, not just looking at rural sides but other places that I am interested in but I wouldn't get chance to those at the moment because I am looking at rural areas just because that applies to me at the moment but I would look at wider ranges of things to politics'. He elaborated in terms of career aspirations, 'Mainly at the moment, I am very interested in Psychology and sort of Child Psychology and things like that but that would also work well with my Kid's Kouncil things because by attending meetings I can see what sort of things that kids want and they sort of go together'. On the topical issue of lowering the voting age to 16, Theo said, 'Well, personally I think that not everybody is aware of all the different parties so I think that the voting age at the moment is good … I think that our own votes would have been useful to include but I would say that I am not sure whether that would be generalisable (*sic*) enough to the whole of the youth around England so I am not sure I would have to have sort of more information'. In terms of citizenship teaching, he said 'Although it is taught once a year at our school, the idea is not taught enough and most people don't know what it is about' (Theo's School holds an annual citizenship day, as opposed to weekly lessons). As to whether more could be done to make young people more aware of politics, he said 'Politics could be made a compulsory lesson once a week, it's important that young people know about politics because it is very important to understanding how our country is ruled and governed'. With regards to his friends being interested in politics, Theo said, 'I have a few friends who are involved in their own councils, etc. One of my friends is on the school council but the majority of my friends don't know a lot about it'.

Another young politico, Jayden,[21] currently at university, was elected on to Bedfordshire Youth Parliament in 2010. In the same year, he also served as a representative on the UK Youth Parliament. From a young age, he had always wanted to get involved with his School Council, eventually leading it and also being a sitting member of the Children's Trust Board. He became interested in politics in 2008 at the start of the recession when he was 15 years old. Whilst not hailing from a political family, his parents have always voted, but they have not always discussed politics at home. On a continuum from one to ten, he rated his interest as ten, stating that this led him to want to study politics and declaring, 'I am enjoying that documentary on the House of Commons'. Issues of concern to him include bullying, cost of transport and lack of places to go for young people (he originates from a small, rural town with 'relatively little to do'). He has campaigned on the issue of saving youth services from budgetary cuts, organised petitions (presented to Central Bedfordshire Council) and spoken about it in the media. He covets a career in politics but not as an MP, preferring to be 'in the background, in the civil service or in local government'. In terms of lowering the voting age, Jayden said, 'Yes, I am in favour', continuing 'I can see the benefits. Many thousands vote in the UK Youth Parliamentary elections so I can't see why not'. He also felt that it 'might encourage voting'. In terms of citizenship teaching, he claimed it to be 'very badly organised and constantly changing for my year group. It changed in the sixth-form; we did general studies, where we did stuff on the AV [electoral system] referendum. Politics wasn't touched until the sixth-form'. He did feel, however, that more should be done to make young people aware of politics, 'My flatmate's girlfriend, for example, hasn't a clue about politics, about how the system works, about manifestoes, etc.'. He finished by commending the House of Commons, especially Speaker Bercow, for allowing them to use the Commons Chamber for UK Youth Parliament annual debates, stating there were now more MPs interested in these and they had even had responses from government departments.

YOUTH PARLIAMENTS

The primary focus of this chapter is youth political participation at the local level. Given that some of the interviewees were, or had been, members of the UK Youth Parliament, it is pertinent to assess what it is and how it operates. The UK Youth Parliament was set up in July 1999. Its first sitting was held in February 2001 in London, and there are now around 300 elected members of the UKYP, which double including Deputy MYPs (Members of the Youth Parliament). Elections are held each year and any young person aged between 11 and 18 can vote and stand. The elected MYPs work with various bodies including School and Youth councils, MPs and local councillors to press for issues of concern to them to be taken on board. As their manifesto claims it is 'Run by young people, for young people, UKYP provides opportunities for 11–18 year-olds to use their voice in creative ways to bring about social change'. Issues concerning the UKYP include the following: the way the young people are portrayed in the media, they have an emphasis on multi-culturalism, citizenship education, an equal minimum wage, accessible transport, sexual health education, challenge to gang culture and opposition to the 'Mosquito' noise-emitting device used to disperse young people who congregate in groups, and so forth.

Youth is not one great amorphous mass; young people are as heterogeneous as the rest of society. There are as many divisions amongst young people as there are unifying aspects. Questions must be asked, however, when we see such low levels of political participation amongst a particular sector of society. The debate in the House of Commons in October 2009 (the first time the Commons was used as a debating chamber by non-MPs, whereby 300 members of the UKYP graced the seats) can surely only be seen as a positive move. Indeed, the seventh annual Youth Parliament debate in the Commons Chamber took place on Friday, 13 November 2015.[22] 'Chaired by the Speaker, John Bercow, the debates over each of the seven years have been dynamic and topics have included youth crime, whether the voting age should be lowered to 16 years of age, and free university education. The 2015 debates covered: the living wage; a curriculum to prepare young people for life; mental health; transport; and tackling racism and religious discrimination. The debates are notoriously dynamic. The 2012 debate, for example, was attended by the Children's Minister, Edward Timpson MP, who said 'We've had energy, eloquence and passion in abundance. You've tested and challenged my views and values and those of all around you. I would challenge anyone here today or watching elsewhere to leave without feeling seriously impressed'.[23] Gerry Stoker seeks to harness the dynamism and potential of the various youth assemblies when he advocates giving 'the UK Youth Parliament, the Northern Ireland Youth Forum, the Scottish Youth Parliament and the Children and Young People's Assembly for Wales the right to call a people's ballot or citizen's initiative referendum on a topic of their choosing' (Stoker 2014: 26; see also Qvortrup 2015, re-the referendum). This could mean that they have the power to effect real political change.

As Shephard and Patrikios (2012) point out, one remedy for low levels of youth involvement has been the setting up of youth parliaments. The Scottish Youth Parliament, for example, came into being on 30 June 1999. Youth parliaments can be seen as rectifying an 'institutional lacuna' by providing young people with an arena in which to 'practice civic and social skills' and a place where young people 'are listened to by politicians' (2012: 1). As Shephard and Patrikios explain, decreasing levels of 'voting, membership of traditional organisations and civic trust can also be linked to the prominence of young participants in the worldwide wave of social unrest that marked 2011 (for example in the "Arab Spring", in the "indignados" movements in Spain and Greece and in various "Occupy" or "99 %" movements)' (Ibid: 2).[24] As they go on to say, these 'developments add a tone of urgency to the need for effective institutional mechanisms that reconnect young citizens with formal politics' (Ibid.). They also attest how through being closely engaged with the roles of national parliamentarians, young people expand their skill sets. They accentuate the Scottish Youth Parliament where, for example, young people have become 'increasingly active participants in agenda setting and policy influence (for example, the "Mosquito" petition and the "Love Equally" campaign)' (Ibid: 17). The Mosquito is a device which emits a high-frequency, penetrating sound designed only to be heard by younger people and which has been used in certain areas to disperse groups of young people on the streets. The Love Equally Campaign was aimed at promoting marriage equality between homosexual and heterosexual couples, where the Scottish Youth Parliament was said to have been instrumental in getting it brought forward. For Shephard and Patrikios, it is imperative that best practice is shared on a pan-European basis in relation to youth parliaments. As they say, 'particularly in the midst of the recent global wave of protest movements and social unrest' (Ibid.). Certainly, youth political participation, as *this* study of Lincolnshire Youth Cabinet illustrates, helps young people to build up their skill sets and feed into the policy-making process.

As Alan Turkie affirms, however, young people need to ensure that their views, and a representative sample of views, are aired. He points out, in his study of the UKYP that 'concerns about tackling racism, sexism or homophobia have not been raised as campaign choices within the UKYP, in spite of strong representation by Black young people, young women and young gay men' (2010: 268) and he, therefore, warns them against mimicking 'flawed adult structures' (Ibid.). This is as issue of which young people should be wary. Perpetuating existing inequalities should not be seen as the way forward. Likewise, McGinley and Grieve, in their study of youth councils in Scotland, believe that the voices of many young people are not being heard. As they contend, 'Youth councils allow limited involvement in decision making, usually at the level of consultation rather than of encouraging young people to drive their own agenda' (2010: 260). This resonates with Chap. 2 and the theoretical ladder of participation, with the debate centring on different rungs or 'degrees' of participation. It could be that, whilst youth councils, parliaments and cabinets do provide an opportunity and a vehicle for political participation, and enable young people to build up their confidence whilst acquiring skills such as public-speaking and committee techniques, they are not the sole approach. Other mechanisms, such as, the 'rights-based approach' (Ibid: 259) advocated by McGinley and Grieve require a more concerted effort to involve and include young people at many levels of the decision-making process. The model that they propose 'recognises and celebrates current capacities and encourages levels of involvement that are meaningful and aspirational' (Ibid.). It will be interesting to see whether these new ways of working and engaging politically, as advocated by McGinley and Grieve, do ever come to fruition or is it the case that existing structures are so ingrained that it would be difficult for the power-brokers to give up some of their stranglehold to actively empower young people in a meaningful and genuine way?

CONCLUSION

Young people are not uninterested in politics but appear less than enamoured by mainstream politics. The 'buzz', for many, comes through an interest in specific issues such as environmentalism and animal rights. It is also a cross-national phenomenon, as Alison Byrne Fields elucidates when writing about young people in the USA. 'Kids in high school are fighting to establish gay-straight alliances. Young people in the Bay Area of California are taking on the juvenile justice system. High school students in New York City are walking out of their classes to demonstrate their anger over a lack of funding for education. Students in Massachusetts are boycotting standardized tests that they see as being unfair to students in underresourced school districts' (Byrne Fields in Dalton 2011: 38). She also illuminates how young people are using their purchasing power to organise boycotts of disreputable companies and organisations and 'buycotts', that is to say purchasing from and being loyal to companies which are making 'a commitment to social responsibility' (Ibid: 39; see also Sloam, 2015). Young people are, self-evidently, the future. Events such as the Commons debates, may serve to spread political interest amongst our young people. It is patronising for adults to believe that they must constantly direct, control and chaperone young people. Young people can be bold, innovative and inspirational. Indeed, Louis Braille was only 15 when he devised the Braille system of writing. As mentioned previously, playwright Shelagh Delaney was only 18 when she wrote *A Taste of Honey*. Likewise, the Glo-Sheet luminescent device was apparently the product of a 10 year old. Delving further into the annals of time, the artist J.M.W. Turner exhibited at the Royal Academy's Summer Exhibition in 1790 when he was only 15, and the Spanish painter Diego Velázquez began his apprenticeship at the age of 11 and painted *Old Woman Frying Eggs* at the turn of 1618 when he would have been 18. Adults do not have a monopoly on creativity and dynamism!

To achieve their goals, young people are, as Byrne Fields (cited in Dalton 2011: 45) states, 'volunteering, organizing their communities, protesting, and boycotting in record numbers. Young people are using media and technology and working across lines of racial and ethnic difference to redefine what it means to be an engaged citizen in the 21st century'. As Sian Griffiths points out, 'Today's teenagers are the most ambitious, career-minded generation in 100 years' (2014: 7). This is according to a report entitled Evolution of the Teenager that was produced for the National Citizen Service which questioned 'the silent generation (aged

72–89), the baby-boomers (54–71), generation X (32–53), generation Y (19–31) and generation citizen [13 to 19]' (Ibid.). Clearly, there is ample reason to be positive about young people and politics, as evidenced both by the National Citizen Survey and these qualitative comments. There is a level of participation that extends beyond the ballot box, and young people's activism at local level is symptomatic of that dynamic approach.

NOTES

1. See http://microsites.lincolnshire.gov.uk/teeninfolincs/ for the latest data.
2. Email to author, 12 August 2013.
3. Interview with author, 11 November 2015.
4. Ibid.
5. Email to author 1 June 2011.
6. Email to author, 23 February 2010.
7. See https://www.speakersschoolcouncil.org/ for more detail, accessed 21 July 2014.
8. Interview with author, 27 May 2011.
9. Ibid.
10. Interview with author, 23 May 2011.
11. Interviews with author, March 2010. Names of all interviewees have been changed for anonymity.
12. Interview with author, 23 January 2012.
13. Interview with author, 23 March 2012.
14. Interview conducted 22 May 2012.
15. Interview with author, 9 March 2010.
16. Interview with author 26 March 2010.
17. Interview with author 16 March 2010.
18. Interview with author, 16 March 2010.
19. Interview with author 29 June 2010.
20. Interview with author, 28 June 2010.
21. Interview with author, 26 February 2015.
22. See UK Youth Parliament website http://www.ukyouthparliament.org.uk/houseofcommons accessed 9 November 2015.
23. Cited on the UKYP website http://www.ukyouthparliament.org.uk/2012/news/youth-parliament-calls-curriculum-overhaul/ accessed 18 September 2015.
24. See Chou (2015) for more detail regarding Occupy.

BIBLIOGRAPHY

Arnstein, S. R. (1969, July). A ladder of citizen participation. *Journal of the American Institute of Planners, 35*(4), 216–224.

Bruter, M., & Harrison, S. (2009). *The future of our democracies: Young party members in Europe.* Basingstoke: Palgrave Macmillan.

Chou, M. (2015). From crisis to crisis: Democracy, crisis and the occupy movement. *Political Studies Review, 13,* 46–58.

Cracknell, R., McGuinness, F., & Rhodes, C. (2011). *General Election 2010.* Research Paper 10/36, House of Commons Library, London.

Dalton, R. (Ed.) (2011). *Engaging youth in politics: Debating democracy's future.* New York: International Debate Education Association.

Dunn, G., & Roach, K. (2013). *Youth unemployment in Lincoln city.* Lincoln: Lincoln City Council.

Gibson, R. K., Lusoli, W., & Ward, S. J. (2005). Online participation in the UK: Testing a 'contextualised' model of Internet effects. *The British Journal of Political and International Relations, 7*(4), 561–583.

Gomm, R. (2009). *Key concepts in social research methods.* Basingstoke: Palgrave.

Gomm, R., Hammersley, M., & Foster, P. (Eds.) (2000). *Case study method.* London: Sage.

Griffiths, S. (2014). Today's teens most driven for a century. *The Sunday Times,* 26 June, p. 7.

Hackett, P., & Hunter, P. (2010). *Who governs Britain? A profile of MPs in the new parliament.* London: The Smith Institute.

Hamel, J. (1993). *Case study methods.* London: Sage.

Hammersley, M. (2008). *Questioning qualitative enquiry.* London: Sage.

Hawkins, O., Keen, R., & Nakatudde, N. (2015, July 28). *General Election 2015.* Briefing Paper, CBP7186, House of Commons, London.

Henn, M., Weinstein, M., & Forrest, S. (2005). Uninterested youth? Young people's attitudes towards party politics in Britain. *Political Studies, 53*(3), 556–578.

Lincolnshire Research Observatory. (2014). *Unemployment in Lincolnshire: August 2014.* Lincoln: Lincolnshire County Council.

Marsh, D., O'Toole, T., & Jones, S. (2007). *Young people and politics in the UK: Apathy or alienation?* Basingstoke: Palgrave.

McGinley, B., & Grieve, A. (2010). Maintaining the status quo? Appraising the effectiveness of youth councils in Scotland. In B. Percy-Smith & N. Thomas (Eds.), *A handbook of children and young people's participation: Perspectives from theory and practice* (pp. 254–261). London: Routledge.

Pitkin, H. F. (1967). *The concept of representation.* Berkeley, CA: University of California Press.

Qvortrup, M. (2015). Power to the people! But how? The different uses of referendums around the world. *Political Studies Review, 13*, 37–45.

Shephard, M., & Patrikios, S. (2012). Making democracy work by early formal engagement? A comparative exploration of youth parliaments in the EU. *Parliamentary Affairs*, 14 May, pp. 1–20 (Advance Online Publication).

Sloam, J. (2015). Political parties are neglecting young people—It's time for unis to step in. *The Guardian*, 25 February. Retrieved September 27, 2015, from http://www.theguardian.com/higher-education-network/2015/feb/25/political-parties-are-neglecting-young-people-its-time-for-unis-to-step-in

Stoker, G. (2014). Political citizenship and the innocence of youth. In A. Mycock & J. Tonge (Eds.), *Beyond the youth citizenship commission: Young people and politics* (pp. 23–26). London: Political Studies Association.

Thomas, G. (2009). *How to do your research project*. London: Sage.

Thomas, P. (2009, April). Between two stools? The government's 'Preventing Violent Extremism' agenda. *Political Quarterly, 80*(2), 282–291.

Travers, M. (2001). *Qualitative research through case studies*. London: Sage.

Turkie, A. (2010). More than crumbs from the table: A critique of youth parliaments as models of representation for marginalised young people. In B. Percy-Smith & N. Thomas (Eds.), *A handbook of children and young people's participation: Perspectives from theory and practice* (pp. 262–269). London: Routledge.

Watson, R. (2010). Bright young thing. *Children and Young People Now*, 23 February–1 March, p. 13.

Wattenberg, M. P. (2012). *Is voting for young people?* (3rd ed.). New York: Longman Pearson.

White, C., Bruce, S., & Ritchie, J. (2000). *Young people's politics: Political interest and engagement amongst 14–24 year olds*. York: Joseph Rowntree Foundation.

Whiteley, P. (2014). Does citizenship education work? Evidence from a decade of citizenship education in secondary schools in England. *Parliamentary Affairs, 67*(3), 513–535.

Yin, R. K. (2009). *Case study research: Design andd methods* (4th ed.). London: Sage. Retrieved September 5, 2011, from http://www.youngwomeninpolitics.com/

CHAPTER 7

Gender and Political Participation

The aim of Chap. 7 is to examine the differing levels of political participation of young men and young women. Based around a number of focus groups, the emphasis is upon gendered political participation. To reiterate the outline furnished in the introductory chapter, key questions include the following: What accounts for this difference? Are young men more politically aware than young women? Do levels of political participation vary between the two groups? The focus of this chapter is primarily upon young women, partly redressing the balance given the fact that political science has, for decades, been a male-dominated discipline (in terms both of the study and the practice)[1] but also giving voice to the concerns of young women. Young women have, traditionally, been the sector of the electorate least likely to cast their vote, and yet, if examination is made of specific policy areas, there are many aspects that ought to be of primary concern to women. Child care provision, the increase in cases of sexually transmitted diseases, issues in relation to women in the workplace, such as the gender pay gap (19.1 per cent in 2014—see the Fawcett Society 2015), are examples of issues which ought to galvanise women to cast their vote. To reiterate, this chapter focuses upon gender differences in relation to political participation and non-participation. Some academics are not enamoured by focus groups but they do have a place in the research

An earlier version of sections of this chapter was published in the *Journal of Youth Studies* entitled 'Young Women and Politics: An Oxymoron?'

J. Briggs, *Young People and Political Participation*, DOI 10.1057/978-1-137-31385-0_7 process, and authors such as David Morgan (1997), Michael Bloor et al. (2001) and Pranee Liamputtong (2011) would certainly agree. The focus group material will be used to supplement the data gleaned from other sources.

Building upon the literature that examines young people and politics, this chapter examines the extent to which young women are interested in politics. The hypothesis is that young women might not necessarily be interested in mainstream party politics but that, when questioned, they are actually interested in political issues. This ties in with the findings of the flourishing literature on young people and politics (see, for example, the work of Henn et al. 2002, 2004, 2005; Kimberlee 2002; Molloy et al. 2002; O'Toole et al. 2003a, b; Phelps 2004; Sloam 2013a, 2015) whereby a similar conclusion is reached here that young people may have turned away from the ballot box and from parliamentary politics but that, when questioned, they are actually interested in political issues. The focus is primarily upon young women as opposed to looking at young people as a generic grouping. Based upon in-depth interviews with young women (18–24-year-olds) in focus groups, this research seeks to find answers to the vexed question of why politics appears to be a turn-off for the majority of young women. In doing so, there are also lessons to be learnt in relation to young men and politics.

INTRODUCTION

There is a general impression that women, and young women in particular, are the least likely to vote and to profess an interest in politics (Electoral Commission 2004a: 8, 31, b; Fawcett Society 2004a,b,c; Williams 2005: 7; Stevens 2007: 51). This research is going to explore, firstly, whether this is the case and, secondly, if so, to explore the reasons as to why this should be. Is it the case that young women, in particular, feel that 'politics' does not relate to their lives and, if so, what can be done to rectify this situation? This is an issue that is and should be of interest to politicians and policymakers alike. The women's vote, or in this case the young women's vote, is not something that should be ignored, taken lightly or taken for granted. Granted, as Tam O'Neil and Pilar Domingo point out, 'women are not a homogenous group with a discernible set of "women's interests"' (2015: 5) but there is significant synergy for them to be treated as a cohesive whole. In 2005, the Fawcett Society ran a campaign to ensure that women's representation was part of the campaign and kept at the forefront of the debate. This included an analysis of the party manifestoes to see whether they were prioritising policies for equality. Likewise, in 2001, the parties, the political pundits and the media were all chasing the mythical 'Worcester Woman', in the swing constituencies, as the key to their electoral success. In the context of campaigns, there has been a focus upon capturing women's vote. Any party capturing the female vote at the 2015 General Election would undoubtedly be successful. Women (comprising 52 per cent of the electorate) have the potential to have a significant impact upon the outcome of the electoral process. If they are encouraged to make the connection between their opinions and formal politics then they, potentially, could be the voice of real and lasting change. As the Sex and Power 2014 Report reveals, it is 'now almost 40 years since the Sex Discrimination Act was passed, over 40 since the Equal Pay Act, and over 80 since women got the right to vote equally with men, yet women all too often are still missing from politically powerful positions in the UK' (Centre for Women and Democracy 2014: 7). Women's voices and physical presence are still sidelined as far as politics is concerned. As mentioned elsewhere, 'Increases in numbers of women politicians have not yet facilitated a significant shift in the masculine values and practices often driving mainstream politics across the UK. Recent announcements by a number of female MPs in Westminster stating their intention not to stand for re-election in 2015 highlights ongoing disillusionment with parliamentary life and its political culture' (Briggs 2014: 32). Those who stood down included the following: on the Labour benches, Dawn Primarolo, Tessa Jowell, Ann Clwyd, Joan Ruddock and Glenda Jackson; and on the Conservative side, Jessica Lee, Laura Sandys and Lorraine Fulbrook. Mary Riddell cites the 'macho, antediluvian culture', an anachronistic throwback that serves to exclude, or at least sideline, women (Riddell, cited in Sanghani 2014). Certainly, for some of the long-serving Labour leavers, this is probably not the case, but Parliament does need to undergo further change if it is to make more women feel welcomed and a sense of belonging.

This chapter examines the extent to which young women are interested in politics. It seeks to ascertain whether young women are interested in mainstream party politics and/or whether they are actually interested in specific political issues. The literature on young people and politics (see, for example, the work of Henn et al. 2002, 2004, 2005; Kimberlee 2002; Marsh et al. 2007; Molloy et al. 2002; O'Toole et al. 2003a,b; Phelps 2004; Sloam 2015) argues that young people may have turned away from the ballot box and from parliamentary politics but that, when questioned, they are actually interested in political issues. As stated, 'while they are clearly interested in many political issues, young women often face gender-specific challenges that limit their political participation and democratic representation' (Briggs 2014: 32). This research adds to the debate because its focus is primarily upon young women as opposed to young people as a generic grouping.

This study looks at the political interests and behaviour of young women in Lincolnshire, using a number of focus groups. The chapter begins by accentuating young people and politics in general. The discussion then moves on to an examination of young women and politics. The methodological approach adopted by the study is outlined before moving on to an exposé of the findings of the research. Finally, the concluding section draws together the findings from the primary data and links this in with current debates in the wider literature.

Young People and Politics

The concept of youth is a relatively recent phenomenon (Osgerby 1998) and links in with factors such as the period of relative affluence that stems from the 1950s and 1960s, echoed in Prime Minister Harold Macmillan's oft (mis)quoted phrase 'You've never had it so good'. It ties in with the growth and development of popular music and the corresponding rise in youth sub-cultures. Inglehart's post-affluence thesis also helps explain the growth of youth as a political concept—the notion that, as people become better off financially, they can turn their attention away from basic economic survival, from thinking about where their next meal is coming from to expressing a concern for issues like animal rights or the plight of others (Inglehart 1977a, b). The origin and development of the various new social movements that stem from this period also contribute to the rise of youth culture. To name a few, young people were heavily involved in the peace protests, the anti-Vietnam protests and the student protests of the 1960s (cf. Todd and Taylor 2004).

It is fair to say, therefore, that the phenomenon of 'youth' constituting a separate and distinct category, set aside from the world of both adults and children, developed significantly in the post-Second World War period. As Osgerby says, 'After 1945 the themes and imagery of "youth" featured within the mass media and impinged upon the public consciousness as never before' (Osgerby 2002a, b: 370). Prior to this time, there was some notion of younger people constituting a distinct category, the 'Peaky Blinders' of Birmingham and the 'scuttling' gangs of Manchester at the end of the nineteenth century, were forerunners of contemporary youth groups (see, for example, Pearson 1983; Osgerby 1998). As Pearson (1983:94) states, 'In Manchester, the gangs were known as "Scuttlers"—a word which went back to the 1880s—and their gang fights and rowdyism as "Scuttling" or "Scuttles"'. Similarly, in Birmingham, 'corner boys and street gangs were known as "Peaky Blinders", or less commonly as "Sloggers"' (Ibid: 96). On a political level, young (male) students have been seen as a dangerous political element since industrialisation began, for example, in 1848, the Springtime of the Peoples revolutions were supported and often led by young students. Thus, instead of being a totally new concept, 'the youth culture of the fifties and the social responses it elicited are more accurately seen as an extension of phenomena long a feature of British society' (Osgerby 1998: 5). The concept of youth existed prior to the Second World War but the 'post-war era saw a range of developments in labour markets, earning power, cultural provision and marketing which, together, served to accentuate considerably the profile of "youth" as an identifiable social category' (Ibid). As stated, by the 1960s, young people had emerged at the forefront of movements of popular protest, such as the anti-Vietnam protests, the student protest and the emerging women's movement.

In relation to politics, there has traditionally been a lack of interest amongst political scientists with reference to young people and politics. Social class used to be the most defining characteristic as far as voting behaviour was concerned, and for many, youth was simply a non-issue (see Weinstein 2004: 176). This changed in the 1960s/1970s, particularly with the emergence and growth of new social movements. New social movement activity appears attractive to young people in particular (See also White et al. 2000; Evans 2003: 92; Henn et al. 2004: 213). Likewise, Hay states, 'Many, especially young, citizens who have chosen either to disengage, or never to engage in the first place, in formal politics are active in informal politics' (Hay 2007: 27). Compare this youth involvement in new social movements with their levels of activity in mainstream politics. Table 7.1 illustrates the level of turnout in general elections of young people in the UK and the electorate as a whole. It is evident that turnout fell sharply in 2001, but the fall was even greater among young voters—a trend that continued in 2005 (despite a slight increase in turnout amongst voters as a whole). In 2010, the trend reversed and there was an increase in turnout of 7 percentage points amongst the 18–24 age group, taking it to 44 per cent. Likewise, overall turnout increased slightly to 65.1 per cent. In 2015, the overall turnout was 66.1 per cent, and turnout of young people was 43 per cent (*Source*: Ipsos MORI 2015). This is higher than the 16 per cent of 18–24-year-olds who said they were 'certain to vote' (Hansard Society 2015: 6). It is fair to say, however, as shown in Chap. 3, low turnout amongst young people is not a country-specific issue. As Wattenberg (2012: 2) asserts, 'political apathy among young people is now so widespread across the world's established democracies makes it improbable that country-specific factors are at the root of the problem'.

In terms of the 2010 UK General Election, as shown in Table 7.1, turnout amongst 18–24-year-olds increased slightly to 44 per cent (up 7 percentage points on the previous general election). Of those who voted, 30 per cent voted Conservative (up 2 percentage points on 2005), 31 per cent voted Labour (down 7 percentage points on 2005), 30 per cent voted Liberal Democrat (up 4 percentage points on 2005), whilst 9 per cent voted for 'others'. It can be seen, therefore, that of the 44 per cent of young people who voted in 2010, the vote was fairly evenly split between the three major political parties—with both the Conservatives and the Liberal Democrats having increased their support amongst young people since the previous general election.

If these figures are disaggregated to take account of gender, it can be seen that 29 per cent of 18–24-year-old men who voted, voted for Conservative; 34 per cent voted for Labour; 27 per cent voted for Liberal; and 10 per cent voted for 'others'. The corresponding figures for female

Table 7.1   Youth turnout in comparison with the electorate as a whole

Year of general election	*18–24-year-old voters turnout (%)*	*Electorate as a whole turnout (%)*
1992	61	77.7
1997	68	71.4
2001	39	59.4
2005	37	61.3
2010	44	65.1
2015	43	66.1

Source: Butler and Kavanagh (1997: 295), Jowell and Park (1998), Electoral Commission (2001: 15), Evans (2003), *The Observer* 8 May (2005):6, Cracknell et al. (2011), Ipsos MORI (2015)

Table 7.2   Young people and the 2010 General Election: How they voted

2010 General Election	Conservative (%)	Labour (%)	Liberal democrats (%)	Others (%)
All 18–24-year-old voters	30	31	30	9
18–24-year-old men	29	34	27	10
18–24-year-old women	30	28	34	9

Table 7.3   Young men and women and turnout

General election	All 18–24-year-olds (%)	18–24-year-old men (%)	18–24-year-old women (%)
2005	37	39	35
2010	44	50	39
2015	43	42	44

Source: Adapted from data provided by Ipsos MORI, *How Britain Voted in 2010*; and Ipsos MORI, *How Britain Voted in 2015*

voters aged 18–24 are, 30 per cent voted for Conservative, 28 per cent voted for Labour, 34 per cent voted for the Liberal Democrats and 9 per cent voted for others. It can be seen, therefore, that young women voters were more attracted to the Liberal Democratic Party than young men (by 7 percentage points) and less attracted to the Labour Party in comparison with young men (by 6 percentage points) (Table 7.2).

In terms of the difference in turnout between young men and young women, Table 7.3 illustrates how the turnout of young women in the 18–24-year-old age bracket remains the lowest turnout. Even though more young women turned out to vote in 2010 than had done so in 2005 (by 4 percentage points), turnout amongst young women aged 18–24 remained the lowest level of turnout amongst all ages categories at the 2010 General Election, with just 39 per cent of young women turning out to cast their vote. The corresponding figures for the 2015 General Election reveal that young women voted in slightly greater numbers than young men (*Source*: Ipsos MORI 2015). Whilst noting the possibility of a margin of error here, this is an interesting turnaround in that young men have usually turned out in greater numbers than young women (Ibid.). Many young women appear equally disconnected with mainstream party politics and participation in elections as their male counterparts, and their

Table 7.4 Young people and the 2015 General Election: How they voted

2015 General Election	Conservative (%)	Labour (%)	Liberal democrats (%)	UKIP (%)	Greens (%)	Others (%)
All 18–24-year-old voters	27	43	5	8	8	9
18–24-year-old men	32	41	4	7	8	8
18–24-year-old women	24	44	5	10	9	8

Source: Adapted from data provided by Ipsos MORI (2015)

attitudes and behaviours tie in with the burgeoning literature on young people and politics (cf. Mycock and Tonge 2012a, b; Sloam 2013a, b, c, 2015).

In terms of how young people voted in 2015, Table 7.4 reveals the breakdown.

There was a 7.5 percentage point swing from Conservative to Labour amongst 18–24-year-olds in 2015. Disaggregated, this rises to 11 percentage point if the focus is upon 18–24-year-old women, yet only a 2 percentage point swing amongst 18–24-year-old men.

Did Young Women Buck the Trend in 2015?

According to data from Ipsos MORI, they did buck the trend, albeit by a small margin. Slightly more young women than young men voted in 2015—44 per cent to 42 per cent, respectively. In terms of how they voted, 44 per cent of the voting 18–24-year-old women voted for Labour, compared with 41 per cent of 18–24-year-old men. In terms of support for the Conservative Party amongst 18–24-year-olds, 32 per cent of 18–24-year-old men voted for the Conservatives, compared with 24 per cent of 18–24-year-old women. Young women, therefore, voted for the Labour Party more than young men. This is an interesting development given that, traditionally, women generally were said to favour the Conservative Party. The Liberal Democrats received the support of 4 per cent of 18–24-year-old men who voted and 5 per cent of 18–24-year-old women. Support for other parties grew amongst 18–24-year-olds at the

2015 General Election, with 23 per cent of young men and 27 per cent of young women who voted voting for parties other than the three main ones.

It is evident that the Labour and Conservative parties were the key parties of choice for young women, but there was significant slippage in support for the Liberal Democrats at the 2015 General Election. This support amongst young women voters was down from 34 per cent in 2010 to 5 per cent in 2015—a statistically significant fall of 29 percentage points (mirrored, to a lesser extent, by the drop in support for the Liberal Democrats amongst young men—down from 27 per cent to 4 per cent, a fall of 23 percentage points). Clearly, many young women had become disillusioned with the Liberal Democrats after five years of Coalition Government. Debate surrounds why this should be, but perhaps the perception that Nick Clegg had performed a *volte-face* in terms of tuition fees contributed to this turnaround. Correspondingly, there has been a significant increase in support for other parties amongst young women voters— up 18 percentage points from 9 per cent in 2010 to 27 per cent in 2015 (again, there was a corresponding increase amongst young men supporting other parties—up 13 percentage points from 10 per cent to 23 per cent). This move away from the three major political parties amongst young women fits with the general shift towards support for minor parties. It appears that the Greens and also the UKIP were the main beneficiaries of this change.

Turnout among young people is also low in 'other' elections. For example, an NOP (National Opinion Poll) estimated that only 16 per cent of young people actually voted in the 2003 Election to the Welsh Assembly (Broughton and Storer 2004: 278). We need to be wary, however, as low turnout does not always mean apathy. Research suggests that young people are interested in specific issues, for example, environmentalism or animal rights (Evans 2003: 92). By attaching greater importance to such issues, the mainstream political parties may see increasing levels of political participation amongst the young. We also need to widen our definition of politics (Buckingham 2000: 204; Henn et al. 2002: 168). The argument here is that young people are not apathetic but they are interested in a different type of politics. According to a MORI poll published in the aftermath of the 2005 General Election, the notion that young people are not bothered about politics is actually a myth. They found that more young people were interested than uninterested in the general election. The MORI survey (cited in the *Observer* 8 May 2005: 7) concludes that

'Young people are not apathetic, but many are disengaged'. On the contrary, other commentators believe that young people are not disengaged from mainstream politics and the views of young and older people are often similar. It could simply be that young people have 'better things to do with their time, such as finding partners, homes and jobs' (Jowell and Park 1998: 15). This issue is examined in the data analysis section to ascertain whether the focus group respondents support the point being made by Jowell and Park.

If turnout figures are an indication of low levels of interest in mainstream politics amongst people at large, then elections are failing to inspire on more general terms (cf. Baston and Richie 2004). Low turnout does not necessarily mean apathy, but the decline in turnout could indicate that it is part of a wider malaise. Young people tend not to see voting as a 'civic duty' in the same way as older people (cf. Goerres 2007; Whiteley 2012), and even where young people have been active (such as contacting a politician or attending a meeting) this is not an indicator that they will also vote (Electoral Commission 2001: 15–18). So, again, young people may be interested in politics and policies, but this does not mean that they will actually vote.

In part, the British Government's Green Paper, *The Governance of Britain* (Stationery Office 2007), is a response to declining levels of turnout in elections and a belief that certain sectors of society are disengaged from the political process. The Paper suggests consideration of proposals such as moving elections to the weekend (the last time this happened in Britain was on Saturday, 14 December 1918). Many proposals concern facilitation of the act of casting one's vote; they do not focus upon re-engaging a disillusioned electorate. The Green Paper acknowledged that certain sectors of society—notably, for example, young people—appear to be alienated from mainstream politics. Russell, in the Political Studies Association's response to the Green Paper, argues that although young people may not be voting in significant numbers, they are not disengaged with politics more generally. He spotlights the work of Dalton (2008a: 92, b), who believes that electoral turnout is not the only factor in measuring the political engagement of young people. Russell emphasises that differential turnout 'between the youngest and oldest sections of the electorate has grown in most established democracies in recent years' (2007: 23). He makes the point that parties focus on issues which they believe will stimulate likely voters as opposed to likely non-voters. Citing Wattenberg (2006), Russell (2007: 23) emphasises how elections focus on issues such as 'pensions, health insurance and prescription drugs' since these are likely to attract the older voters.

To reiterate, one outcome of the Green Paper was the setting up of the Youth Citizenship Commission, headed by Jonathan Tonge. Part of its remit was to examine ways of getting young people's participation in politics to increase, including consideration as to whether the voting age should be lowered to 16, a proposal favoured by the Liberal Democrats. The Isle of Man and Jersey enfranchised 16-year-olds in 2006 and 2007, respectively, and, as noted in Chap. 5, 16- and 17-year-olds were able to vote in the referendum on Scottish independence (September 2014). This aligns with other moves such as the reduction in the candidacy age in the UK from 21 to 18 years, which came into being in July 2006.

Research has shown a gender gap in terms of young people and political activism, with young men more likely to have broken the law, in addition to taking part in direct action and demonstrations, whereas women were more likely to have donated money to a cause or written to politicians and newspapers (Electoral Commission 2004a: section 3.28–3.29, b). Young men were more likely to say that they would vote in a general election (65 per cent compared to 55 per cent). It is clear, therefore, that there might be an activism gap but that this is not the same across all areas. The Electoral Commission's survey found women to be more cause-orientated than men (being more likely to sign a petition or boycott products, for example), whereas men were more campaign-orientated (more likely to contact politicians, to join or work for a political party). One surprising result too was that where a constituency had a female MP, women were more likely to be politically active—a result that should fuel calls for more female MPs to be (s)elected. It could be that a female MP acts as a role model and inspires women in that constituency.

YOUNG WOMEN

The relative absence of young women, from discussions about youth in general, is well documented (Osgerby, *op. cit.*: 50; Bhavnani 1991: 28–1). The gendered dimension has been less often discussed, but young women and politics is an equally fascinating subject. In terms of politics, young women have traditionally been less likely to vote than young men (Williams 2005). Stokes' examination of women in contemporary politics illuminates the assumption that because young women have participated in politics to a lesser degree than young men this means that they are not interested.

She cites how research counteracts the view that women are less interested and informed than their male counterparts (Stokes 2005: 51–53). Women may, therefore, be no less interested and informed than men, but they have, in the past, been less active (cf. Krook and Childs 2010, for detail about women and political power). In terms of participation levels, in 2015, only 29.38 per cent of MPs were female, 25.0 per cent of the members of the House of Lords (cf. Keen 2015), 31.5 per cent of local councillors,[2] 34.9 per cent of Members of the Scottish Parliament (MSPs), 41.7 per cent of Assembly Members (AMs) of the Welsh Assembly, and 41.0 per cent of UK Members of the European Parliament (MEPs)—fewer than half in every representative body. Indeed, the only body where 50 per cent was achieved was in the Welsh Assembly at the 2003 elections, so Wales has witnessed a decrease since that pinnacle. As Meryl Kenny elucidates, 'An unprecedented high of 191 women MPs (29 per cent) were elected to the House of Commons on the 7 May, an increase of 48 from the immediate post-2010 election results' (Kenny 2015: 12). This is not exactly cause for celebration, as Kenny continues, 'Women are more than half of the population but less than a third of MPs, 41 per cent of UK MEPs, 34 per cent of MSPs, 42 per cent of AMs, and 19 per cent of MLAs. The 2015 election results put the UK in only 36th place worldwide for women's representation' (Ibid.). As the *Sex and Power 2015* Report puts it, 'there have only ever been 450 women MPs—still well short of a full Parliament's-worth, and still (just) below the number of men elected in 2015 [459]' (Centre for Women and Democracy 2015: 8). An examination of women's lifestyle patterns may reveal that the reasoning behind women's relative lack of activism is that they still retain primary responsibility for caring commitments in our society (be that of children and/or of the elderly people) and are the main fulfillers of household domestic duties (cf. Mackay 2001; Annesley et al. 2007; Squires 2007; Stevens 2007). Hardly surprising, therefore, that women have little time left to indulge their interest in politics and political affairs in a more practical and active vein. Kenny sees the problem as outwith women's control, 'the central issue is one of demand rather than supply—in other words, women aren't the problem, parties are' (Kenny, *Op. Cit*: 13). The remedy is positive action, 'the continuing exclusion of women from British politics is a serious democratic deficit that demands action—the time has come to consider legislative quotas for women in order to deliver real change' (Kenny, Ibid: 15). The new Women's Equality Party, created in 2015, has also called for a gender quota system (Mason and Watt 2015: 8). Party leader Sophie Walker says, 'We have 30 million women in this country. I think it's highly unlikely you would struggle to find 325 brilliant ones to become MPs' (Walker quoted in Ibid.). The fact that the newly elected Canadian Prime Minister Justin Trudeau has appointed equal numbers of men and women to his cabinet has also fuelled the debate about quotas (Annesley et al. 2015). Campaigning organisations such as the former *300 Group*, and also *50:50 Parliament* have also focused upon the issue of the under-representation of women.

There are clearly factors which continue to limit the election of women and their elevation to positions of power within British political institutions and parties. It should be of some considerable concern to those interested in the health of our democracy that more young women are currently not seeking to participate in politics. There is a need for young women to have their levels of political awareness raised to encourage greater political participation, particularly given the continued existence of such issues as sexual discrimination and sexism within society, domestic violence that predominantly involves males using force against women[3] and of the continuing gender pay gap. Currently, men in full-time work still earn, on average, 14.2 per cent more than women in full-time work; 9h November, Equal Pay Day, is set as the symbolic date from which women start working for free until the end of the year given the pay gap. Comparing all workers, the pay gap is 19.1 per cent, the European Union average is 16.4 per cent (Fawcett Society 2015). David Cameron has pledged to force large companies to reveal the gender pay gap within their organisations, a move which may pressurise firms to pay women more.

Women's life experiences have undergone change over recent years. They are, for example, more likely to remain in education or to enter paid employment (Jowell and Park 1998: 10)—factors which may contribute to the politicisation of young women. Indeed, there are more female full-time undergraduates than males at UK universities, with 55 per cent of current female cohort compared to 45 per cent male (Ratcliffe 2013). However, disaggregation of the data in relation to youth unemployment reveals that young women are more likely to be unemployed than young men (BBC 2013). Such factors are generational and may well contribute to a future politicisation of young women who could be a powerful political voice. This noted, in circumstances where they do not enter either the world of work or academia, so-called lifestyle choices such as young motherhood should also mean that women want and need to concern themselves with political issues and questions. As Baker, editor of *Cosmopolitan* magazine, stated, young British women do care about political issues even if the statistics tell us that they are not voting. She asserted that young women were 'prepared to hit the streets to protest against war in Iraq, were incensed about street safety, abortion, contraception, the treatment of rape victims and the lack of STI clinics ... and yet they did not appear to equate those problems with the men (and it is still largely men) in parliament who made such decisions on their behalf' (Baker 2005: 7). One young woman who has acted politically and can be said to have potentially made a difference is 17-year-old Fahma Mohamed, an active campaigner against female genital mutilation (FGM)—it is estimated that 24,000 girls are at risk of female genital mutilation. As Alexandra Topping states, the then Education Secretary, Michael Gove, claims that he will write to all schools outlining the struggle against FGM. 'The education secretary's pledge was given as he met 17-year-old student Fahma Mohamed, the face of the campaign, and praised her for her "inspirational" work' (Topping 2014: 1). Fahma met Gove in February where a petition of about 250,000 signatures was presented. Gove's pledge to act demonstrates that young people can make a difference. Young women are, therefore, aware of and interested in political issues but are often not making the connection with mainstream politics. Beckwith articulates the fact that women are not solely women but that they possess a whole host of socio-economic characteristics, for example, age, race, ethnicity (2005: 128–129, 135). Clearly, there is scope for further research relating to women and politics.

Childs (2004, 2006) has examined whether female representatives 'do' politics in a manner different to their male counterparts and the impact of the presence of women in politics. In terms of voting, the traditional view has been that women are more Conservative than men in their voting preferences. More recent research does not support this view, Norris (1996: 333) claims that it is more accurate to talk in terms of a 'gender-generation gap' whilst Stokes (2005: 59) argues that men and women vote in similar proportions—with older women remaining more Conservative than men but with younger women being more left-wing. Norris cites a 20 percentage point gender gap at the 1992 General Election with 53 per cent of 18–24-year-old women voting Labour and only 33 per cent of 18–24-year-old men doing the same (1996: 336). Likewise, at the 1997 General Election 'Labour had developed a ten-point lead among women in the youngest generation' (Norris 2000: 45). This is not just an issue relating to British politics. Burrell, writing about the American political system, posits that women are a powerful political force and that part of the issue relates to notion of the gender gap (2005: 32).

This gender gap was evident in Britain at the 2005 General Election with 'women more likely to vote than men' (Whiteley 2012: 40), with 66 per cent of men turning out to vote, compared with 70 per cent of women. Here, more women voted Labour than men (38 per cent women compared with 34 per cent men). As regards the Conservatives, women voted 32 per cent, compared with 34 per cent men. The gender split for the Liberal Democrats in 2005 was women 22 per cent, compared with men 23 per cent (Worcester 2005, p.6). Women, who were once likely to be Conservative supporters, are now slightly more supportive of Labour. It used to be the case that women were more Conservative but this was not necessarily deemed to be related to their gender. In part, it was linked with the fact that women tended to constitute a much larger proportion of church-goers (traditionally, a pro-Conservative supporting sector of society) and, in addition, due to the greater longevity of women in comparison to their male counterparts. Research-based evidence supports this theory given that women are now more Labour supporting than male voters. The political parties would do well to focus upon winning the support of women because they are 'more likely than men to turn out and vote and are more ready to switch from one party to another' (*The Guardian*, 22 February 2005). Labour has focused on women's concerns in areas such as equal pay, childcare and development policy (Annesley et al. 2007: 231). Likewise, David Cameron appears to be taking this issue on board, focusing on work–life balance and recruiting more women into politics (Annesley et al. 2007: 232). There is evidence that the parties *are* trying to woo women voters (Lovenduski 2005: 150–151; Stevens 2007: 63). Having said this, Cameron's reshuffle of July 2014, which boosted the number of women in the cabinet from three to five, with three others also able to attend cabinet meetings, was met with derision from some quarters (cf. Williams 2014: 24). It was regarded by some as blatant electioneering and a concerted effort to woo the female voter. Conversely, a poll carried by OnePoll for vInspired, a charity that aims to increase turnout amongst young people, reveals that the reshuffle has 'boosted young people's interest in politics and made it more likely they will vote' (Watts 2014). In particular, '17 per cent of young women said they would be more likely to vote if there were more women in Parliament' (Ibid.). The role model effect of more women in positions of power should not be underestimated. Similarly, the view that women in power may be more empathetic to the wishes and views of the public at large might also hold sway.

As illustrated in Table 7.1, in terms of young people and the 2005 General Election, the youth vote declined to 37 per cent. It is difficult to disaggregate this figure in order to ascertain the percentage of young women that turned out to vote. It is clear, however, that the numbers were alarmingly low—as in 2001, only around one-third of 18–24-year-old young women actually turned out to cast their vote and exercise their 'civic duty' in 2005. As stated, this figure increased to 44 per cent in 2010 and remained fairly static in 2015, at 43 per cent (compared to 78 per cent of the over 65s) but it still constitutes fewer than half of those eligible. Politicians need to take action to re-engage these young women.

METHODOLOGY

Based upon in-depth interviews with young women in three focus groups, this research seeks to find answers to the vexed question of whether and why politics appears to be a turn-off for the majority of young women. The term 'young' is interpreted to mean 18–24-year-olds. With this in mind, three groups of young women in the 18–24-year-old category were interviewed across a two-month period towards the end of 2005. The three groups were selected on the following basis: one group comprised eight young women who meet regularly at a Youth Centre in Lincoln, the second group was a group of eight female politics students at the University of Lincoln and the third group was a group of eight students studying subjects other than politics. All three focus groups were asked a range of general questions as to what they understood by the term politics, whether they were interested in politics and how often they discussed politics. They were also asked to comment on a number of controversial statements such as the monarchy should be abolished, there should be compulsory AIDS testing and abortion is a woman's right to choose.

The focus group approach offered the best research method as far as this project was concerned. As Burnham et al. (2004: 106) state, 'Focus groups are groups composed of carefully selected individuals brought together to discuss a specific topic'. They argue that focus groups clearly 'have a specific purpose, an appropriate size (usually considered to be between six and ten people), composition and method of proceeding' and that people are chosen because they 'have characteristics in common which relate to the issues to be discussed by the group' (2004: 106–107). The focus group is then an extremely useful tool for the political researcher (Litosseliti 2003) and was used to great effect for the purposes of this project. The group dynamics were clearly in evidence at all three of the focus group meetings. Participants developed a degree of confidence to air their views and to bounce ideas off one another to an extent that other research methods may not have facilitated, for example, a doorstep survey would not have elicited the same in-depth responses. The focus group interviews were transcribed and then a content analysis was undertaken. The key themes were emphasised (voting/understanding of 'politics'/ interest in politics/whether they believe young men or young women are more interested/discussion of specific issues) and comparisons were made across the three focus groups. The groups were labelled C for Community, P for Politics and E for Education, and each interviewee was given a number—for example, C#1.

Based upon the three focus groups and the relatively sparse related literature, this study has discovered that the majority of young women profess to have little or no interest in mainstream politics. It is the case, however, that when pressed further on a number of political issues, problems and policies, the young women are, in fact, interested in these issues. It is evident that they fail to make the connection between what they perceive as politics and these 'other' interesting issues that initially do not appear to be overtly political (or not political in the sense of not overtly identifying with what might be termed mainstream politics). As will be examined later, they fail to make the connection between the 'personal' and the 'political'.

The interviews all took place in Lincolnshire towards the end of 2005. The politics of the area is as follows; in May 2005, of the 77 seats on Lincolnshire County Council, 45 were Conservative, 21 Labour, eight Liberal Democrat and there were three Independents. At the Parliamentary level, six Labour MPs and six Conservative MPs were elected at the 2005 General Election. This research cannot claim to be representative of the UK as a whole but does provide a firm basis upon which to build in subsequent research. The first group was a community group of young women, including a couple of young mothers, the second group was made up of young women studying politics at university (including one young mother) and the third group was with young women in the educational system but who were not studying politics (including two young mothers). In essence, many of their replies were remarkably similar, and the results do not appear to have been affected by the fact that two of the groups were in education and one group was not. It appears that many of the issues faced by young women currently are the same, regardless of whether they remain in the educational system or not. The young women studying politics were better versed in the terminology but, nonetheless, the views and opinions of all three groups were remarkably consistent.

FINDINGS

The results from the focus groups conducted for this research certainly accord with the findings of Henn et al. in that it is suggested that young women are interested in politics. They are interested in specific issues and *are* concerned about topics that may be loosely categorised as belonging to the realm of new social movements. These include such factors as women's rights, animal rights and concern for the wider environment.

The young women interviewed for the purposes of this chapter were not totally uninterested in mainstream party politics; indeed, as will be shown, the majority of them (14 out of 24) voted in the previous general election. They made a number of pertinent observations about politics and policy issues and, even though the majority of those interviewed did vote, they expressed dissatisfaction with the contemporary political process. It will be problematic not only for the young women themselves but also for society as a whole if the views and opinions of this sector are sidelined and/or ignored altogether. They are the next generation of mothers, career women, part-time workers and carers, amongst other categories.

The research investigated, firstly, whether they had voted; secondly, what they understand by 'politics'; thirdly, how interested they would say they are in politics; fourthly, whether they think that young women are less interested in politics than young men. Finally, the interviewees were asked for their views on a range of issues. Firstly, in terms of whether they had voted, the young women studying politics had a greater propensity to vote. Six out of the eight in this focus group had voted in the 2005 General Election. Of the two who did not vote in this group, one (Interviewee: P#7) was a citizen of Jersey and said she had not been eligible to vote in the 2005 General Election and the other one (P#8) said she was not registered but was not attracted to any party. In terms of the group consisting of women in education but not studying politics, four had voted in the general election and four had not. Of the four who had not, three were too young to vote. One (E#6) said, 'I will definitely vote and that's in all elections'. The final one (E#8) said she would vote and she also mentioned the suffragettes as role models. The outcome was equally split in the focus group of young women in the community group, with four having voted and four having declined to exercise their democratic right. One (C#5) who did not vote said, 'I don't understand it. I can't go and put a vote against something I don't understand'. Another (C#6) said, 'I don't know nothing about politics and I don't have time'. When asked whether the activities of the suffragettes might influence her to vote, she replied, 'Well, I've heard about all that, I have. What I mean is, I probably would go but I just forget and I'm not very organised'. The two others (C#7; C#8) who had not voted simply felt that none of the political parties had anything to offer them.

Secondly, the focus groups were questioned as to what they understood by the term 'politics'. The women's community group came up with a number of interesting responses including (C#1) 'Old men stuck in a room arguing with each other over silly things ... I say old men but there are a few ladies now ... to be fair'. Another (C#2) said 'Elections for your house captain at school and things like that'. One young woman (C#3) testified how the intricacies of the electoral system had baffled her,

[Denise] was trying to explain to us because we couldn't all understand why Labour had got voted in if they didn't have as much chairs or something as the others? ... I always thought it was people put their votes in the boxes and whoever got the most votes in them boxes got elected.

She went on to say,

So, I think it's misleading really because even if you've got a basic understanding of politics, people say, "Do your vote, it counts" [but] then it kind of doesn't count.

It is significant that this young woman, who professed to have little interest in and knowledge of the political system, appears to grasp some of the anomalies of the First Past the Post electoral system.

Of the young women in education but not studying politics, one (E#1) said that politics to her conjured up notions of 'governing. To me it's the Government and how a country is run and all issues affecting that like economics, religion. It all mixes in with politics and current issues'. Another (E#2) said, 'It's the society. Each country has a different political system related to the social structure'. A third (E#3) said, 'I don't understand you know right-wing and left-wing. I don't understand any of that ... but I am interested in the different areas and being able to make a change'. Another

(E#4) related politics to her family situation, having a family member in the armed forces going to Iraq in the near future, 'My brother's in the army. His friend's been to Iraq and that's what I think of when I think of politics'. Yet another said that when she thinks of politics she thinks of 'Tony Blair'. One young woman (E#5) said politics to her means, 'Government, parties, manifestoes, legislation'. The young women studying politics had a greater propensity to see politics as all-encompassing. As one (P#1) stated, 'Politics is everything. It's life. It's everything you do'. Another (P#7) said, 'It means voting. It means different opinions. Politics in Jersey means a lot of campaigning for each candidate. It means making policies that affect everything'. Another (P#2) said, 'Politics means everything. Its really important and a part of everything. It's central in the meaning of things'.

Thirdly, in terms of how interested these young women claimed to be in politics, as might be expected, those studying politics cited much higher levels of interest in politics. One (P#1) claimed to be at point ten on a scale of one to ten. Another (P#2) said 'Very interested' and that travel during her gap year had made her 'want to know more about other countries and how to change things'. The other six politics students all claimed to be 'very interested' too. In terms of those young women in education, one (E#1) claimed to be at point eight or nine on a scale of one to ten (with ten being the most interested) but she added, 'I am interested but not very knowledgeable'. Yet another (E#2) stated, 'I would put myself at seven'. Another (E#6) said, 'I am not interested as a rule no but I do get quite heated about ID cards'. She continued, 'I am for them one hundred per cent and I hate it when people say "I don't want to be on anyone's computer" because you are anyway. You're on so many computers, driving license, bank, college, NHS'. Another (E#5) said, 'I am not really interested as a rule but I do have an opinion on certain things but generally I am not interested'. One young woman (E#4) said, 'I'd say point five because everybody has an opinion on some things. I wouldn't go out of my way to discuss politics but I would have a say'. Another (E#3) said, 'Nine or ten [on the scale] because I like to keep up-to-date with recent issues. I read the *Times* and I watch the news'. The final two women (E#7; E#8) in the education group said they were not interested in politics.

In terms of the women in the community group, only three said they were potentially interested in politics. One (C#1) said, 'I would if I could say I knew more about it but it's a kind of thing where if you don't know a lot about something then you tend not to bother with it'. Another (C#2) echoed these sentiments with the comment, 'If we knew more about it then there might be a point'. Yet another (C#5) said, 'If it wasn't so boring on the telly ... then I might be interested'. One (C#4) woman believed that, 'Most people moan about stuff and don't do anything about it'. Another (C#7) said 'I wouldn't say I was interested, no'. She did acknowledge, however, that 'Politics comes into everyday things but I don't sit down and go "Let's discuss politics" but it does come into a lot of things so yes'. So, the young women studying politics expressed most interest in politics but it is perhaps noteworthy that those not studying politics were not completely apathetic and many expressed high levels of political interest—especially those within the education system.

Fourthly, the 18–24-year-old respondents were then questioned as to whether they believe that young women are, in fact, less interested in politics than young men. One woman (C#7) from the community group said she believed that young women are less interested 'because we don't have the time, we're busy sorting all the house out. Not to be sexist or anything but the majority of us are'. This certainly accords with Jowell and Park's (1998) theory that young people have other ways of filling their time, such as finding homes, partners and jobs. It is possible that Jowell and Park's thesis is even more applicable to young women. Another (C#8) said, 'We're doing the school runs and the after-school clubs [when] the kids are in bed, we just want to sit and don't want to be hassled with other stuff'. A third (C#6) stressed the merits of their community group for allowing them the time to discuss issues, 'if they came to groups like this where they haven't got the children ... they can just sit and discuss what's important to them ... I think that's more helpful and then you haven't got to worry about other things'. In terms of the women in education, one young woman (E#2) felt that social class was a bigger factor in the equation in comparison with gender, 'I think it depends on class because the people I know both men and women are very interested but that's generally a middle class background ... I have a few friends that are working class and they don't seem as bothered'. The impact of social class on young female voters is an issue that would benefit from greater exploration in future research. Another respondent (E#6) stated, 'I'm not quite sure. Overall, I think men are more interested'. This view was counteracted by another young woman (E#8), when she stated, 'The young men that I know aren't really interested in politics but the women care about what goes on'. She went on to say, 'I think women are more sensible than men. Men have one point of view and won't sway from that view whereas women take in everything that everybody else is saying'. Another young woman (E#3) stated, 'All my mates [females] are far more interested in politics than their partners or their male friends. They [female friends] have an opinion whereas the men don't always'. Her peer (E#4) felt that it was more to do with your position in life, 'If you're 21 and have kids and a house then a woman does care more about things like taxes, tax credits … it depends what your situation in life is like'. She emphasised her point, 'It's not just about whether you're young. It's about your life experiences'. This, again, accords with Jowell and Park (*op. cit.*). In terms of the women studying politics, one (P#5) said 'I think young women and young men are equally apathetic'. Another (P#6) stated, 'I've always found women to be more interested but not necessarily younger women'. They disclosed the dearth of women studying politics on their course as a possible indicator of women being less interested in politics than men. One (P#2) described encountering criticism after labelling herself a feminist. Another (P#3) stated that, in her opinion, 'young women are ever so slightly more interested [in politics] because they are more interested in certain issues, for example, abortion at the moment. Guys can detach themselves more'. Another (P#4) believed that 'It's generational … 18–24 year olds at the moment are very different from previous generations'. She went on to say that 'politics is still a man's world but less so than it was'. It appears, therefore, that opinion is divided as to whether young women are more interested in politics than young men.

Finally, the interviewees were asked for their views on a range of 'political' issues. It is noteworthy that even those who had expressed relatively little interest in politics *per se* were able to offer comment on most of the issues. The young women were asked to comment on statements such as the following: Tony Blair is doing a good job, the monarchy should be abolished, abortion is a woman's right to choose, hunting should be banned, AIDS tests should be compulsory, animals have rights too. In terms of whether Tony Blair is doing a good job, one woman (P#3), from the politics group, stated 'I think Gordon Brown is … I wouldn't say that [Blair] is a bad prime minister but then I wouldn't like to say he's a good one either'. It is worth flagging up that, out of the eight politics students, only two (P#1, P#2) agreed with the statement. In terms of the women in education, one (E#1) stated, 'I think he's doing the best he can but, to some people, that's not the case'. One (E#2) stated, 'He's not doing a good job with the war in Iraq'. Another (E#3) stated, 'He should choose his cabinet ministers more carefully' [a reference to the then recent departure from the cabinet of David Blunkett].

The women in the community group were also critical of Blair's role in Iraq; one (C#2) stated, 'I think he probably was doing a good job until he brought us to war in Iraq and that kind of killed it for him'. Abortion was a key issue with all the women. The consensus was that it is a woman's right to choose. One woman (C#5) in the community group expresses it thus, 'men can just walk away whenever they want'. A young woman in education (E#2) stated, 'It's people's right to choose—although I don't agree with [abortion] personally'.

The hunting debate divided the women. Two women in the education group, emanating from rural communities, were very much pro-hunting. One (E#2) stated, 'this is one thing that I am definitely in favour. All those people are going to lose their jobs. The dogs are just trained for fox hunting'. Another (E#5) stated, 'I don't agree with animal testing but I do agree with fox hunting. It's part of our tradition and culture. I don't condone cruelty to animals but I am biased because I do agree with fox hunting'.

Living in the country did not automatically mean being pro-hunting, one young woman (E#3) said,

> I live in the country. All my family have been on hunts but I don't agree with it. Drag hunting is such a viable option … We gave up hanging, let's give up fox hunting!

To reiterate, it is clear that whilst young women may not necessarily express an interest in mainstream politics, they do offer opinion when questioned on a range of topics. It appears to be the case that they are not apathetic have some interest in political issues but they fail to see the connection between political/controversial issues and mainstream party politics.

It is also apparent that part of the issue is that the young women are not making the connection between the personal and the political. The feminist mantra, 'the personal is political', does not appear to impact their perceptions of what constitutes politics. The majority of them are casting their vote in a general election (6 out of 8 of those studying politics, 4 out of 8 of those in education and 4 out of 8 of the young women in the community group out of the total 24 interviewees; therefore, 14 voted and 10 did not). The difficulty is that even though the majority of the women *are* voting, they are not engaging with mainstream politics on any other level.

Future research could focus upon the contrast in political knowledge and interest across both genders to facilitate more direct comparisons. Earlier research, such as that by Nestlé Family Monitor (2003), looking at young people's attitudes towards politics, and White et al.'s (2000) research into young people's political interest and engagement, is now a little dated. More recently, Newman (2013) showcased a study which revealed that British women know less about politics than British men—with women being more likely to answer 'don't know' to questions about politics than men, and also women still perceiving politics as being a 'man's world' and tending to feel disconnected from that world.

The key findings from a perusal of the literature and from these focus group interviews are that young women may not necessarily be interested in mainstream party politics but that they do have opinions on particular topics and could be said to have an interest in political issues if not necessarily wanting to take this further—be that to actually voting or to a more extensive form of political participation. It is pertinent to remind ourselves of the feminist mantra that 'the personal is political' (cf. Annesley et al. 2007: 36). Part of the issue here is encouraging these young women to recognise that the realm of what constitutes politics extends far beyond what is usually labelled as such. There needs to be a movement away from a focus upon traditional definitions of what constitutes politics to a wider/all-encompassing definition that will enable the lifestyles and concerns of these young women to be addressed as politically relevant. Their lifestyles, activities, opinions and concerns are/ought to be of interest to our politicians and policymakers. One way forward might be for citizenship classes to focus upon the lived experiences of young women. By empowering young women through the development of gender-related citizenship knowledge and skills, low levels of female representation could be redressed. Young women, encouraged to make their voices aired and heard in schools and local communities, could finally challenge long-established notions that the world of politics, to use the old adage, is a 'man's world'. Despite the Fawcett Society's efforts in 2005, Labour's campaign coordinator, Alan Milburn, was 'criticised for refusing to campaign specifically on women's issues and to attract the disillusioned female vote' (Annesley et al. 2007: 10–11). It is society's loss if we continue to have approximately two-thirds of the young women in Britain failing to engage with mainstream politics. Having said this, Ruth Picker's research that examines young women's political participation across Europe found that 'differences based on national political cultures and different oppor-tunity structures are often stronger than differences based on gender. Country trends overrode in many instances differences between young women and men, so that youths within countries were more alike than young women and men across countries' (Picker 2008: 115). This is an interesting dimension in relation to young women and politics and pro-vides a possible niche for further study.

The young women interviewed for this research are unrepresentative to the extent that the majority claim to have voted in the previous general election (14 out of 24) and so the 58 per cent turnout is significantly higher than the 37 per cent turnout for the 18–24-year-old age group as a whole at the 2005 General Election or, indeed, the 43 per cent in 2015 (75 per cent of the young women studying politics voted, compared with 50 per cent of those in the education group and 50 per cent of those in the community group). The women may have voted, but when questioned, they stated this does not mean that they are engaging with formal poli-tics. They expressed significant dissatisfaction with politicians and politi-cal parties in general. They were more animated and interested when the discussion moved to specific issues. Abortion, fox-hunting and the role of the monarchy were all issues, amongst other, that inspired these young women to express their opinions. It would be interesting, in a further study, to examine the extent to which these issues are actually discussed in Parliament. A cursory perusal of Hansard illustrates that these issues *are* broached in Parliamentary debates. Perhaps the issue is that politicians are simply not getting this message across to the people and, specifically, to young women.

A survey conducted in 2015 by the Young Women's Trust found that the 'first generation' of the twenty-first-century young women (aged 18–30), 'are worried about money, housing and whether they have the abilities to get a job … they are pessimistic about the future' (2015: 3). In an apparent backward step *vis-à-vis* older women, they regard 'many tradi-tionally male roles and professions [as being] out of their reach' (Ibid: 5). Recommendations from the Young Women's Trust include more help to get women into the workplace, stricter enforcement of the national mini-mum wage and training in confidence-building techniques. These results paint a worrying picture of how young women view their lives and oppor-tunities and reveal that there is work to be done in this area.

CONCLUSION

The value of this research is that, although based on a relatively small-scale study, it does give us some insight into what these young women think about politics and how they see it relating to their lives. They expressed some understanding of what politics is about—although the community group was most negative in their interpretation of politics. In terms of interest in politics, only three out of eight in the community group said that they were interested. This compares with all the politics students who claimed to be very interested and four of the education group. All three groups, however, were vocal and opinionated on a number of political issues. Future research, involving additional resources (time/finances), could access more focus groups, for example, women's refuges. It would also be beneficial to conduct focus groups with male participants to see whether their views accord with those of the women. Further research would also benefit from a more explicit focus upon issues such as housing, fiscal policies and European work-directive issues. Clearly, areas that accord with Jowell and Park's (1998) belief are that young people are concerned with finding a partner, a job and a home. In addition, a comparison of these findings with similar focus groups made up of young men, or older women or men, in an effort to assess the gender-generational divide in more detail (Russell et al. 1992; Norris 1996), whilst outside the scope of this research, would be beneficial for future research. Social class is another variable that would benefit from greater exploration. At the 2010 General Election, according to Toynbee (2008: 33), 'Despite citizenship classes, only 23 % of 18–24 year-olds say they'll vote'. The reality was slightly higher than that at 44 per cent, and 39 per cent if we disaggregate and just focus upon how many young women voted.

A so-called Mumdex Report based on a poll of 11,000 mothers (orchestrated by the supermarket chain, *Asda*) reveals that although 81 per cent claim that they intend to vote (63 per cent of mums under 30) and 82 per cent believe it is important to get their voice heard, only 2 per cent claim to feel represented by politics. As the Report says, 'mums under 30 are not quite as committed to voting, with one in five of them—more than twice as many as any other age group—saying they are undecided about voting in 2015' (*Asda* Mumdex 2014: 11). In terms of political engagement, 88 per cent believe politicians are not good at engaging with mums and with issues that matter to mums, and 71 per cent think policies tend to focus upon male concerns. In all, 81 per cent think politicians are out of touch, two-thirds think there should be more women in positions of political power, 68 per cent think e-petitions are a good way to get your voice heard and 65 per cent have signed an e-petition. A substantial 85 per cent of respondents believe that women's contribution to the economy is not valued. It is pertinent to note that 48 per cent of mums aged under 30 would like more digital ways of voting and connecting with their elected representatives. The survey also reveals that 'Younger mums need action—directness—immediacy; for them, what's important is the impact policies can have on the costs they are facing day-to-day' (*Asda* Mumdex 2014: 11). The survey also highlighted the fact that mums undertake an average of 10.8 hours of unpaid work every week—this is in addition to the paid employment and childcare commitments and includes care for the elderly people, disabled, and voluntary work amongst other aspects, an estimated saving to the national coffers of £37.2 billion (*Source*: *Asda* Mumdex 2014). Given the outcome of the 2015 General Election and the part that young women played in that, all politicians should dwell upon these facts and neglect women's votes and opinions at their peril.

NOTES

1. See Bochel and Briggs (2000); Childs and Cowley (2011); Stokes (2005).
2. Email correspondence with Michael Thrasher, local government expert, 18 August 2015.
3. See the UK Government's 'This is abuse' campaign—http://thisis-abuse.direct.gov.uk/ accessed 18 August 2015.

BIBLIOGRAPHY

Annesley, C., Beckwith, K., & Franceschet, S. (2015). What is 'merit' anyway? On using gender quotas in cabinet appointments. *UK PSA Women and Politics Specialist Group* Blog, 5 November. London: Political Studies Association UK.

Annesley, C., Gains, F., & Rummery, K. (2007). *Women and New Labour*. Bristol: The Policy Press.

Asda Mumdex. (2014, May 8). *The Mumdex Report*. Leeds: Asda. Retrieved May 22, 2014, from http://your.asda.com/system/dragonfly/production/2014/05/02/16_29_26_23_ASDA_MUMDEX_R10_REPORT_V15_nocrop_1_.pdf

Baker, S. (2005). We care about politics and our vote matters. *The Guardian*, 13 March, p. 7.

Baston, L., & Richie, K. (2004). *Turning out or turning off? An analysis of political disengagement and what can be done about it*. London: Electoral Reform Society.

BBC. (2013). Young and jobless forever: What do the numbers tell us? 31 October. Retrieved January 30, 2015, from http://www.bbc.co.uk/news/business-24708170

Beckwith, K. (2005, March). A common language of gender? *Politics and Gender*, *1*(1), 128–137.

Bhavnani, K. K. (1991). *Talking politics: A psychological framing of views from youth in Britain*. Cambridge: Cambridge University Press.

Bloor, M., Frankland, J., Thomas, M., & Robson, K. (2001). *Focus groups in social research*. London: Sage.

Bochel, C., & Briggs, J. E. (2000, May). Do women make a difference? *Politics*, *20*(2), 63–68.

Briggs, J. E. (2014). Young women and politics: Developing engagement for the 21 century. In A. Mycock & J. Tonge (Eds.), *Beyond the youth citizenship commission: Young people and politics* (pp. 32–36). London: Political Studies Association.

Broughton, D., & Storer, A. (2004). The Welsh Assembly Election of 2003: The triumph of 'Welfarism'. *Representation*, *40*(4), 266–280.

Buckingham, D. (2000). *The making of citizens: Young people, news and politics*. London: Routledge.

Burnham, P., Gilland, K., Grant, W., & Layton-Henry, Z. (2004). *Research methods in politics*. Basingstoke: Palgrave Macmillan.

Burrell, B. (2005). Gender, presidential elections and public policy: Making women's votes matter. *Journal of Women, Politics and Policy*, *27*(1/2), 31–50.

Butler, D., & Kavanagh, D. (1997). *The British General Election of 1997*. Basingstoke: Macmillan.

Centre for Women and Democracy. (2014). *Sex and Power 2014: Who runs Britain?* Leeds: Centre for Women and Democracy.

Centre for Women and Democracy. (2015). *Sex and Power 2015: Who runs Britain?* Leeds: Centre for Women and Democracy.

Childs, S. (2004, October). A British gender gap? Gender and political participation. *The Political Quarterly*, *75*(4), 422–424.

Childs, S. (2006). The complicated relationship between sex, gender and the substantive representation of women. *European Journal of Women's Studies*, *13*, 7–21.

Childs, S., & Cowley, P. (2011). The politics of local presence: Is there a case for descriptive representation? *Political Studies*, *59*, 1–19.

Cracknell, R., McGuinness, F., & Rhodes, C. (2011). *General Election 2010*. Research Paper 10/36, House of Commons Library, London.

Dalton, R. (2008a). Citizenship norms and the expansion of political participation. *Political Studies, 56*, 76–98.

Dalton, R. (2008b). *The good citizen: How a younger generation is reshaping American politics.* Washington, DC: CQ Press.

Electoral Commission. (2001). *Election 2001.* London: Politico's Publishing.

Electoral Commission. (2004a). *Age of electoral majority: Report and recommendations.* London: Electoral Commission.

Electoral Commission. (2004b). *Gender and political participation.* London: Electoral Commission.

Evans, G. (2003). Political culture and voting participation. In P. Dunleavy et al. (Eds.), *Developments in British politics 7* (pp. 82–99). Basingstoke: Palgrave Macmillan.

Fawcett Society. (2004a). *Women voters and the conservative party.* Retrieved April 24, 2008, from http://www.fawcettsociety.org.uk/documents/Women_and_Conservatives_Oct04.pdf

Fawcett Society. (2004b). *Winning women's votes: Labour's key to the next election.* Retrieved April 24, 2008 from http://www.fawcettsociety.org.uk/documents/Women_and_Labour_Sept04.pdf

Fawcett Society. (2004c). *Women voters and the Liberal Democrats.* Retrieved April 24, 2008, from http://www.fawcettsociety.org.uk/documents/Women_and_Lib_Dems_Sept04.pdf

Fawcett Society. (2015). *Equal Pay Day.* Retrieved November 9, 2015, from http://www.fawcettsociety.org.uk/our-work/campaigns/equal-pay-day-2/

Goerres, A. (2007, February). Why are older people more likely to vote? The impact of ageing on electoral turnout in Europe. *British Journal of Politics and International Relations, 9*(1), 90–121.

The Guardian. (2005). Kennedy to woo women. 22 February.

Hansard Society. (2015). *Audit of political engagement 12.* London: Hansard Society.

Hay, C. (2007). *Why we hate politics.* Cambridge: Polity Press.

Henn, M., Weinstein, M., & Forrest, S. (2005). Uninterested youth? Young people's attitudes towards party politics in Britain. *Political Studies, 53*(3), 556–578.

Henn, M., Weinstein, M., & Wring, D. (2002, June). A generation apart? Youth and political participation in Britain. *British Journal of Politics and International Relations, 4*(2), 167–192.

Henn, M., Weinstein, M., & Wring, D. (2004). Alienation and youth in Britain. In M. J. Todd & G. Taylor (Eds.), *Democracy and participation: Popular protest and new social movements* (pp. 196–217). London: Merlin.

Inglehart, R. (1977a). *The silent revolution: Changing values and political styles among Western publics.* Princeton, NJ: Princeton University Press.

Inglehart, R. (1977b). *Modernization and post-modernization: Cultural, economic and political change in 43 countries.* Princeton, NJ: Princeton University Press.

Ipsos MORI. (2015). *How Britain voted in 2015*. Retrieved August 21, 2015, from https://www.ipsos-mori.com/researchpublications/researcharchive/3575/How-Britain-voted-in-2015.aspx?view=wide

Jowell, R., & Park, A. (1998). *Young people, politics and citizenship: A disengaged generation?* London: The Citizenship Foundation.

Keen, R. (2015, June 19). *Women in parliament and government*. Briefing Paper, SNO1250. London: House of Commons.

Kenny, M. (2015). Why aren't there more women in British politics? *Political Insight*, September, pp. 12–14.

Kimberlee, R. H. (2002). Why don't British young people vote at general elections? *Journal of Youth Studies, 5*(1), 85–98.

Krook, M. L., & Childs, S. (2010). Women, gender and politics: An introduction. In M. L. Krook & S. Childs (Eds.), *Women, gender and politics: A reader* (pp. 3–20). Oxford: Oxford University Press.

Liamputtong, P. (2011). *Focus groups methodology: Principles and practice*. London: Sage.

Litosseliti, L. (2003). *Using focus groups in research*. London: Continuum.

Lovenduski, J. (2005). *Feminizing politics*. Cambridge: Polity Press.

Mackay, F. (2001). *Love and politics: Women politicians and the ethics of care*. London: Continuum.

Marsh, D., O'Toole, T., & Jones, S. (2007). *Young people and politics in the UK: Apathy or alienation?* Basingstoke: Palgrave.

Mason, R., & Watt, N. (2015). Call for quotas to bring gender parity to politics. *The Guardian*, 14 October, p. 8.

Molloy, D., White, C., & Hosfield, N. (2002). *Understanding youth participation in local government*. London: DTLR.

Morgan, D. L. (1997). *Focus groups as qualitative research* (2nd ed.). London: Sage.

Mycock, A., & Tonge, J. (2012a). The party politics of youth citizenship and democratic engagement. *Parliamentary Affairs, 65*, 138–161.

Mycock, A., & Tonge, J. (2012b). Alex Salmond's Bannock's bairns. *Open Democracy*, 20 February. Retrieved November 20, 2012, from http://opendemocracy.net

Nestlé Family Monitor. (2003). *Young people's attitudes to politics*. Croydon: Nestlé UK.

Newman, C. (2013). British women know less about politics than men—But why? *The Telegraph*, 3 July. Retrieved May 12, 2016, from http://www.telegraph.co.uk/women/womens-politics/10154822/British-women-know-less-about-politics-than-men-but-why.html

Norris, P. (1996). Mobilising the 'Women's vote': The gender-generation gap in voting behaviour. *Parliamentary Affairs, 49*(2), 333–342.

Norris, P. (2000). Gender and contemporary British politics. In C. Hay (Ed.), *British politics today* (pp. 38–59). Cambridge: Polity.

O'Neil, T., & Domingo, P. (2015, September). *The power to decide: Women, decision-making and gender equality*. London: Overseas Development Institute.

O'Toole, T., Lister, M., Marsh, D., Jones, S., & McDonagh, A. (2003). Tuning out or left out? Participation and non-participation among young people. *Contemporary Politics, 9*, 45–61.

O'Toole, T., Marsh, D., & Jones, S. (2003). Political literacy cuts both ways: The politics of non-participation among young people. *The Political Quarterly, 74*(3), 349–360.

Osgerby, B. (1998). *Youth in Britain since 1945*. Oxford: Blackwell.

Osgerby, B. (2002). "The good, the bad and the ugly": Post-war media representations of youth. In A. Briggs & P. Cobley (Eds.), *The media: An introduction* (2nd ed., pp. 369–382). Harlow: Pearson Education.

Osgerby, B. (2002). Youth. In A. Briggs (Ed.), *The media: An introduction* (2nd ed., pp. 368–382). Harlow: Pearson Education.

Pearson, G. (1983). *Hooligan: A history of respectable fears*. London: Macmillan.

Phelps, E. (2004). Young citizens and changing electoral turnout, 1964–2001. *Political Quarterly, 75*(3), 238–248.

Picker, R. (2008). Young women's political participation in Europe: Closing the gap? In R. Spannring, G. Ogris, & W. Gaiser (Eds.), *Youth and political participation in Europe* (pp. 105–119). Opladen: Barbara Budrich Publishers.

Ratcliffe, R. (2013). The gender gap at universities? Where are all the men? *The Guardian*, 29 January. Retrieved January 30, 2015, from http://www.theguardian.com/education/datablog/2013/jan/29/how-many-men-and-women-are-studying-at-my-university

Russell, A. (2007). Youth and political engagement. In A. Russell & G. Stoker (Eds.), *Failing politics? A response to The Governance of Britain Green Paper* (pp. 22–25). Newcastle: Political Studies Association.

Russell, A. T., Johnston, R. J., & Pattie, C. J. (1992). Thatcher's children: Exploring the links between age and political attitudes. *Political Studies, 40*, 742–756.

Sanghani, R. (2014). The real reasons female Tory MPs are quitting Parliament. *The Telegraph*. Retrieved June 12, 2014, from http://www.telegraph.co.uk/women/womens-politics/10588196/The-real-reasons-female-Tory-MPs-are-quitting-Parliament.html

Sloam, J. (2013a). The 'outraged young': How young Europeans are reshaping the political landscape. *Political Insight, 4*(1), 4–7.

Sloam, J. (2013b). 'Voice and equality': Young people's politics in the European Union. *West European Politics, 36*(4), 836–858.

Sloam, J. (2013c). Young people are less likely to vote than older citizens, but they are also more diverse in how they choose to participate in politics. *London School of Economics and Political Science* Blog, London. Retrieved November 7, 2013, from http://blogs.lse.ac.uk/europpblog/2013/07/19/young-people-are-less-likely-to-vote-than-older-citizens-but-they-are-also-more-diverse-in-how-they-choose-to-participate-in-politics/

Sloam, J. (2015). Political parties are neglecting young people—It's time for unis to step in. *The Guardian*, 25 February. Retrieved September 27, 2015, from http://www.theguardian.com/higher-education-network/2015/feb/25/political-parties-are-neglecting-young-people-its-time-for-unis-to-step-in

Squires, J. (2007). *The new politics of gender equality*. Basingstoke: Palgrave Macmillan.

Stationery Office. (2007). *The Governance of Britain*. Cm 7170, 3 July. London: The Stationery Office.

Stevens, A. (2007). *Women, power and politics*. Basingstoke: Palgrave Macmillan.

Stokes, W. (2005). *Women in contemporary politics*. Cambridge: Polity.

Todd, M. J., & Taylor, G. (Eds.) (2004). *Democracy and participation: Popular protest and new social movements*. London: Merlin Press.

Topping, A. (2014). Gove to write to all schools as he backs anti-FGM fight. *The Guardian*, 26 February, p. 1.

Toynbee, P. (2008). One small electoral change could rouse the sulking, apathetic hordes. *The Guardian*, 28 March, p. 33.

Wattenberg, M. P. (2006). *Is voting for the young?* New York: Longman.

Wattenberg, M. P. (2012). *Is voting for young people?* (3rd ed.). New York: Longman Pearson.

Watts, J. (2014). David Cameron's Cabinet reshuffle 'made young more likely to vote'—Poll suggests. *The London Evening Standard*, 28 July. Retrieved July 29, 2014, from http://www.standard.co.uk/news/london/david-camerons-cabinet-reshuffle-made-young-more-likely-to-vote-9632851.html

Weinstein, M. (2004). Political activity and youth in Britain. In M. J. Todd & G. Taylor (Eds.), *Democracy and participation: Popular protest and new social movements* (pp. 176–195). London: Merlin Press.

White, C., Bruce, S., & Ritchie, J. (2000). *Young people's politics: Political interest and engagement amongst 14–24 year olds*. York: Joseph Rowntree Foundation.

Whiteley, P. (2012). *Political participation in Britain: The decline and revival of civic culture*. Basingstoke: Palgrave Macmillan.

Williams, Z. (2005). Is there any such thing as the women's vote? *New Stateswoman*, 4 April, pp. 6–9.

Williams, Z. (2014). This phoney reshuffle will keep things just the same. *The Guardian*, 14 July, p. 24.

Worcester, R. (2005). Women's support gave Blair the edge. *The Observer*, 8 May, p. 6.

Young Women's Trust. (2015). *The clock turns back for young women*. London: Young Women's Trust Retrieved from www.youngwomenstrust.org.

CHAPTER 8

Conclusion

The *teen players* who are the subject of this book, the young people and the concept of political participation, are of increasing interest to politicians, policymakers and academics alike. With organisations like the Youth Citizenship Commission, discussion around the teaching of citizenship in schools and the divisive question of whether or not the voting age should be lowered to enable 16- and 17-year-olds to participate in elections, there is certainly plenty for the expert and the layperson to debate. This final chapter summarises the key findings of the investigation into young people and levels of political participation. It analyses the lessons to be learnt from this comprehensive investigation into young people and political participation. What can our politicians, policymakers and political scientists glean from this study? Should the voting age be lowered to 16 in line with a few other countries? Does participation at local level and at a younger age, such as via youth cabinet and youth parliament participation, lead to a long-term interest and involvement in politics? Can measures be taken in order to encourage more young women, in particular, to participate in the political process? In terms of policy transfer, are there lessons to be gleaned from other European countries in relation to young people and political participation?

The first chapter set the scene and the parameters of debate of the book by defining what is meant by the concept of youth and how this has changed over the years. This chapter introduced the topic of young people and political participation. Examination was made of what consti-

© The Author(s) 2017

J. Briggs, *Young People and Political Participation*,
DOI 10.1057/978-1-137-31385-0_8

tutes youth, the growth and development of youth, historical background, youth as consumers and purchasing power. The rise of youth culture and the duality of youth (whereby young people are regarded both as the future and a source of optimism but also as a troubling phenomenon and a sector of society to be feared) were also assessed. This chapter sets the scene in terms of facilitating understanding of what the concept of youth entails and examining the situation from a historical perspective. It is pertinent to note that youth is not a new phenomenon and that notions such as ephebiphobia (fear of youth/teenagers) have existed for a significant amount of time. This, scene-setting, chapter provides a logical starting point before proceeding to look at youth in contemporary society.

Chapter 2 provided the theoretical background to the book. The focus of Chap. 2 is upon political participation in general terms. The theoretical underpinnings in relation to political participation are examined in this chapter. What is meant by political participation? How have political scientists and political philosophers attempted to define participation? Is there a difference between participation where one's aims are achieved or are there benefits to be gained through having participated so that it does not necessarily matter if the goals are not attained? John Stuart Mill made reference to the benefits of participation over and above merely achieving one's policy goals, and this fits in with the Ancient Greeks and their concept of the 'Good Life'. Reference is also made to theoretical perspectives such as Sherry Arnstein's 'Ladder of Participation', whereby there are gradations of participation, the higher-level rungs on the ladder involving greater degrees of participation than others. In this chapter, comparisons were also made with the wider society. Examination was made of differing levels of political participation between the different generations. The concept of political participation is clearly of keen interest and relevance to political scientists and it was interesting to focus upon how this relates to young people.

Chapter 3 turned attention to the wider international arena, where the focus is upon a comparative approach. Young people and political participation on a pan-European basis are examined here. Utilising quantitative data gleaned from a variety of sources, this chapter provides a quantitative analysis of political participation levels in all 28 countries of the European Union. Comparisons were made between different types of political participation and also between differing levels of governance. It was interesting to investigate whether, for example, young people in Denmark are more willing to participate in politics than, say, the youth of

Portugal. If so, why should this be the case? Why does the youth of one particular nation appear to be more galvanised and politically active than, say, the young people of another nation? Questions such as the proportion of young people being of the opinion that it is a citizen's duty to vote and whether this has altered over time are investigated, alongside other pertinent questions about young people and political participation/ non-participation. Answers are provided to questions such as these. James Sloam divulges how young people across Europe, where they do look to mainstream politics, are often turning to new political parties, many of which are 'populist (the Five Star Movement in Italy), nationalist (the True Finns in Finland) or extremist with an anti-immigrant or even anti-Islamic rhetoric (Geert Wilders in the Netherlands)' (2013a: 5). Young people, often those of low socio-economic status, are turning to these parties in increasing numbers.

Chapter 4 investigates the usage of social media by young people. This chapter examined new media and political participation and focused upon political participation levels amongst young people, primarily in the UK, but using a comparative approach, where appropriate. Again, political participation was examined at differing levels of governance and, in addition, differing types of participation were compared. The usage of new technology, in particular Web 2.0 technology (such as social networking sites like *Facebook*™, *Bebo*™ and *MySpace*™, and the use of microblogging sites such as *Twitter*™), was examined in order to ascertain the extent to which these new approaches facilitate and encourage greater political participation amongst young people. As James Sloam points out, the 'repertoires of political engagement have become more diverse: from consumer politics, to community campaigns, to international networks; from the ballot box, to the street, to the internet; from political parties, to social movements and issue groups, to social networks' (2013a: 5). He underlines how protest has been 'facilitated by the rise of the internet and social media (including Twitter and Facebook)' and cites the example of 'the 12 March Movement in Portugal [which] began with a group of young people writing a blog and organising a Facebook event and quickly led to demonstrations by hundreds of thousands of Portuguese citizens in Lisbon, Porto and other major cities' (Ibid.). The potential of the Internet, social networking sites and new technology, in general, to reach out to a mass audience is boundless. International borders, financial constraints and middle-aged politicians are not necessarily barriers to political participation when new technology enters the equation.

Chapter 5 focused upon the topical question of whether or not the voting age should be lowered to the age of 16. This is particularly apposite given the fact that 16- and 17-year-olds were able to vote in the referendum on Scottish independence, held on 18 September 2014, and that 16- and 17-year-olds in Scotland will be able to vote in Scottish Parliamentary and local elections from 2016. The debate surrounding whether 16- and 17-year-olds ought to be able to vote in the UK-wide referendum on continued membership of the European Union has also focused attention. This chapter involved a detailed analysis of the key arguments for and against lowering the voting age to 16. In part, the focus is upon a case study of Austria where the voting age was lowered to 16 in 2007 (the first country out of the then 27 members of the European Union to do so for national elections). In addition, detailed investigation is made of the situation closer to home in Jersey, Guernsey and the Isle of Man where the voting age has been lowered to 16 years too. There is a vocal campaign in the UK to lower the voting age to 16 (cf. the *Votes at 16* Coalition), but many oppose this; both sides of the discussion are subject to in-depth analysis in this chapter. Two more examples from mainland Europe are incorporated into the study. These are Germany and Bosnia. The reason this chapter investigates these two countries is that, firstly, with respect to Germany, it constitutes an interesting case study because there 16-year-olds can vote in some municipal elections in some states. Bosnia is chosen as the second country, the reason for this second selection is that, in Bosnia, 16-year-olds can vote if they are employed. The various bodies that support lowering the voting age to 16, and the key arguments that they espouse, are examined in detail. Equal consideration is given to the arguments propounded by those opposed to the idea of lowering the voting age. Analysis is provided as to why the majority of young people have not expressed support for this idea. Opinion tends to be polarised on this topic, and this is what makes it such an interesting issue and worthy of detailed examination. It is not intended that the book becomes a vehicle for arguing in favour of lowering the voting age, but, rather, that it illuminates the key arguments on both sides of the debate.

Chapter 5, therefore, discussed briefly, the notion of the right to vote, the history of the franchise, who can and cannot vote, current debates about extending the franchise, such as whether or not voting should be compulsory and in relation to prisoners' rights, before it proceeded to analyse the lowering of the voting age to 16. Arguments exist both for and against lowering the voting age to 16 years. One of the most consistent and vocal opponent of lowering the voting age is David Denver. He refutes the key arguments that have been espoused in relation to lowering the voting age. In terms of arguing for parity with other ages at which rights are acquired, he says that there is 'no inconsistency in arguing that rights in different spheres of activity should be conferred at different ages' (2013: 36). Just because one can marry at 16 does not mean it follows logically that one should be able to vote. Likewise with paying taxes, he clarifies how the proportion of 16- and 17-year-olds paying taxes is minimal and that 'resident aliens, visiting tourists, children spending their pocket money on sweets or iTunes downloads also pay tax' (Ibid.), but that we are not arguing for them to have the vote. Denver also dismisses the citizenship argument, the notion that citizenship lessons mean we have a more educated and engaged youth cohort by saying that 'we have had compulsory PE for long enough but this has not prevented soaring levels of obesity among young people' (Ibid: 37). He also feels that a lowering of the voting ages would simply expand the section of non-voters, and because children grow up they get to vote in due course. Concluding that, in general, 'children below the age of 18 do not have enough experience of life, have too few responsibilities and have too short a memory of governments or public affairs to make informed decisions affecting the country's future' (Ibid.). Denver is unequivocal in his opposition to lowering the voting age to 16 and 17 year olds. Andrew Russell is another commentator who has clearly articulated the arguments against lowering the voting age. Dismissive of the line that 16- and 17-year-olds can leave home and marry with parental consent, Russell states, 'in 2012 more than 90 % of 16–17 year olds lived with their parents and were staying at home for longer than previous generations did' (Russell 2014). He also flags up the fact that 'few pupils left at 16 and they are no longer allowed to do so. And according to official figures, 92 % of 16–17 year-olds now stay on' (Ibid.). Conversely, those who argue in favour of lowering the voting age cite the notion of 'rights' as one of their key points. Thus, proponents of lowering the voting age devote less attention to arguments such as whether 16- and 17-year-olds live with their parents, whether they work or whether they remain in full-time education.

This right to the franchise was rolled out to 16- and 17-year-olds in the 2014 independence referendum in Scotland. Some argue that this change was brought about, not due to rights but because Alex Salmond, Scotland's then First Minister, believed they would vote 'Yes' to independence. Granted, the numbers of newly enfranchised 16- and 17-year-old age group in Scotland was relatively small, the interesting issue, however, was that research, undertaken by Lindsay Paterson and colleagues from the University of Edinburgh, revealed that Salmond may have made a mistake. Their findings showed that many of these young people might have been more inclined to vote 'No' when they had the opportunity to vote on 18 September. It seems that Denver may, indeed, be proven correct. The researchers questioned more than 1000 youth aged 14–17 years (some of the 14-years-olds would have been 16 by the time of the referendum) and they discovered that 21 per cent would vote yes, 19 per cent were undecided and 67.2 per cent wanted more information ahead of making their decision. Of the interviewees, 94 per cent were aware of the referendum and 69 per cent said they were going to vote. In terms of whether they would vote for independence, 60.3 per cent said 'No', 20.9 per cent said 'Yes' and 18.8 per cent were undecided. Clearly, the parties in Scotland had their work cut out to ensure that young people felt that they had enough information at their disposal for them to be able to make an informed decision. It was crucial, therefore, that additional information was forthcoming, both from the political parties themselves and from other bodies, in order that young people, alongside their older counterparts, were able to make informed, knowledgeable decisions. In the referendum itself, more than 120,000 youth aged 16- and 17 years in Scotland were able to vote—this was out of an electorate of 4 million people. As Carrell stated, 'Excluding undecideds, the poll showed opposition to independence at 74 % versus 26 % in support' (2013). This was an extremely wide margin against independence and would certainly have provided Alex Salmond with data upon which to reflect. The poll also revealed that young people were more opposed to independence than their parents. With regards to gender, the research poll also revealed a divide, just as with their adult female counterparts, 'a smaller proportion of girls backed independence, with just over 17% of girls planning to vote yes compared with 25 % of boys' (Ibid.). As Paterson acknowledged, polls do change over time. This poll of young people did, however, certainly furnish some very interesting data, and it was fascinating (in Chap. 5) to see what happened in reality.

Youth political participation at the local level was the subject of Chap. 6. Comparative data were used here but, in addition, a useful addendum to this chapter was the case study of Lincolnshire Youth Cabinet. Based upon qualitative methodology, namely, in-depth interviews, the latter part of this chapter utilises a study of members of Lincolnshire Youth

Cabinet. In particular, the reasons these young people participate in politics to a much greater extent than their peers are investigated. The chapter assessed the types of policy areas upon which young politicos prefer to focus. Investigation was also made of their motivations and whether the reality meets their original expectations. Discussion also centred on the career pathways that these young people hope to pursue in the future and the extent to which 'politics' features in their future career plans.

Chapter 7 focused upon the concept of gender and political participation. Using focus groups, Chap. 7 examined the differing levels of political participation of young men and young women. It looked at what accounts for this difference and whether young men are more politically aware than young women. It also investigated whether levels of political participation vary between the two groups. Young women have, traditionally, been the sector of the electorate least likely to cast their vote, and yet, if the focus is upon specific policy areas, there are many aspects that ought to be of primary concern to women. Child care provision, the increase in cases of sexually transmitted diseases, issues in relation to women in the workplace, such as the gender pay gap, are examples of issues which ought to galvanise women to cast their vote. To reiterate, this chapter focused upon gender differences in relation to political participation and non-participation. Few young women are participating in mainstream politics, only 44 per cent of 18- to 24-year-old women voted in the 2015 General Election, a figure that ought to have our politicians and policymakers extremely worried for the future of democratic participation. Clearly, where power is located, women are either absent or present in relatively small numbers. In answer to the question of 'Who runs Britain?', and interpreting the extent of female political participation, it would be difficult to over-emphasise the role played by women. If this situation is to change, the role played by the current generation of younger women becomes increasingly important. Young men may not necessarily be participating in mainstream politics but, when the spotlight turns to young women, that situation is magnified exponentially when considered over time.

The focus was primarily upon young women as opposed to looking at young people, as a generic grouping future research could focus upon the views of young men too. Based upon in-depth interviews with young women (18–24-year-olds) in focus groups, this research sought to find answers to the vexed question of why politics appears to be a turn-off for the majority of young women. In doing so, there were also lessons to be learnt in relation to young men and politics. Marsh, O'Toole and Jones, in their study of young people and politics, focus upon the relative exclusion of women from political life and that central to 'the justification of such exclusions was the normative separation between the public and the private' (2007: 153). For their respondents too, there was a clear link between gender and class, as they say their 'female respondents lived gender, but they did so differently, largely dependent on their access to economic, social and cultural capital' (Ibid: 214). Clearly, the topic of young women and political participation is worthy of further investigation, and this sector of society is potentially doubly disadvantaged when examined from the perspective of political capital. They lose out politically by virtue of the fact that they are female and they also face challenges due to the reality that they are young! This book recommends that the Westminster All-Party Parliamentary Group for Women in Parliament should establish an inquiry on Young Women in Politics in order to explore the reasons for and rectify the relative absence of young women from local and national politics.

ARE YOUNG PEOPLE INTERESTED IN POLITICS?

In terms of what has been unearthed via this book on young people and political participation, a number of key points can be articulated. Evidence reveals that young people *are* interested in politics—probably more so than many observers, and possibly even themselves, realise. Part of the issue is getting them to recognise what constitutes politics. If politics is presumed to be a wider classification than mainstream, party politics, than politics with an upper case 'P', then they do appear to be more enamoured by this aspect. They are interested in issues as opposed to political parties, and environmental concerns and animal rights are two of the key areas in which young people have a passionate interest. Our politicians have their work cut out in getting the majority of young people to have an interest in party politics on a wide scale. This scepticism and lack of interest has been exacerbated by the Parliamentary expenses scandal which, as mentioned previously, emerged in 2009 (a furore which has impacted the perceptions of not only young people but also older generations). There is a palpable lack of trust in politicians and corresponding lack of respect for the role of an MP and also, to a lesser extent, local politicos. Politicians are seen as self-interested as opposed to altruistic, interested in self-gain instead of changing society for the better. This is rather a sad indictment of twenty-first-century politics and sadly negates much of the good work that many politicians, undoubtedly, undertake in their quest to, as they see it, improve society. The ramifications of the expenses scandal will reverberate beyond the current cohort of politicians.

In February 2014, the Office for National Statistics published the results of its Measuring National Well-being Survey (see Randall 2014). According to the Survey, 42 per cent of 16–24-year-olds claimed that they had no interest in politics whatsoever. It also revealed that the UK had the lowest proportion of young people who had voted in an election. For Richard Driscoll, a teacher of A level Government and Politics, the survey is misleading in that, as he says, it does not reveal 'what proportion of the 42 % of young people with no interest in politics have ever signed an e-petition or taken part in a protest. They may well have done so, but simply do not see this act as a political one' (Driscoll 2014, http://www. psa.ac.uk/insight-plus/blog/ons-survey-wrong-young-people-do-have-interest-politics). For Driscoll too, part of the issue is the perception of what is politics and what constitutes a political act. As he continues, 'Those who profess apathy may still engage in political activity. For example, the increase in student tuition fees undoubtedly brought considerable apathy from young people towards the main political parties. But the very fact that so many turned out to protest against these rises would suggest that political engagement is rife' (Ibid.). Driscoll believes that 'Initiatives such as the e-petition procedure have given young people the opportunity to really get involved in issues of importance to them'. He cites the successful example of '17 year old Fahma Mohamed asking schools to raise the awareness of female genital mutilation' (Ibid.) and garnering support from Secretary of State for Education, Michael Gove (as mentioned in Chap. 7). In an earlier survey, the British Social Attitudes Survey (2013), it is noticeable that 'in nearly every aspect of political engagement reported, younger people lag behind older members of the electorate' (Lee and Young 2013: 71–72). Older people were more likely than younger people to be more closely aligned to a political party and also to regard voting as their civic duty. In the 2014 *Measuring National Well-being—Governance* Survey, whilst the findings are as outlined by Driscoll above, there is room for optimism perhaps given that the suggestion is that young people may be more likely to participate in politics in less formal ways, for example, using their purchasing power to boycott certain products (Randall 2014).

Continuing these grounds for optimism, Jonathan Birdwell and Mona Bani outline Generation Y, explaining that 'Generation Y, known in the US as the Millennials. Generation Y is the generation born between the years 1980 and 2000' (2014: 33). They say that 'despite some disillusionment—young people do not necessarily subscribe to the "do not vote" philosophy of Russell Brand, as demonstrated in his interview on *Newsnight* in October 2013' (Ibid: 54–55). They interviewed a significant number of teachers and found that 59 per cent of the teachers they interviewed felt that 'the current generation were either more likely or as likely as previous generations to "sign political petitions or take part in a boycott"' (Ibid: 57). In addition, 88 per cent of the teachers surveyed by Demos thought that young people were 'more engaged in volunteering for organisations and good causes than their own generation was when they were teenagers' (Ibid: 58). Thus, reiterating the belief that although young people 'are not engaging with traditional forms of political engagement, they are using alternative means to express themselves and engage with the world around them' (Ibid: 59). The poll paints an extremely positive picture about today's youth, namely, that they are keen to volunteer and that they genuinely care about social issues. This *Demos* survey provides a positive outlook in terms of young people and political participation.

Young people, as with everyone else over the age of 18, have to be registered to vote if they are to participate in mainstream politics. In February 2014, a £4.2 million fund was launched by the government to try to encourage young people to register to vote. The charity UK Youth is to work alongside local councils and other bodies in a concerted effort to get more young people on to the electoral register. It was estimated that at least one in four young adults, approximately 800,000, were not registered to vote (see Morris 2014c: 10). A ComRes survey, carried out for the Electoral Reform Society in early 2014, found that 'Hundreds of thousands of 18- to 21-year-olds have lost the right to vote by failing to add their names to the electoral register [and] that at least one in four young people could be missing from the register' (Morris 2014a: 5). These startling figures are blamed on the fact that from summer 2014, a new voter registration system, brought in by the Electoral Registration and Administration Act 2013, means that each individual has to sign up—rather than household registration being the norm.

Likewise the Youth Citizenship Commission, set up under the Labour Government in 2008, felt that encouraging electoral registration was crucial in terms of fostering political engagement amongst young people (see Mycock and Tonge 2014) and facilitating their involvement in formal politics through the most basic act of voting.

An interview with a leading expert in the field of youth political engagement, Andrew Mycock,[1] elicited the following response in terms of whether young people are interested in politics, 'Young people are interested in politics and many continue to engage and participate in various ways with politicians and the political system more widely. They are active in their schools and communities and have a keen interest in issues that relate to or affect them. As with other generational cohorts, they are, however, mainly interested in issues which directly impact on them. It is clear though that established forms of engagement are less attractive than de-aligned, single-issue campaigning and that social media is the dominant form of political activity'. Mycock clearly reveals the extent to which young people are politically engaged and the way in which they often use new forms of communication, such as social media, to participate politically. He continues by illustrating how the economic crisis has facilitated political engagement, 'The recent austerity programme initiated by the Coalition Government has encouraged numerous examples of young people engaged in campaigning and other forms of direct action which highlight a more dynamic and developed sense of citizenship which goes beyond the act of voting. However, lower patterns of voting in recent elections and falling membership of political parties has allowed for commentators and political élites to represent wider problems of democratic engagement through the prism of youth. Whilst some local and national governmental initiatives to develop representative institutions, such as youth and school councils, should be welcomed, there remains a lack of preparedness to address the root causes of youth political disconnection'.

Mycock puts forward an interesting analysis in that there does seem to be a lack of effort to dig deeper and examine the underlying issues where young people remain disengaged. He continues by unmasking problems within the political parties themselves, 'Political parties are hierarchical and ageist, often excluding young people from decision-making and representative roles whilst overlooking their interests in policy terms. Politicians remain wedded to an insular political culture and language which is exclusory and elitist. There is a need to trust the views and choices of young people and open up our political institutions to greater inter- and intra-generational debate'. Mycock has illuminated a key issue and one which the political parties themselves would be well advised to address in the near future. Parties need to reach out to young people and to focus upon properly thought-out measures that will enable them to achieve genuine participation as opposed to mere lip-service, tokenism or therapy. They need to fully incorporate young people into their party machinery by allowing them genuine decision-making powers and not simply keeping them on the sidelines. Piers, an interviewee in Chap. 6, kept referring to making politicians and political parties more 'open minded'. This is precisely what is needed; parties need to permit genuine participation from the young people themselves. In addition, young people have to be able to influence policy. Granted, from a pragmatic point of view, politicians tend to focus upon the interests and concerns of those most likely to turn out at the polls, that is, older people. This, on the face of it at least, is the rational approach but they ignore the opinions and interests of young people at their peril. Youth is, quite literally, the future. Their issues and concerns must not be ignored or even sidelined by the politicians. This would create untold problems for future political stability.

SHOULD THE VOTING AGE BE LOWERED TO 16 YEARS?

A key issue examined within this book is the question of whether or not the voting age should be lowered to 16 years. This is particularly topical given the momentum that does seem to have gathered pace for policy change in this area. Change which has seen the voting age lowered in Austria, Jersey, the Isle of Man and Guernsey, amongst others, and which saw 16- and 17-year-olds able to vote in the Scottish independence referendum (held on 18 September 2014) in the year of the 700th anniversary of the Battle of Bannockburn, and in the Scottish Parliamentary elections held on 5 May 2016. It was interesting to see what proportion of eligible 16- and 17-year-olds decided to use their vote and also, now, whether the momentum gathers pace to such an extent that the government has no option but to roll the vote out to 16- and 17-year-olds across the UK as a whole.

Some commentators see early voting as being an important aspect in relation to political participation and engagement more generally. As Kozeluh and Nitsch have pointed out in relation to the 2005 Viennese local elections, which was the first time that 16- and 17-year-olds could vote, they found that early voting had a stabilising, legitimising effect and that it will probably 'increase the chance of continued voting' (2006: 147). Likewise, Filzmaier and Klepp, who also investigated young Austrian voters in terms of whether or not they distrust politics and whether different groups of young people are more susceptible to extremism, found that there is a correlation between interest in politics and political knowledge and 'social and educational backgrounds' (2009: 352–353).

Certainly, the question of whether or not the voting age should be lowered is an issue that divides opinion. Andrew Mycock underlines some the key issues, 'Votes at 16 should only be considered after the radical revision of the structure and content of democratic politics in the UK. If lowering the voting age was a panacea to such issues, young people between the ages of 18–24 would have continued to vote in large numbers after 1969'. Mycock exposes an issue that many other commentators (cf. Cowley and Denver 2004) have pronounced, that lowering the voting age will not necessarily lead to higher levels of electoral turnout. In fact, it may simply exacerbate the problem, leading to even more people not voting. As Mycock states, 'Lowering the voting age is a symptom-led response which fails to address the causes of lower turnouts and political engagement amongst young people'.

As the Youth Citizenship Commission found, the general direction of the age of maturity has increased over the past few decades. It appears an odd message to suggest to young people that they are not mature enough to make many decisions about their lives but are mature enough to vote. Votes at the age of 16 'would, at present, create a two-tier citizenship whereby some citizens have more rights than others'. As Mycock proceeds to state, however, this 'does not mean that the voting age should not be lowered in the future, more that there needs to be a more holistic approach to debates about young people and politics. There remains no groundswell amongst young people for lowering the voting age and this suggests issues of political cynicism and non-participation go beyond low turnout in electoral politics'. For Mycock, therefore, it is not simply about permitting 16- and 17-years-olds to vote, it is about focusing upon measures to encourage and enhance their political engagement. This is where the Youth Citizenship Commission has been instrumental in focusing the debate upon how young people can become more politically engaged and where the debate about the teaching of citizenship in schools becomes even more meaningful.

COMPULSORY VOTING

For some commentators, the key to avoidance of differential turnout, whereby certain sectors of society, such as young people, are dropping off the political radar, is to introduce a system of compulsory voting.

Compulsory voting is a misnomer as the electorate cannot be physically forced to cast their vote. It is more accurate to label it compulsory turnout in that people can be coerced into participating. There has to be the inclusion on the ballot paper of a section entitled 'None of the Above' (NOTA) so that those who are dissatisfied with all the political parties and candidates on offer can express their view by ticking the relevant option. There are those who feel that compulsory voting would facilitate the real and genuine political participation of young people. By being 'forced to participate', their views would be heard and it may also have an educative effect. The fact that they would have to vote may mean that young people are galvanised into finding out about what the political parties stand for and about the key tenets of the policies that they espouse. This educative effect may lead to a more politically engaged electorate (cf. Briggs and Celis 2010) and may lead to greater participation in other areas of political life—not just in terms of voting. As Martin Wattenberg states, 'Political scientists have been far too cautious in recommending compulsory voting despite what we know about the seriousness of the turnout problem among young people and how well this solution works to correct it' (2012: 202). For Wattenberg, compulsory voting is the key response to low levels of youth political participation. He also believes that attitudes will change towards compulsory voting once it becomes established, just as it has done with, say, compulsory wearing of seatbelts in cars or the ban on smoking in public places—an observation that relates to the UK political scenario just as much as it relates to Wattenberg's USA. In relation to attitudinal change, Wattenberg states, 'attitudes and behaviour can change as people become more aware of a problem; and once such changes are put into motion, politicians feel compelled to take actions that they never would have even considered a decade earlier' (Ibid: 203). A detailed discussion of compulsory voting is out with the scope of this book but, suffice to say, attitudinal change *is* important and, just as it is highly likely that future generations will look aghast at historical accounts of parents being legally able to smack their children, so too, the figure of only 43 per cent of 18–24-year-olds voting in a UK general election (as happened in 2015, or worse still, 37 per cent, as occurred in 2005) will elicit cries of derision. Perhaps the time is right for compulsory voting to be introduced in order to redress the balance with regards to youth political participation?

PRISONERS AND THE VOTE

The issue of whether the franchise should be lowered to the age of 16 also resonates with the current debates surrounding the question of whether or not prisoners should be allowed to vote. As White notes, the disenfranchisement of prisoners 'dates back to the Forfeiture Act 1870 and was linked to the notion of "civic death"' (2013: 4). This is where they would lose the right to vote when they were serving a sentence exceeding 12 months. This had effect until the Criminal Law Act 1967 amended the 1870 Act so that only those convicted of treason were disenfranchised. In 1969, however, the Representation of the People Act, led to 'convicted persons [being] legally incapable of voting during the time that they were detained in a penal institution' (Ibid: 5). Under current law, only prisoners on remand are entitled to vote. Prime Minister David Cameron has been unequivocal in arguing against giving prisoners the vote, stating at Prime Minister's Questions on 24 October 2012, 'I do not want prisoners to have the vote, and they should not get the vote ... prisoners are not getting the vote under this Government' (Ibid: 40). A comparative analysis is interesting; in some countries a ban on voting depends on the crime committed (e.g. France) or on the length of sentence (as in Austria), or they are only allowed to vote in certain elections (Ukraine). It is significant to note that in many other European countries, at least 18 nations, prisoners do have the right to vote, regardless of their crime. If policy transfer and European parity are taken into consideration, will it be only a matter of time, regardless of the Prime Minister's viewpoint, before the UK goes in the same direction?

YOUTH PROTESTS

Clearly young people have issues that are of key concern. There have been flashpoints in the recent past. The student protests being a case in point where significant numbers of young people came together to protest against the removal of the EMA and the rise in higher education tuition fees (amongst other aspects). In addition, there were also the riots of August 2011, although opinion is divided over the extent to which these were political and whether this was simply a case of people jumping on the bandwagon. As Andrew Mycock states, 'The August 2011 riots were a mixture of localised issues linked to the shooting of Mark Duggan and national issues relating to government's treatment of a generation of young people'. Mycock's analysis focuses upon the national issues. 'The narrative developed by the Coalition Government since coming to power in May 2010 sought to frame the future prospects of the UK in a determinedly pessimistic hue. This sense of despair was particularly acute amongst young people. The riots of 2011 were a response to the cutting of various educational support programmes including the EMA, the huge hike in university tuition fees, and a lack of sympathy for the dramatic rise in youth unemployment'. He proceeds to state that, for 'many of those rioting, their actions were a mixture of frustration, opportunism and anger. The Government's response was to denigrate the most excluded in our society without coming to terms with the complex motivations for the rioting'. Mycock's final analysis will strike a chord with many other political observers when he states that 'I believe that this lack of appreciation will see rioting of 2011 repeated again soon'. Unless and until young people are able to participate politically in a meaningful and valued manner it is likely that Mycock's worrying prediction will come to fruition. The events of 2011, shocking as they were, provide us with a stark reminder that young people must not be sidelined, ignored or patronised. Their 'voice' is as worthy and vital as older generations. It should be listened to, respected, valued and, where appropriate, acted upon.

As Sloam (2007: 565) explains, 'Young people are interested in politics, but not in the political process, though their interest is not matched by a deep understanding of how things work'. For Sloam, the answer is 'a combination of better information and education, greater integrity and more engagement from key (local and national) political actors, and more effort to engage young people (especially at the local level) and listen to issues that really concern them' (Ibid.). More recently, Sloam describes how the interests of the young 'have been viewed as insignificant of even expendable (witness the Liberal Democrat u-turn on tuition fees). Whilst benefits for older people—such as pensions—have often been protested or even increased, benefits and services for the young have been drastically reduced' (2013a: 4). He explains how many young people have, therefore, turned their backs on mainstream politics and 'turned to alternative political parties that focus upon single issues (such as the Pirate Parties), present a populist message (for example, Beppe Grillo's Five Star Movement in Italy) or adopt an extreme position (for example, against immigrants)' (Ibid: 5). There is a view that the young people who do participate politically tend to be representative of a '(thwarted) aspirational group' (Ibid.) and that other young people who do not engage in protest are doubly excluded.

Political parties should not neglect the political power of young voters. Bruter and Harrison, in their study of young party members in Europe, have pointed out that young people 'are the future of old-style politics, and without their participation, some fear that our current model of governance might reach a point of no return' (2009: 2). Parties need the new blood of young people to enable them to rejuvenate and continue into the future. Indeed, Shiv Malik (2013: 12) affirms and Ipsos MORI reports the increase in support for the Conservative Party under David Cameron by Generation Y (those born after 1980)—especially when some older voters have either gone over to UKIP or decided to become floating voters. Malik states that the pre-war generation have left the party despite the Tories 'raising pensions, and protecting universal old age benefits, such as free bus passes and winter fuel payments, in the midst of swingeing cuts' (Ibid.). As Paul Chaney attests, age is important in a world which 'by 2050, older people will outnumber the population of children (0–14 years) for the first time in human history' (2013: 456). Sloam has illustrated how protest politics 'runs the risk of spilling over into extremist politics and even violence' and how despite the financial cuts, it is imperative that politicians across Europe 'spread the burden more fairly across generations' (2013a: 7). Granted, the demographic trend is towards an increasingly older population. All the more reason, therefore, that our policymakers do not neglect the wishes, demands and policy preferences of the younger generations—who are, after all, quite literally the future!

Thinking about what that future entails, the Youth Citizenship Commission, set up in 2008 to investigate youth political engagement, made a number of recommendations and, as two of its leading members, Jonathan Tonge and Andrew Mycock, state, they expect in 'future years ... to see electoral registration in schools, the devolved institutions determining the age of franchise in their countries; improved and effective citizenship education; formal channels of communication established between local authorities and young people, replicated at national level by government departments and movement towards a programme of civic service' (2010: 198). At the time of the 2015 General Election, it was 18 years since the last time that more than 50 per cent of young people voted in a general election. This particular coming of age—albeit in a negative sense—is hardly a cause for celebration. Hopefully, measures such as those suggested by the Youth Citizenship Commission will go some way towards redressing this balance. A proper programme of political education is required if we are to equip young people with the skills and confidence to participate politically. History shows us that 2015 was not the harbinger of a significant increase in the number of young people voting, but there is still plenty of scope for optimism.

As mentioned, a key conclusion relates to the question of whether or not the voting age should be lowered to enable 16- and 17-year-olds to participate in elections. Opinion is divided and, whilst respectful of the viewpoint of eminent academics such as David Denver and Philip Cowley, the momentum gathered pace with the Scottish independence referendum of September 2014 and the Scottish Parliamentary Elections of 2016. Despite the voting age remaining at 18 for the 2016 referendum on continued European Union membership, it can only be a matter of time before the voting age will be extended to 16 and 17 years.

As this research has illustrated, young people have a great deal to give and to gain from political involvement. They often bring a fresh perspective, a new vision and a different approach to politics. Existing structures and political personnel must be wary of simply paying lip-service to their voices, votes and vision. In order for real, meaningful participation to occur, young people must be able to air their views and they must be taken seriously. There is a great deal of room for optimism *vis-à-vis* the future if the young people who were interviewed as part of this research are anything to go by. They have exciting ideas and bring a fresh approach to political life. Those who ignore or sideline today's youth do so at their peril. Not only do they risk marginalising a significant part of the population, they also potentially exclude some very interesting and exciting ideas from getting on to the political agenda. Jon Savage reminded us that, autumn 2014 saw 'the 70th anniversary of the invention of the teenager. Since the end of the Second World War, the American ideal of the informed, democratic consumer has proved a highly durable and workable rite of passage between childhood and adulthood' (Savage 2014: 19). Young people are an important sector of society for various reasons, not simply because they have helped to shape the past but also because they constitute the future.

Looking to that future, perhaps the fact that Terence Smith became the UK's youngest mayor in May 2016 (as Mayor of Goole at the age of 19) and with his express desire to be a 'young people's champion' (Johnston 2016), will prove inspirational for young people and encourage their greater political participation on a formal and informal basis.

NOTE

1. Interview with author, 10 June 2013. Dr Mycock played a leading role in the influential Youth Citizenship Commission. The YCC was set up in 2008 to look at ways of developing young people's understanding of citizenship and to increase their political participation.

BIBLIOGRAPHY

Birdwell, J., & Bani, M. (2014). *Introducing generation citizen.* London: Demos.

Briggs, J. E., & Celis, K. (2010). For or against: Compulsory voting in Britain and Belgium. *Social and Public Policy Review, 4*(1), 1–33.

British Social Attitudes 30. (2013). The younger electorate: What's the future? NatCen Social Research. Retrieved February 25, 2014, from http://www.bsa-30.natcen.ac.uk/read-the-report/politics/the-younger-electorate-what%E2%80%99s-the-future.aspx

Bruter, M., & Harrison, S. (2009). *The future of our democracies: Young party members in Europe.* Basingstoke: Palgrave Macmillan.

Carrell, S. (2013). Scottish teenagers likely to reject independence. *The Guardian,* 3 June.

Chaney, P. (2013). Electoral competition, issue salience and public policy for older people: The case of the Westminster and regional UK elections 1945–2011. *British Journal of Politics and International Relations, 15,* 456–475.

Cowley, P., & Denver, D. (2004). Votes at 16? The case against. *Representation, 41,* 57–62.

Denver, D. (2013, April). Votes at sixteen? Surely not! *Political Insight, 4*(1), 36–37.

Driscoll, R. (2014). *The ONS survey is wrong: Young people do have an interest in politics.* London: Political Studies Association. Retrieved May 15, 2014, from http://www.psa.ac.uk/insight-plus/blog/ons-survey-wrong-young-people-do-have-interest-politics

Filzmaier, P., & Klepp, C. (2009). Far more than Voting at the age of 16: Empirical findings on youth and civic education. *Osterreichische Zeitschrift Für Politikwissenschaft, 38*(3), 341–355.

Johnston, C. (2016). Terence Smith is youngest mayor in UK—Aged 19. 13 May. Retrieved May 13, 2016, from www.theguardian.com

Kozeluh, U., & Nitsch, S. (2006). "Voting means to grow up!" An analysis of the voting behaviour of 16 to 18 year old juveniles at the Viennese local elections in 2005. *SWS-Rundschau, 46*(2), 126–149.

Lee, L., & Young, P. (2013). A disengaged Britain? Political interest and participation over 30 years. In *British Social Attitudes 30.* London: NatCen Social Research.

Malik, S. (2013). Cameron's tough stand on welfare may be winning over Generation Y. *The Guardian*, 19 June, p. 12.

Marsh, D., O'Toole, T., & Jones, S. (2007). *Young people and politics in the UK: Apathy or alienation?* Basingstoke: Palgrave.

Morris, N. (2014a). Thousands of young people won't get a vote. *i-newspaper*, 5 February, p. 5.

Morris, N. (2014c). £4m fund to find 'missing' young voters. *i-newspaper*, 6 February, p. 10.

Mycock, A., & Tonge, J. (Eds.) (2014). *Beyond the youth citizenship commission: Young people and politics*. London: Political Studies Association.

Randall, C. (2014). *Measuring national well-being—Governance*. London: Office for National Statistics. Retrieved February 25, 2014, from http://www.ons.gov.uk/ons/dcp171766_352561.pdf

Russell, A. (2014). The time has come—But not for votes at 16. *Manchester Policy Blogs: Westminster Watch*. Retrieved April 21, 2014, from http://blog.policy.manchester.ac.uk/featured/2014/04/the-time-has-come-but-not-for-votes-at-16/

Savage, J. (2014). Time up for the teenager? *RSA Journal*, Issue 1, 16–19.

Sloam, J. (2007, January). Rebooting democracy: Youth participation in politics in the UK. *Parliamentary Affairs, 60*(4), 548–567.

Sloam, J. (2013a). The 'outraged young': How young Europeans are reshaping the political landscape. *Political Insight, 4*(1), 4–7.

Tonge, J., & Mycock, A. (2010). Citizenship and political engagement amongst young people: The workings and findings of the youth citizenship commission. *Parliamentary Affairs, 63*(1), 182–200.

Wattenberg, M. P. (2012). *Is voting for young people?* (3rd ed.). New York: Longman Pearson.

White, M. (2013). Political anger and apathy a reflection of voter "kidiocy". *The Guardian*, 27 December. Retrieved January 14, 2014, from http://www.theguardian.com/politics/2013/dec/27/political-anger-apathy-voter-kidiocy

BIBLIOGRAPHY

Agger, B. (2009). The pulpless generation: Why young people don't protest the Iraq war (or anything else), and why it's not entirely their fault. *Cultural Studies/Critical Methodologies, 9*(1), 41–51.

Annesley, C. (2010). Gender, politics and policy change: The case of welfare reform under new labour. *Government and Opposition, 45*(1), 50–72.

Austin, E. W., Vord, R. V. d., Pinkleton, B. E., & Epstein, E. (2008). Celebrity endorsements and their potential to motivate young voters. *Mass Communication and Society, 11*(4), 420–436.

Barnes, S. H., Kaase, M., Allerbeck, K. R., et al. (1979). *Political action: Mass participation in five Western democracies.* Beverly Hills, CA: Sage.

Baty, P. (2005). Young people's political apathy is a myth. *Times Higher Education Supplement,* Issue 1685, January, p. 4.

BBC Action Briefing Network. (2004). Votes for 16 year olds. 4 November. Retrieved from http://www.bbc.co.uk/dna/hub/A2519327

BBC News. (2013). Scottish independence: Study suggests most 16/17 year olds would vote 'no'. 2 June. Retrieved June 6, from http://www.bbc.co.uk/news/uk-scotland-scotland-politics-22745855

Bean, C. (1991, September). Participation and political protests: A causal model with Australian evidence. *Political Behavior, 13*(3), 253–283.

Bendit, R., & Hahn-Bliebtreu, M. (Eds.) (2008). *Youth transitions: Processes of social inclusion and patterns of vulnerability in a globalised world.* Leverkusen: Barbara Budrich.

Bennett, C. (2010). One thing the parties agree on—Keep women out. *The Observer,* 9 May, p. 39.

© The Author(s) 2017
J. Briggs, *Young People and Political Participation,*
DOI 10.1057/978-1-137-31385-0

Bennett, C. (2012). Rude, impulsive, sulky ... still, let our 16-year-olds vote. *The Observer*, 14 October.

Benyon, J. (2012, April). England's urban disorder: The 2011 riots. *Political Insight*, 3(1), 12–17.

Berry, C. (2008). Labour's lost youth: Young people and the labour party's youth sections. *Political Quarterly, 79*(3), 366–376.

Berry, C. (2014). Vote early and vote often: Reinforcing the unwritten rule of representative democracy. In A. Mycock & J. Tonge (Eds.), *Beyond the youth citizenship commission: Young people and politics* (pp. 14–17). London: Political Studies Association.

Bessant, J. (2014). The political in the age of the digital: Propositions for empirical investigation. *Politics, 34*(1), 33–44.

Bite the Ballot. (2014). Retrieved February 21, 2014, from http://bitetheballot. co.uk/

Blossfeld, H.-P., Hofäcker, D., & Bertolini, S. (Eds.) (2011). *Youth on globalised labour markets*. Leverkusen: Barbara Budrich.

Boyd, D. (2014). *It's complicated: The social lives of networked teens*. New Haven and London: Yale University Press.

Briggs, J. E. (1998). *Strikes in politicisation*. Aldershot: Ashgate.

Briggs, J. E. (2010, April). Generation i-Pod: From apathy to engagement. *e-Pol, 3*(2), 3–5. Manchester: Political Education Forum.

Buckingham, D. (1999). Young people, politics and news media: Beyond political socialisation. *Oxford Review of Education, 25*(1), 171–184.

Bynner, J., Romney, D., & Emler, N. (2003). Dimensions of political and related facets of identity in late adolescence. *Journal of Youth Studies, 6*(3), 319–335.

Cairney, P., & McGarvey, N. (2013). *Scottish politics* (2nd ed.). Basingstoke: Palgrave Macmillan.

Campbell, R., & Childs, S. (2010). Wags, wives and mothers ... but what about women politicians? *Parliamentary Affairs, 63*(4), 760–777.

Campbell, R., & Lovenduski, J. (2005). Winning women's votes? The incremental track to equality. In P. Norris & C. Wlezian (Eds.), *Britain Votes 2005* (pp. 181–197). Oxford: Oxford University Press.

Carman, C. (2010). The process is the reality: Perceptions of procedural fairness and participatory democracy. *Political Studies, 58*, 731–751.

Carnegie Young People Initiative. (2008). *Empowering young people: Final report of the carnegie young people initiative*. Dunfermline: Carnegie UK Trust.

Children and Young People's Unit. (2002). *Young people and politics: A report on the Yvote?/Ynot? project*. London: Children and Young People's Unit.

Childs, S. (2004, October). A British gender gap? Gender and political participation. *The Political Quarterly, 75*(4), 422–424.

Citizenship Foundation. (2012). *Voting age: Reduction to 16*. Retrieved July 25, 2012, from http://www.citizenshipfoundation.org.uk/main/page.php?76

Citrin, J., & Elkins, D. J. (1975). *Political disaffection among British university students.* Research Series Number 23, Institute of International Studies, Berkeley.

Cochrane, K. (2006). We imagine teenagers will simply vote for any party that legalises drugs or changes working hours to, say, 1pm to 4.30pm. *New Statesman, 135*(4783), 23.

Cockburn, T. (2010). Children and deliberative democracy in England. In B. Percy-Smith & N. Thomas (Eds.), *A handbook of children and young people's participation: Perspectives from theory and practice* (pp. 306–317). London: Routledge.

Coleman, S., & Rowe, C. (2005). *Remixing citizenship: Democracy and young people's use of the Internet.* London: Carnegie Young People's Initiative.

Conge, P. J. (1988, January). The concept of political participation: Toward a definition. *Comparative Politics, 20*(2), 241–249.

Copus, C. (2010). The councillor: Governor, governing, governance and the complexity of citizen engagement. *British Journal of Politics and International Relations, 12,* 569–589.

Crick, B. (1986). *In defence of politics.* London: Penguin.

Crick, B. (1992). *In defence of politics* (4th ed.). London: Penguin.

Crick, B., & Porter, A. (1978). *Political education and political literacy.* London: Longman.

Crick Report. (1998). *Education for citizenship and the teaching of democracy in schools: Final report of the advisory group on citizenship.* London: Qualifications and Curriculum Authority.

Cutts, D., & Widdop, P. (2013). Was labour penalised where it stood all women shortlist candidates? An analysis of the 2010 UK general election. *British Journal of Politics and International Relations, 15,* 435–455.

Dalton, R., & Kuechler, M. (Eds.) (1990). *Challenging the political order: New social and political movements in Western democracies.* Cambridge: Polity.

Davies, A. (1998). Youth gangs and masculinity in the late Victorian period. *Journal of Social History, 32*(2), 349–369.

Davis, C. (2013). *SPSS step by step: Essentials for social and political science.* Bristol: Policy Press.

della Porta, D. (2013). *Can democracy be saved?* Cambridge: Polity Press.

Devereux, C., Drummond, G., & Harvard, C. (1995). *M-Power: Young voter registration campaign.* London: British Youth Council.

Digital Democracy Commission. (2015). *Open up! Report of the speaker's commission on digital democracy.* London: Digital Democracy Commission.

Dionne, E. J. (2004). *Why Americans hate politics.* London: Simon and Schuster.

Diplock, S. (Ed.). (2001). None of the above: Non-voters and the 2001 election. *Hansard Society Briefing.* London: Hansard Society.

Dobson, A. (2007). *Green political thought* (4th ed.). London: Routledge.

Doheny, S., & O'Neill, C. (2010). Becoming deliberative citizens. *Political Studies, 58,* 630–648.

Electoral Commission. (2003, February 27). *Electoral Commission to review minimum voting age.* Retrieved from http://www.electoralcommission.org.uk/news-and-media/news-releases/electoral-commission-media-centre/news-releases-reviews-and-research/electoral-commission-to-review-minimum-voting-age

Electoral Commission. (2003). *How old is old enough? The minimum age of voting and candidacy in UK elections.* London: Electoral Commission.

Elmhirst, S. (2011). The lost generation. *New Statesman,* 21 February, pp. 33–36.

European Social Survey. (2012). Retrieved April 2014, from http://www.europeansocialsurvey.org/

Evans, G. (2003). Political culture and voting participation. In P. Dunleavy et al. (Eds.), *Developments in British politics 7* (pp. 82–99). Basingstoke: Palgrave Macmillan.

Evans, P., & Krüger, A. (2013). *Youth and community empowerment in Europe: International perspectives.* Bristol: Policy Press.

Farthing, R. (2010). The politics of youthful antipolitics: Representing the "issue" of youth participation in politics. *Journal of Youth Studies, 13*(2), 181–195.

Faulks, K. (2006). Education for citizenship in England's secondary schools: A critique of current principle and practice. *Journal of Education Policy, 21*(1), 59–74.

Ferreira, P. M. (2007). Youth and democracy in Portugal. *Org and Demo, 8*(1–2), 69–92, translated from Portuguese using online software.

Fishkin, J. S., & Laslett, P. (Eds.) (2003). *Debating deliberative democracy.* Oxford: Blackwell Publishing.

Fitgerald, R., Graham, A., Smith, A., & Taylor, N. (2010). Children's participation as a struggle over recognition. In B. Percy-Smith & N. Thomas (Eds.), *A handbook of children and young people's participation: Perspectives from theory and practice* (pp. 293–305). London: Routledge.

Flanagan, C., Finlay, A., Gallay, L., & Kim, T. (2012). Political incorporation and the protracted transition to adulthood: The need for new institutional inventions. *Parliamentary Affairs, 65,* 29–46.

Forbrig, J. (Ed.) (2005). *Revisiting youth political participation: Challenges for research and democratic practice in Europe.* Strasbourg: Council of Europe.

Frazer, E. (2007). Depoliticising citizenship. *British Journal of Educational Studies, 55*(3), 249–263.

Free the Children. (2014). Retrieved March 10, 2014, from http://www.freethechildren.com/

Furlong, A., & Cartmel, F. (2007). *Young people and social change.* Milton Keynes: Open University.

Garcia Albacete, G. (2014). *Young people's political participation in Western Europe: Continuity or generational change?* Basingstoke: Palgrave Macmillan, forthcoming.

Gavin, N. T. (2010). Pressure group direct action on climate change: The role of the media and the Web in Britain—A case study. *British Journal of Politics and International Relations, 12*, 459–475.

Gibbs, A. (1997). Focus groups. *Social Research Update, 19* (Winter issue). Retrieved May 2011, from http://sru.soc.surrey.ac.uk/sru19.html

Gibson, S. (2011). Dilemmas of citizenship: Young people's conceptions of un/employment rights and responsibilities. *British Journal of Social Psychology, 50*, 450–468.

Goebert, B., & Rosenthal, H. M. (2002). *Beyond listening: Learning the secret language of focus groups.* New York: John Wiley.

Golding, W. (1954). *Lord of the flies.* London: Faber and Faber.

Gonzalez-Ricoy, I. (2012). Depoliticising the polls: Voting abstention and moral disagreement. *Politics, 32*(1), 46–51.

Goodwin, J., & Jasper, J. M. (2009). *The social movements reader: Cases and concepts* (2nd ed.). Oxford: Wiley-Blackwell.

Goodwin, J., & Jasper, J. M. (Eds.) (2015). *The social movements reader: Cases and concepts* (3rd ed.). Oxford: Wiley-Blackwell.

Grant, W. (2000). *Pressure groups and British politics.* Basingstoke: Palgrave Macmillan.

Greenberg, J. (2010, Spring). "There's nothing anyone can do about it": Participation, apathy and "successful" democratic transition in postsocialist Serbia. *Slavic Review, 69*(1), 41–64.

Greenberg, J. (2014). *After the revolution: Youth, democracy, and the politics of disappointment in Serbia.* Stanford, CA: Stanford University Press.

Griffiths, N., & Egan, B. (2002). Give Wayne Rooney the vote. *New Statesman,* 4 November.

Groundwater-Smith, S., Dockett, S., & Bottrell, D. (2015). *Participatory research with children and young people.* London: Sage.

Guernsey Legal Resources. (2012). Retrieved February 18, 2012, from http://www.guernseylegalresources.gg/article/96983/Reform-Guernsey-Amendment-Law-2007

Hancox, D. (Ed.) (2011). *Fight back! A reader on the winter of protest.* London: Open Democracy.

Hansard Society. (2011). *Audit of political engagement 8.* The 2011 report. London: Hansard Society.

Hansard Society. (2013). *Audit of political engagement 10.* London: Hansard Society.

Harrison, L., & Deicke, W. (2000). Capturing the first time voters: An initial study of political attitudes among teenagers. *Youth and Policy, 67*, 26–40.

Hart, R. (1997). *Children's participation: The theory and practice of involving young citizens in community development and environmental care.* New York/London: Unicef/Earthscan.

Hawkins, A. (2010). Men vote for Mars, women vote for Venus. *Total Politics,* 19 February.

Held, D. (2006). *Models of democracy* (3rd ed.). Cambridge: Polity Press.

Helm, T. (2016). EU referendum: Poll shows young voters could hold key in June vote. *The Guardian,* 2 April. Retrieved from http://www.theguardian.com/politics/2016/apr/02/eu-referendum-young-voters-brexit-leave

Henn, M., & Foard, N. (2012). Young people, political participation and trust in Britain. *Parliamentary Affairs, 65*(1), 47–67.

Henn, M., & Foard, N. (2014a). Social differentiation in young people's political participation: The impact of social and educational factors on youth political engagement in Britain. *Journal of Youth Studies, 17*(3), 360–380.

Henn, M., & Weinstein, M. (2006). Young people and political (in)activism: Why don't young people vote? *Policy and Politics, 34*(3), 517–534.

Hirzalla, F., & van Zoonen, L. (2011). Beyond the online/offline divide: How youth's online and offline civic activities converge. *Social Science Computer Review, 29*(4), 481–498.

HM Government. (2010). *An agenda for youth engagement: Government response to the recommendations of the youth citizenship commission.* London: Cabinet Office. Retrieved January 4, 2011, from http://www.cabinetoffice.gov.uk/media/333826/youthengagement.pdf

Hooghe, M., Dassonneville, R., & Marien, S. (2015). The impact of education on the development of political trust: Results from a five-year panel study among late adolescents and young adults in Belgium. *Political Studies, 63,* 123–141.

Hoskins, B., & Kerr, D. (2012). *Final summary and policy recommendations: Participatory citizenship in the European Union.* Brussels: European Commission.

Howker, E., & Malik, S. (2010). *Jilted generation: How Britain has bankrupted its youth.* London: Icon Books.

http://www.5050parliament.co.uk/. Retrieved September 21, 2015.

http://www.bbench.co.uk. Retrieved September 21, 2015.

http://bitetheballot.co.uk/verto/. Retrieved April 24, 2015.

http://www.democracymatters.org.uk. Retrieved October 3, 2015.

http://www.guardian.co.uk/technology/2012/may/15/twitter-uk-users-10m. Retrieved November 16, 2012.

http://www.itpro.co.uk/624724/silver-surfers-dominate-uk-web-use. Retrieved November 18, 2012.

http://mashable.com/2012/03/21/twitter-has-140-million-users/. Retrieved November 16, 2012.

http://www.mylifemysay.org.uk. Retrieved October 3, 2015.

http://www.salon.com/2012/11/15/in_uk_twitter_facebook_rants_land_some_in_jail/. Retrieved November 16, 2012.

http://www.telegraph.co.uk/technology/internet/7862234/Silver-surfers-increase-by-one-million-over-the-last-year.html. Retrieved November 18, 2012. Published June 30, 2010.

http://www.thepoliticsproject.org.uk. Retrieved October 3, 2015.

Inman, P. (2013). Surprise rise in pay gap as men grab lion's share. *The Guardian*, 13 December.

Inthorn, S., & Street, J. (2011). "Simon Cowell for prime minister?" Young citizens' attitudes towards celebrity politics. *Media, Culture and Society, 33*(3), 479–489.

James, C. (2014). *Disconnected: Youth, new media, and the ethics gap*. Cambridge, MA: MIT Press.

Jenkins, J. C., & Klandermans, B. (1995). *The politics of social protest*. London: UCL Press.

John, P., Cotterill, S., Moseley, A., Richardson, L., Smith, G., Stoker, G., et al. (2011). *Nudge, nudge, think, think: Experimenting with ways to change civic behaviour*. University of Manchester, University of Southampton and University College London.

John, P., Fieldhouse, E., & Liu, H. (2011). How civic is civic culture? Explaining community participation using the 2005 English citizenship survey. *Political Studies, 59*, 230–252.

Johnston, R., & Pattie, C. (2003). The growing problem of electoral turnout in Britain? Voluntary and involuntary non-voters in 2001. *Representation, 40*(1), 30–43.

Kelly, U. (2003). *Bradford-Keighley youth parliament—The first year*. Bradford: Bradford University Department of Peace Studies.

Kerr, D. (2014). Enhancing the political literacy of young people—A shared responsibility. In A. Mycock & J. Tonge (Eds.), *Beyond the youth citizenship commission: Young people and politics* (pp. 44–47). London: Political Studies Association.

Kisby, B. (2009). Social capital and citizenship lessons in England: Analysing the presuppositions of citizenship education. *Education, Citizenship and Social Justice, 4*(1), 41–62.

Kisby, B., & Sloam, J. (2012). Citizenship, democracy and education in the UK: Towards a common framework for citizenship lessons in the four home nations. *Parliamentary Affairs, 65*, 68–89.

Kisby, B., & Sloam, J. (2014). Promoting youth participation in democracy: The role of higher education. In A. Mycock & J. Tonge (Eds.), *Beyond the youth citizenship commission: Young people and politics* (pp. 52–56). London: Political Studies Association.

Lane, R. (1959). *Political life: Why people get involved in politics?* Glencoe: The Free Press.

Lau, J. C. (2012). Two arguments for child enfranchisement. *Political Studies, 60,* 860–876.

Laurie, P. (1965). *The teenage revolution.* London: Anthony Blond.

Lee, B. (2014). Window dressing 2.0: Constituency-level web campaigns in the 2010 UK general election. *Politics, 34*(1), 45–57.

Lijphart, A. (1999). *Patterns of democracy.* New Haven, CT: Yale University Press.

Loncle, P., Cuconato, M., Muniglia, V., & Walther, A. (Eds.) (2012). *Youth participation in Europe: Beyond discourses, practices and realities.* Bristol: The Policy Press.

Lusoli, W. (2005). A second-order medium? The Internet as a source of electoral information in 25 European countries. *Information Polity, 10*(3–4), 247–265.

Malone, M. (Ed.) (2011). *Achieving democracy: Democratization in theory and practice.* London: Continuum.

Marien, S., Hooghe, M., & Quintelier, E. (2010). Inequalities in non-institutionalised forms of political participation: A multi-level analysis of 25 countries. *Political Studies, 58,* 187–213.

Marsh, A. (1977). *Protest and political consciousness.* London: Sage.

Matsusaka, J. G. (2005). Direct democracy works. *Journal of Economic Perspectives, 19*(2), 185–206.

McDonnell, J. (2010). We are many. *New Statesman Political Studies Guide,* 29 November, p. 12.

McRobbie, A. (1991). *Feminism and youth culture.* Basingstoke: Macmillan.

Milbrath, L. W., & Goel, M. L. (1977). *Political participation: How and why do people get involved in politics?* (2nd ed.). Chicago: Rand McNally.

Mill, J. S. (2005). *On liberty.* New York: Cosimo. First published in 1859.

Milliken, M. (2001). Enfranchising young people: The case for a youth parliament. *Child Care in Practice, 7,* 157–163.

Morgan, D. L. (1996). Focus groups. *Annual Review of Sociology, 22,* 129–152.

MORI. (2002). Children's attitudes to politics. Retrieved from http://www.mori.com/polls/2002/atl.shtml

Morris, N. (2012). Give 16-year-olds the right to vote, Government told. *i-newspaper,* 11 October, p. 5.

Mortimore, R., Skinner, G., & Mludzinski, T. (2013). "Cameron's problem with women": The reporting and reality of gender-based trends in attitudes to the Conservatives 2010–11. Paper presented to the *Political Studies Association Annual Conference,* Cardiff, March.

Mycock, A., & Tonge, J. (2007). The future of citizenship. In A. Russell & G. Stoker (Eds.), *Failing politics? A response to The Governance of Britain Green Paper* (pp. 18–21). Newcastle: Political Studies Association.

Newton, J. (2001, March). Can citizenship education affect voting levels and patterns? In V. Gibbons (Ed.), *The people have spoken. UK elections: Who votes and who doesn't.* Hansard Society Report.

Norris, P. (2001). *Digital divide: Civic engagement, information poverty and the Internet worldwide.* Cambridge: Cambridge University Press.

Norris, P. (2004). Will new technology boost turnout? In N. Kersting & H. Baldersheim (Eds.), *Electronic voting and democracy.* London: Palgrave.

O'Loughlin, B., & Gillespie, M. (2012). Dissenting citizenship? Young people and political participation in the media-security nexus. *Parliamentary Affairs, 65*(1), 115–137.

O'Toole, T. (2003). Engaging with young people's conceptions of the political. *Children's Geographies, 1*(1), 71–90.

O'Toole, T., & Gale, R. (2013). *Political engagement amongst ethnic minority young people: Making a difference.* Basingstoke: Palgrave Macmillan.

Ofsted. (2006). *Towards consensus? Citizenship in secondary schools.* Manchester: Ofsted.

Park, A. (1999). Young people and political apathy. In R. Jowell, J. Curtice, A. Park, K. Thomson, & L. Jarvis (Eds.), *British social attitudes: The 15th report* (Vol. 16). Aldershot: Ahsgate.

Parliamentary Archives. HL/PO/PU/1/1918/7&8G5c64.

Parliamentary Archives. HL/PO/PU/1/1928/18&19G5c12.

Pattie, C., Seyd, P., & Whiteley, P. (2004). *Citizenship in Britain: Values, participation and democracy.* Cambridge: Cambridge University Press.

Pearson, G. (2006). The generation game. *The Guardian,* 8 November, p. 4 (Society section).

People's Century. Part 21, *1968,* Youth Movement, BBC DVD, 9mins, 3 seconds to 9 minutes 35 seconds. Retrieved July 27, 2014, from http://www.youtube.com/watch?v=tBjZRh4KOOI

Percy-Smith, B., & Thomas, N. (Eds.) (2010). *A handbook of children and young people's participation: Perspectives from theory and practice.* London: Routledge.

Phelps, E. (2012). Understanding electoral turnout among British young people: A review of the literature. *Parliamentary Affairs, 65,* 281–299.

Phillips, A. (1995). *The politics of presence.* Oxford: Clarendon Press.

Pirie, M., & Worcester, R. (2000). *The big turn-off.* London: Adam Smith Institute.

Putnam, R. (2000). *Bowling alone: The collapse and revival of American community.* New York: Touchstone Books.

Pykett, J., Saward, M., & Schaefer, A. (2010). Framing the good citizen. *British Journal of Political and International Relations, 12,* 523–538.

Quintelier, E. (2007). Differences in political participation between young and old people. *Contemporary Politics, 13*(2), 165–180.

Quintelier, E. (2008, December). Who is politically active: The athlete, the scout member or the environmental activist?: Young people, voluntary engagement and political participation. *Acta Sociologica, 51*(4), 355–370.

Ramamurthy, A. (2013). *Black star: Britain's Asian youth movements.* London: Pluto Press.

Richards-Schuster, K., & Checkoway, B. (2009, Winter). Youth participation in public policy at the local level: New lessons from Michigan municipalities. *National Civic Review, 98*(4), 26–30.

Roper, L., & Smith, S. (1975). The evolution of Juvenile delinquency in England, 1890–1914. *Past and Present, 67*(1), 96–126.

Ruggiero, V., & Montagna, N. (2008). *Social movements: A reader.* London: Routledge.

Rummens, S., & Abts, K. (2010). Defending democracy: The concentric containment of political extremism. *Political Studies, 58,* 649–665.

Russell, A., Fieldhouse, E., Purdham, K., & Kaira, V. (2002). *Voter engagement and young people.* London: The Electoral Commission Research Report.

Ryan, P. (1995). The bubble gum vote. *Quadrant Magazine, 39*(6), 87.

Saha, L., Print, M., & Edwards, K. (Eds.) (2007). *Youth and political participation.* Rotterdam: Sense Publishers.

Samms, C. (1995). *Global Generation X: Their values and attitudes in different countries.* London: Demos.

Scottish Youth Parliament. (2011). *Change the picture.* Edinburgh: Scottish Youth Parliament.

Simmons, R., & Thompson, R. (2011, October). Education and training for young people at risk of becoming NEET: Findings from an ethnographic study of work-based learning programmes. *Educational Studies, 37*(4), 447–450.

Sloam, J. (2008). Teaching democracy: The role of political science education. *British Journal of Politics and International Relations, 10*(3), 509–524.

Sloam, J. (2012a). Introduction: Youth, citizenship and politics. *Parliamentary Affairs, 65,* 4–12.

Sloam, J. (2012b, January). 'Rejuvenating democracy?' Young people and the 'Big Society' project. *Parliamentary Affairs, 65*(1), 90–114.

Sloam, J. (2012c). New voice, less equal: The civic and political engagement of young people in the United States and Europe. *Comparative Political Studies,* online 3 September, pp. 1–26.

Sloam, J., & Kisby, B. (2015, May 19). *Education, equality and participation.* Sheffield: The Crick Centre. Retrieved September 18, 2015, from http://www.crickcentre.org/blog/education-equality-and-participation/

SNP in move to lower voting age to 16. (2008). *Herald Scotland,* 13 June.

Spannring, R., Ogris, G., & Gaiser, W. (Eds.) (2008). *Youth and political participation in Europe.* Opladen: Barbara Budrich Publishers.

Speaker's Commission on Digital Democracy. (2014). Retrieved July 27, 2014, from http://www.parliament.uk/business/commons/the-speaker/speakers-commission-on-digital-democracy/ddc-news/

Speaker's Conference on Parliamentary Representation. (2010). *Speaker's conference on parliamentary representation: Final report, HC 239-1*. London: House of Commons.

Speaker's School Council Awards. (2014). Retrieved July 21, 2014, from https://www.speakersschoolcouncil.org/

Stewart, D. W., Shamdasani, P. N., & Rook, D. W. (2007). *Focus groups: Theory and practice*. London: Sage.

Tapscott, D. (1997). *Growing up digital: The rise of the Net Generation*. New York: McGraw-Hill.

The Times. (2010). Where have all the women politicians gone? *Letters' Page*, 14 May.

Theis, J. (2010). Children as active citizens. In B. Percy-Smith & N. Thomas (Eds.), *A handbook of children and young people's participation: Perspectives from theory and practice* (pp. 343–355). London: Routledge.

Tisdall, E. (2010). Governance and participation. In B. Percy-Smith & N. Thomas (Eds.), *A handbook of children and young people's participation: Perspectives from theory and practice* (pp. 318–329). London: Routledge.

Tonge, J. (2009). Revitalising politics: Engaging young people. *Representation, 45*(3), 237–246.

Topf, R. (1998). Beyond electoral participation. In H. Klingemann & D. Fuchs (Eds.), *Citizens and the state*. Oxford: Oxford University Press.

Tormey, S. (2015). *The end of representative politics*. Cambridge: Polity Press.

Turkle, S. (2011). *Alone together: Why we expect more from technology and less from each other*. New York: Perseus.

UK Youth Parliament. Retrieved April 30, 2014, from http://www.ukyouthparliament.org.uk/about/

Verba, S., & Almond, G. (1963). *The civic culture*. Boston: Little, Brown.

Verba, S., & Nie, N. (1972). *Participation in America: Social equality and political democracy*. New York: Harper and Row.

Verba, S., Nie, N. H., & Kim, J. (1978). *Participation and political equality*. Cambridge: Cambridge University Press.

Votesat16 Campaign. Retrieved from July 25, 2012, from http://www.votesat16.org/

Votesat18blogspot. Retrieved July 25, 2012, from http://votesat18.blogspot.co.uk/

Votes cast for teenagers. (2003). *The Guardian*, 15 October. Retrieved from http://www.guardian.co.uk/politics/2003/oct/15/voterapathy.uk/print

Vromen, A. (2003a). "People try to put us down…": Participatory citizenship of "Generation X". *Australian Journal of Political Science, 38*, 78–99.

Vromen, A. (2003b). Traversing time and gender: Australian young people's participation. *Journal of Youth Studies, 6,* 277–294.

Vromen, A. (2007). Judging cyber optimism: Youth-led participation and the internet. In L. Saha, M. Print, & K. Edwards (Eds.), *Youth and political participation* (pp. 133–151). Rotterdam: Sense Publishers.

Wall, J. (2012). Can democracy represent children? Towards a politics of difference. *Childhood, 19*(1), 86–100.

Wall, J., & Dar, A. (2011). Children's political representation: The right to make a difference. *International Journal of Children's Rights, 19,* 595–612.

Watson, T. (2001, March). Abolishing the democratic deficit—Time for compulsory voting? In V. Gibbons (Ed.), *The people have spoken. UK elections: Who votes and who doesn't.* Hansard Society Report.

Wattenberg, M. P. (2016). *Is voting for young people?* (4th ed.). New York: Routledge.

Werbner, P., Webb, M., & Spellman-Poots, K. (Eds.) (2014). *The political aesthetics of global protest: The Arab spring and beyond.* Edinburgh: Edinburgh University Press.

White, C. (2001, March). Young people's attitudes. In V. Gibbons (Ed.), *The people have spoken. UK elections: Who votes and who doesn't.* Hansard Society Report.

White, I., & Horne, A. (2014). *Prisoners' voting rights—In brief.* London: Commons Library Standard Note. SN/PC/01764, 8 July. Retrieved July 11, 2014, from http://www.parliament.uk/business/publications/research/briefing-papers/SN01764/prisoners-voting-rights

White, I., & Young, R. (2007). *Compulsory voting.* London: House of Commons. Standard Note: SN/PC/954.

White, J., & Ypi, L. (2010). Rethinking the modern Prince: Partisanship and the democratic ethos. *Political Studies, 58,* 809–828.

Whiteley, P. (2010). *The student vote in 2010.* London: Opinionpanel Research.

Whiteley, P., Clarke, H., Sanders, D., & Stewart, M. (2001). Turnout. *Parliamentary Affairs, 54,* 775–788.

Wilkinson, H. (1996). But will they vote? The political attitudes of young people. *Children and Society, 10*(3), 242–244.

Wilks-Heeg, S. (2012). *There is still a very long way to go before votes at 16 at general elections becomes a reality.* London: Democratic Audit UK. Retrieved October 17, 2013, from http://www.democraticaudit.com/?p=306

Williams, S. (2013). Retrieved October 16, 2013, from http://stephenwilliams.org.uk/en/page/campaigns-votes-at-16

Wintour, P. (2006). Brown backs votes at 16 in radical shakeup of politics. *The Guardian,* 27 February.

Worcester, R., Mortimore, R., Baines, P., & Gill, M. (2011). *Explaining Cameron's coalition: How it came about—An analysis of the 2010 British general election.* London: Biteback.

Wring, D., Henn, M., & Weinstein, M. (1998). Lowering the age of assent: Youth and politics in Britain. *Fabian Review, 110*(4).

Wring, D., Henn, M., & Weinstein, M. (1999). Young people and contemporary politics: Committed scepticism or engaged cynicism? In J. Fisher et al. (Eds.), *British elections and parties review* (Vol. 9, pp. 200–216). London: Frank Cass.

Young Women's Trust. (2015). *The clock turns back for young women.* London: Young Women's Trust Retrieved from www.youngwomenstrust.org.

Youth Citizenship Commission. (2008a). *Old enough to make a mark? Should the voting age be lowered to 16?.* Consultation paper. London: Youth Citizenship Commission.

Youth Citizenship Commission. (2008b). *Youth engagement—A literature review.* Prepared by Edcoms. London: Youth Citizenship Commission.

INDEX

Printed by Printforce, the Netherlands